BRITISH COLUMBIA
ALMANAC

British Columbia
ALMANAC

written & edited by Mark Forsythe

host of *BC Almanac* on CBC radioONE

ARSENAL PULP PRESS

VANCOUVER

BRITISH COLUMBIA ALMANAC
Copyright © 2000 by Canadian Broadcasting Corporation except where indicated

Second printing, 2001

All rights reserved. No part of this book may be reproduced or used in any form
by any means – graphic, electronic or mechanical – without the prior written permission
of the publisher, except by a reviewer, who may use brief excerpts in a review, or in the
case of photocopying, a license from the Canadian Copyright Licensing Agency.

ARSENAL PULP PRESS
103-1014 Homer Street
Vancouver, B.C.
Canada V6B 2W9
www.arsenalpulp.com

The publisher gratefully acknowledges the support of the Canada Council
for the Arts and the B.C. Arts Council for its publishing program, and the
support of the Government of Canada through the Book Publishing Industry
Development Program for its publishing activities.

Book design by Lisa Eng-Lodge
Production Assistant Judy Yeung
Editorial Assistant Laura Lemay
Photographs, unless otherwise noted, by Mark Forsythe
Photographs on pages 8, 58, 112, and 162 from Photodisc
Printed and bound in Canada

BC Almanac, its logo, and the logo of the Canadian Broadcasting Corporation used with
permission of the Canadian Broadcasting Corporation.

Efforts have been made to locate copyright holders of source material wherever possible.
The publisher welcomes hearing from any copyright holders of material used in this book
who have not been contacted.

CANADIAN CATALOGUING IN PUBLICATION DATA:
Main entry under title:
British Columbia Almanac

 ISBN 1-55152-087-7

1. British Columbia. I. Forsythe, Mark.   II. Almanac (Radio program)
FC3818.B74 2000   971.1   C00-911005-4
F1087.B74 2000

INTRODUCTION

BC Almanac is CBC Radio One's window on British Columbia. We prop it open with a microphone between noon and 2 pm each weekday, telling stories about BC people, issues, and events – from the plight of commercial fishers to the challenges of urban sprawl. From harvest celebrations to the painfully slow progress of land claim negotiations. Our broadcast links people and communities through a daily "Open Line" – a forum for ideas and opinion. We also like to have fun exploring BC places, hearing stories of colourful BC characters, or sharing our listeners' interests in all things British Columbian.

As host of *BC Almanac*, I get to speak with British Columbians across the province every day – from Atlin to White Rock, Tofino to Fernie. It's not a one way street either; CBC Radio One listeners tend to let you know exactly what they're thinking, from politics to pronunciation (as in "take the soy out of Osoyoos"), fish farming to gray whale sightings. They're integral to each broadcast.

The name Almanac popped into former host Stan Peters' head during a brainstorming session more than twenty years ago. It stuck. The program had a decidedly agricultural/consumer bent then, and through successive hosts – Lucy McNiell and Cecilia Walters – broadened its scope. But we're still conscious of those roots and attempt to relay the rural concerns of Peachland or Fraser Lake to the Lower Mainland and the rest of the province.

This almanac celebrates place through the voices of our listeners; from the mystic Skeena River to a small urban creek providing refuge in Burnaby. There are stories of arrival – from across Canada and around the world – and essays from regular contributors to our "In Search of BC" series – from ethnobotanist Nancy Turner to historian Jean Barman. Master gardener Brian Minter, outdoors columnist Jack Christie, birder Dick Cannings, and astronomer David Dodge all offer up unique perspectives on pursuing their passion in BC. Whether you're a CBC Radio listener or not, you'll recognize their love for this place perched on the edge of the Pacific, and learn from them as I do each day.

BC Bookworld's Alan Twigg gave me a gentle nudge to follow through on the idea for this book; and the incredibly motivated and talented people at Arsenal Pulp Press made it happen: Blaine Kyllo, Brian Lam, Laura Lemay, Lisa Eng-Lodge, and Jaye Lyonns. The folks you don't hear on the radio make the daily *BC Almanac* broadcast possible: associate producers Elizabeth Hoath, Joan Webber, and Sheryl MacKay find the guests and background me on the stories, producers Laura Palmer or Volkmar Richter keep us on track, while technician Clive Bottomley brings it all to life on the air from Studio 31. Our daily broadcast is launched by journalist Susan McNamee, bringing us news from around the province. Contributions from reporters in the Lower Mainland, Victoria, Kelowna, Nelson, Prince George, and Prince Rupert reflect BC back to itself; we also extend our view beyond the Rockies through CBC's renowned national and international coverage. Thanks for putting up with me while I was otherwise occupied stitching together this almanac. My wife Catherine, and sons Ryan and Devon have been patient, too. Finally, thanks to the CBC British Columbia listeners, it's a privilege to be with you each day at 12:08 p.m.

Net proceeds from this book will be directed to BC's Children's Hospital Foundation to fund urgently needed equipment, research, and programs at the hospital.

Send a copy to a friend.

Mark Forsythe
Vancouver, August 2000

Self-portrait at Mile Zero.

P rince George winters often lead to mysterious cases of cabin fever – a state where people have been known to hasten spring's arrival by shoveling snow off their front lawn. I spent most of my twenties in the Spruce Capital and admit to losing my mind more than once.

Although the ice had gone off Bednesti Lake just the previous day, I launched the canoe for a paddle at our log cabin. My centre of balance had shifted slightly from the previous fall, the consequence of one too many helpings of Christmas pudding. Carving a turn, I leaned too far left and next thing water was pouring over the gunwales in icy, slow motion. My brief life didn't quite flash before my eyes, more like, "My God, am I dumb." A thick Cowichan sweater made treading water rather precarious, but I did get an arm around the Chestnut canoe and began kicking and half-crawling toward shore. A neighbour observing all this leaped into his boat and rowed to the rescue; as he towed me into shore all I could muster through blue lips was a sheepish "Th-th-thangs." My wife Cathy stoked our cabin's wood stove, wrapped me in blankets, and poured hot fluids into me, all the while with a look usually reserved for a disobedient puppy. I got the message. These days my vernal excitement revolves around watching rhubarb leaves unfurl in our backyard garden.

Come spring, you can't wipe the smile from Chilliwack gardener Brian Minter's

Spring

BRITISH COLUMBIA VITAL STATISTICS

Coat of Arms
The Union Jack symbolizes BC's colonial origins. The wavy blue and silver bars and the setting sun represent BC's geography, settled between the Pacific Ocean and the Rocky Mountains.

Motto
Translates as "Splendour without dimishment."

face. Once winter's outflow winds have stopped nipping at Minter Gardens, the man is unstoppable. Dig. Plant. Prune. His expert gardening tips are featured throughout our almanac. Spring potatoes have been known to send chef Brad Ovenell-Carter into rapture. As he lifts the barbecue lid on a new season, we include his scrumptious recipe for the perfect steak and grilled potatoes with aïoli.

Our mascot Quoth, the raven, can be heard squawking most seasons, but bird biologist Dick Cannings listens for meadowlarks to confirm spring's arrival in the Okanagan Valley. Travel writer Caryl Dolinko reminds us where British Columbians love to take flight for an early season holiday. Artist and writer Michael Kluckner traded city life for country living, and now observes the season's changes with pitchfork and paintbrush in hand. Maritime historian David Griffiths will again be diving BC waters searching out shipwrecks, treasure, and another story to tell for our "In Search of BC" series.

BC Almanac shakes off winter with a trip to the Columbia Valley where the sun's return is being slowly etched in green. A visit to the Kootenay Trout Hatchery near Cranbrook includes a chance to hold tiny endangered white sturgeon, soon to be released in Idaho's Kootenai River. Part of a recovery partnership with the Kootenai Tribal Hatchery at Bonner's Ferry, these fish will swim back across the border into Kootenay Lake to live out the next 100 years. BC's spring ignites with cherry blossoms, sandhill cranes landing in Telkwa, and the annual Vancouver Children's Festival; a fresh batch of evocative letters also arrive from listeners reveling in the new season, and of their special BC place.

River Reverie

The Bella Coola River is my river. I grew up beside it, on it, and occasionally in it. The upstairs window of my childhood bedroom overlooked the river, only 200 feet away across a hayfield. I observed that river daily and grew to know it as only children know the details of their surroundings.

The Bella Coola was not a majestic river; it was too small for that, and too changeable. In winter it almost went to sleep, sometimes covered by a blanket of ice swept free of snow by a bitter east wind from the Chilcotin plateau.

Spring tides broke the ice, and warming water invited oolichans from the sea to spawn. Bella Coola Indians poled dugout canoes to the riffles and pounded heavy stakes into the river bottom. To the stakes they hung v-shaped nets with open mouths facing upstream. The oolichans, weak swimmers, came in with the tide and then drifted back with it, many of them into the maw of the nets. The activity was accompanied by hordes of hysterical gulls and supervised by eagles perched in the cottonwood trees. After ten days in stink boxes on the river bank, the oolichans were rendered to oolichan grease.

In May, the river changed from clear to opaque as melting glaciers coloured it with rock flour. It flowed dependably all summer, conveying salmon to their home streams to spawn.

In the fall, the Bella Coola River seemed to repent its responsible summer behaviour. After new snow had crept down the mountains, warm rains melted it all in a rush. The river went wild. It tore spruce and cottonwood trees out by the roots. It rolled them over and tipped them end to end and tossed them into log jams. It rolled boulders along its bed, emitting a low rumble. Charged with mud, it smelled like a newly-ploughed field.

Soon the weather turned cold. The river immediately shrank back into its bed, as though ashamed of its undisciplined outburst. Its water was clear and pure. It was a modest river.

Leslie Kopas
Vancouver

Flag
BC's flag was adopted in 1960, and duplicates the design of the coat of arms.

Flower
Pacific dogwood *(Cornus nauttallii)*

Gemstone
jade

Bird
Steller's jay *(Cyanacitta stelleri)*

Tree
Western red cedar
(Thuja plicata donn)

SPRING THAW IN TERRACE

Sarah de Leeuw

Sarah de Leeuw is the BC Almanac community correspondent in Terrace.

Ask a Terrace old-timer about Queensway, and his hardened, cracked fingers will drum on the nearest available surface. His shoulders will roll forward underneath the stained, checkered lumberjack shirt, and a look of concentration will figure upon a face already hazy behind the freshly lit cigarette.

A jumbled story will pour out, one covering various families, fishing trips, the failures of different governments of the day, the airport, and finally, after a long wait, a few sparse details about Her Royal Majesty herself, slowly making her way along the road which now, in name at least, bears tribute to her trip.

Queensway — paved purely for the wheels of Queen Elizabeth's car, to ensure her ride was smooth all those years ago — is now a thin, twisting band of pitted and potted pavement. It winds beside small houses with

Quoth the Raven
BC Almanac *finds an Animal Mascot*

The Vancouver Grizzlies have a basketball-dunking mascot named "Grizz," the Prince George Cougars hockey team unleash "Rowdy Cat" for home games; what's a radio program without a mascot? We issued a challenge to our listeners: what animal best symbolizes the province's character? It must be found everywhere in the province, and be a creature people can relate to. Nominations poured in for the Kermode bear, salmon, even the slimy banana slug. Some of our favourites:

Gillian Ewart rose to the bait so to speak: "My nomination is none other than the spirited, powerful, and highly intelligent salmon. Among the First Nations of BC, the salmon has not only been a source of legend and myth, but it has also been a staple of the diet 'since time immemorial.' When settlers and fur traders arrived in what we now call BC, First Nations shared the plentiful and succulent fish with the newcomers. Through the years, the salmon has provided many BCers an income, a tasty meal, and a sport. The salmon's beauty has inspired people to paint, write, and recreate its spirit in many ways. Give thanks to this amazing creature that connects all British Columbians in some way."

C.M. Sampson of Kyuquot is a gardener with a love for the "second largest slug in the world; that great gastropod, the banana slug. Gardeners who regularly battle the more aggressive non-native species of slug (imported from Europe and Asia), may tend to overlook the contribution of the native slug species in the wild, where they help to break down organic matter, as well as keep other populations of small pests in check."

The wild goose was recommended by an anonymous listener, for three reasons: 1) Shared Leadership. Wild geese fly in a V formation. The amazing thing is that the role of the lead goose is rotated among the flock. The leader has to work harder breaking the air currents setting a course and the others have it a little easier. 2) Support for the fallen. If one of the flock gets sick, hurt, or too tired, some of the flock will stay with the one in need. When they're ready they'll rejoin the flock. 3) Honking from behind. When you see a flock go by it's usually because you hear them first. These noisy geese aren't crticizing their leader, they're just saying 'Hey, good job. Keep it up.'"

Ron Armstrong of Victoria is smitten by the cougar: "The cougar is found throughout BC; that's an important criteria. I have a particular bias towards cats. Lithe. Graceful. One thing I've read is it's efficient – likes to make a quick sharp kill for its dinner and then disappear back into the trees. An animal that is so agile, clever, strong, and obviously likes to spend time recreating – that's British Columbians."

painting by Joanne Beaulieu

And the winner: the trickster raven.

Dan Emerson of Burnaby wrote: "There is no sound in the world like a raven chatting with another in a mist-shrouded west coast forest."

Marion Oak phoned from Kamloops: "The raven is highly intelligent, just like *BC Almanac* [Flattery will get you in our book – Ed.], it's also part of our First Nations' cultural heritage and is often known as the trickster which brings it up to present day – it fits really well with our political system! The raven also has a sense of humour, and best of all, just like *Almanac* it covers all of BC."

Eleven-year-old Laura Marchak of Golden convinced us: "The raven was a special symbol for the natives; to them he is the creator of the world. He is found all around BC and even on the Island. Their call is a symbol of winter, of survival, and adaptation. Also, he is a big, graceful flyer that when caught in the sunlight shines black and blue. He reminds me of wilderness, his cry to some is lonely but in a way warm. To me he is the perfect mascot for British Columbia."

Listeners eagerly pitched in with suggestions for a suitable name: Edgar, Raspy, Nevermore, but the one that soared above the rest was "Quoth" – as in "Quoth the Raven, 'Nevermore.'"

geese outside, a trailer park or two, a boarded up grocery store (busted up Coca-Cola sign and all), the band offices of the Kitsilas Nation, and a Kitsilas carving shed out of which come world-renowned totems, masks, and figures.

All this hugging the banks of the Skeena River. The road seems to cling to cottonwood stands, thin, black-branched veins with a hush of green buds against an early spring sky. Queensway leads up and around, transforming into a tributary of Highway 16, which in turn forms a central artery of the small northwest town of Terrace, following the railway and crossing the Skeena, splitting the community between one side and "the other side of the tracks."

Spring thaw is welcomed in part by the roar of logging trucks making their way to local mills along the highway, clumps of muddy ice falling behind them, exploding on newly dusty streets. The parking lots in front of cinder block buildings and lines of small strip malls come alive with sweepers, getting the sand and gravel of winter anti-slip efforts just about cleaned away.

In the air, spring smells of pollen and moist earth. The sky fills with sounds of Canada geese, rivers rise, and pussy willows peek out. With longer days, people are out biking and mountains glow with white peaks of late snow dustings.

Follow the river and road farther, farther than any member of a royal family has made it, and you will encounter seasonal occurrences like the oolichan runs, tent cities of mushroom pickers, tree planters' trucks parked for early morning coffee breaks, and the seemingly endless line of tourists making their way from the Alaskan ferries.

This life, this awakening with spring, is not one much of British Columbia can visualize.

In recent years, media coverage of the north has been about exodus, with stories of shut-down mills, downturns in the economy, social and economic difficulties. Renewal is a faraway concept. A land of mud-encrusted, rusted-out pickup trucks, a town circled with mountains, avalanches, and green rivers, is something more of tourist guides and summer holiday plans than of reality and daily living.

Terrace residents who hear their geography, events, and stories told on *BC Almanac* feel more real in the eyes of our province — recognized in a small but important way. For each show that covers local events, residents hear their town alongside current and newsworthy items.

And there's a certain sense of majesty in that.

BC and the Birds
Dick Cannings

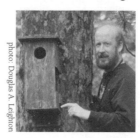

photo: Douglas A. Leighton

Dick Cannings is the resident bird brain at BC Almanac.

I was fortunate to grow up in the Okanagan Valley in a family that encouraged me to wander "across the fence," into the grasslands and ponderosa pines. My brothers and I spent countless hours chasing grasshoppers, throwing speargrass at each other, and occasionally sitting on a patch of prickly pear cactus. Not surprisingly, many of my earliest memories are of birds, of finding a curlew nest in the bunchgrass, scaring up a short-eared owl from a clump of wild rose, and watching tiny Calliope hummingbirds in their spectacular courtship displays. But the sound that ties me to that landscape, as it does to many who grew up on the grasslands of western Canada, is the song of the meadowlark. As soon as the snow had left the ground in early February, the meadowlarks would be there, singing that beautiful song in the first warm mornings of spring, their bright chests as yellow as the buttercups underfoot.

In part because of the meadowlarks, spring is easily my favourite season. I enjoy the other seasons as well of course — the smell of warm sagebrush after a summer rain and the brilliance of scarlet sumac in the fall. I even like a couple of months of crisp winter snow, but am glad that by mid-February the first signs of spring appear in the valley. And for me, the stages of spring are defined by the birds returning from winter homes, each species with a different story to tell. While we think of these as "our" birds coming back, most of them only spend four or five months of the year in Canada, so should perhaps be considered tropical species that dash north to raise their young, enticed by the long Canadian summer days and bumper crops of mosquitoes and other buggy food.

The first to come back are usually the bluebirds and meadowlarks, brightening the brown grasslands after a quick trip up from California. Rufous hummingbirds leave the Sierra Madre in February and reach the British Columbia coast in mid-March, following the salmonberry flowers north. Clouds of wheeling sandpipers arrive in April, having flown all the way from South America and still only half way to their Arctic breeding grounds. The real insect eaters, such as the flycatchers, warblers, and nighthawks, arrive in May. All these birds flying north each spring make British Columbia one of the most diverse areas in North America for nesting bird species, rivalling California and far surpassing subtropical Florida in species richness.

British Columbia is a fabulous place to enjoy the splendours of nature. I have returned to live in the Okanagan Valley, and was awoken today by the first Nashville warbler of the year singing from the creek below my house. We moved here in part so that my children can grow up to appreciate the same sounds and smells that I remember so clearly, but the grasslands are smaller now than when I was a boy, and most of the marshes I mucked around in looking for frogs and turtles are gone entirely. I only hope that we can learn to leave enough habitat for all the plants and animals of our province, so that there will always be mudflats for the sandpipers, forests for the warblers, and bunchgrass for the meadowlarks.

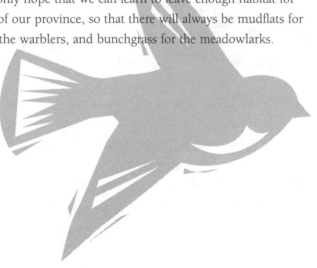

BC BIG TREES

Red Alder (*Alnus rubra*)
Skedans, Louise Island, Haida Gwaii
Massive base, multiple branched crown
Circumference: 7.1 metres
Height: 16.6 metres
Average crown spread: 23.5 metres

Information and image courtesy BC Conservation Data Centre's Big Tree Register: www.elp.gov.bc.ca/rib/wis/cdc.

THE CREW THAT CHASES, CHASES, CHASES

What does it take to stitch together two hours of timely public affairs radio every day? A steady flow of ideas, coffee — and a great crew. I am the on-air presence for a team that's mostly hidden from listeners; Elizabeth Hoath, Joan Webber, and Marcie Gray are behind-the-scenes journalists who thrive on the challenge of a daily deadline. After the 8 am story meeting — chaired by program producer Laura Palmer — the race is on to locate guests for that day's program. It might mean finding a patient stuck in the middle of a doctor's dispute and someone else to provide analysis, a resident living on contaminated soil and the oil company being held responsible, or a forest firefighter sweating it out with an out-of-control blaze. After reaching a potential guest, pick their brains to determine if they really are the right person, then ask them to do it all over again on-air. It takes persistence and pluck to pull it all together. Every day.

Some of the most remote places I have been to in BC have actually been in the Greater Vancouver Regional District. After working for years as a professional archaeologist, remoteness to me refers to the remoteness of time, rather than of place. As a result, I worked on sites that go back 10,000 years at the Glenrose and St Mungo Canneries in Surrey. The St Mungo was excavated at the south end of the Alex Fraser Bridge, and represents three thousand years of salmon fishing in BC. Another remote site I excavated was at the foot of Pitt River Road in Port Coquitlam. Here, between 200 and 800 years ago, occupants of this site used the sandy deposits to construct steaming pits to cook berries called frog berries, or false lily of the valley (Maianthemum dilatatum). First Nations people from the area didn't use these berries, but the Haida did. I suspect I uncovered a real mystery here at the confluence of the Pitt and Fraser Rivers.

Mike Broderick

An Eagle Story

Nine years ago, my family spent a few weeks at our cabin on Hornby Island. We were having some family time together because my older brother, who was twenty-five, was terminally ill with cancer and would pass away in a few weeks. He was desperately trying to catch a salmon. He was, you could say, obsessed. He would get up at dawn and fish well into the night. Unfortunately, he wasn't having any luck and our hearts were sinking along with his.

One afternoon, he noticed an eagle diving into the ocean to catch its dinner. To his amazement, and the eagle's misfortune, the fish plucked from the ocean was too heavy and the bird dropped it near where my brother was standing on the bluff. The salmon was in perfect condition, marked only where the talons had been. Angus brought it home and we were all very grateful to the eagle for our supper. My brother had finally "caught" his salmon!

Fiona Curry
Black Creek

I have been fortunate to become a legal immigrant to Canada. I was the recipient of probably one of the last visas to be sent out during the last few days of the twentieth century, actually holding my visa in my hands on December 29, 1999.

Phew, my head is the right size after all, I thought.

Looking at the criteria one is assessed on when applying for a landed immigrant visa, I can understand the importance of being able to speak one of the official languages.

I can see the need for an assessment of the vocational skills of the applicant to see if they will fit into the work force, and that a certain level of education will mean that they may be more able to find employment.

I can understand the security check to see if the immigrant was a mass murderer in their own land and I can appreciate that a medical examination may show any illnesses that could become problems later.

But what if their head is too small, or too big?

Head measuring is part of the medical examination. Other tests include blood, urine, weight, flexibility, heart rate, eyes, and ears.

I had just had my hair cut very short before my head was measured. Had I known that having the appropriate head size was a factor in having a successful application, I may have waited for my hair to grow back before going for the medical.

But there is no mention in the application literature that points would be added or taken off for head size. Nor does it say what the appropriate head size is.

It occurred to me later that if I had to go to an interview at the Canadian High Commission in London only to be told, "Sorry, Mr Bell. You cannot come to Canada as your head is too large (or too small)." Or would it be a letter: "We regret to inform you that your application has been refused due to your cranial circumference." I wonder how many disappointed applicants have faced this scenario.

In the end my head was apparently the right size, or perhaps the doctor thought my hair would grow back and the immigration officer wouldn't notice. Anyway, here in Rossland we are either skiing (and wearing hats) or mountain biking (and wearing helmets) so all is well.

Anthony Bell
Rossland

ROGERS PASS AVALANCHE
MARCH 5, 1910

Sixty-two trainmen and labourers perished two kilometres west of Rogers Pass, when their engine was hit by an avalanche and hurtled 500 metres into Bear Creek. Over 600 volunteers used pick axes and shovels to dig through ten metres of snow in the search for survivors.

Information courtesy Environment Canada.

17

BRIAN MINTER'S SPRING GARDENING TIPS: MARCH

There's still time for pruning
There is still time to prune fruit trees, shade trees, and ornamentals. Small fruits, some flowering shrubs, and evergreens can be pruned now as well. If the trees are still dormant or just breaking, lime sulphur and dormant oil can still be used at half strength.

Taking care of your lawn
There is still time to burn off the moss. Use a moss-killer chemical, then rake out the dead moss and fertilize with a fast-acting nitrogen for a quick green-up. To keep your lawn green, apply a slow release fertilizer, six to eight weeks later. Wait until the weather warms up and the weeds are actually growing before applying a weed killer.

How Does Your Garden Grow?

"Brian, will you marry me?" That plea was heard during our gardening "Open Line" not so long ago. Green thumb guru Brian Minter was on the air – as he is every second Thursday – and took it all in stride. He chuckled, blushed, then answered another question accompanying it: "What can I plant for some extra fall colour?"

The minute he blows into the studio (usually rushing back from the plant auction), our telephone lines light up. His recall and knowledge continue to amaze. Whether the question relates to battling blight, choosing a shade-loving shrub, or slaying slugs, Brian weighs each carefully and in seconds offers up a crisp solution. The query can come from a novice balcony gardener or a seasoned pro; Brian treats them all with respect, good cheer, and a sense of discovery. And he'll usually toss in the plant's Latin name for good measure!

We've plucked some of his favourite gardening tips for the four seasons of this almanac. Thanks, Brian.

* * *

Over the past sixteen years, I've had the privilege to be a part of the most fun hour on *BC Almanac* – the Gardening Hour. It's a time where we put aside all our daily routines, problems, and concerns to concentrate on what really is important in this world – our gardens!

As we all struggle to grow the best tasting peas, the sweetest-smelling sweetpeas, awsome apples, and "dawlias" the size of dinner plates, we run into little glitches along the way and that's when I get to play "plant doctor."

Folks often compliment me on my apparent vast knowledge of plants and the things that go wrong with them. Well, it's just that I've probably made more mistakes than most people, but I've learned from them. I'm also one of the few "old school" people who have done it all – from growing both greenhouse and nursery plants, floral design, landscaping, retailing, helping to run a show garden, lecturing and writing, to radio and television broadcasting. I was also fortunate to be "plant coached" by many of the wonderful older, well-known gardeners who often took me under their wing.

One of my best sources of information has been the outstanding *BC Almanac* audience who have become friends. I always get faxes, letters, and emails with information about plants, pest solutions, and a whole range of good stuff.

Speaking of *Almanac* listeners, wherever I travel in the province to speak, it's like old home week. The warmth, the friendship, and the sharing of great gardening stories is something quite special. Folks you've never met are instant friends. From landing in the fog on a float plane in the Gulf Islands and taking off in hurricane force winds out of tiny airports, to standing out in -30°C January weather in a sports jacket in the Peace River country, there are many wonderful memories and, hopefully, many more to come.

To keep abreast of the rapidly changing world of gardening, I travel a great deal. Europe has been a great source of so many new plants, as well as incredible ideas from ancient gardens and estates. Attending many lectures and reading and sharing information with the gardening "movers and shakers" around the world is also essential to really comprehend how gardening is changing to meet the needs of people.

In today's fast-paced world of high technology and stress, our gardens have become more important than ever as an escape. They're a place to relax, to fulfill all our senses, and to touch nature. It's a special world, and I'm proud to be a part of it.

MARCH EVENTS

Maillardville Festival Du Bois
(Coquitlam Festival of the Woods)

Mission BC Vocal Jazz Festival

New Westminster Jazz Festival

Saltspring Island Spring Festival

Prince George Dance Festival

Tofino Pacific Rim Whale Festival

The Return of Spring on a Small Farm

Michael Kluckner

Michael Klucker is a writer and artist living in Langley.

In the city, and in much of modern animal husbandry, one season moves seamlessly into the next, illuminated by electric light and enclosed by walls. "Everything comes and goes/marked by lovers and styles of clothes," wrote Joni Mitchell. By contrast, traditional agriculture, for all its hard work and meagre rewards, connects the human animal with the so-called lesser ones that are still plugged in to the rhythms of the planet. On the farm, even the simplest tasks gain greater meaning because they are part of the cosmic cycle. On second thought, I think that's just a rationalization. I'll try restating it: old-fashioned farms have their own rhythm, which is sometimes meaningful and other times is a straitjacket. "Do you live on a hobby farm?" well-meaning people have asked. "No, it's a forced-labour camp," I'm provoked to reply.

The change of the seasons is never more evident than when the earth begins to shift from the tranquility of winter. With the onset of spring the pace quickens. The chickens return to full egg production and, as they contemplate motherhood, become ever more devious at hiding their eggs. The ducks swim about in arabesques before stopping face to face; they bob their heads in courtship, before the drake jumps on top of the hen, forcing her underwater for what seems like an eternity. The geese become remarkably docile and dreamily arrange heaps of straw into nests with their beaks. The sheep stand in the sun with their noses lifted in the air toward the scent of spring. The frogs emerge from their hibernation in the mud and begin to croak. Songbirds nest, and raucous Canada Geese pass through on their way north.

John Heywood's epigram about making hay when the sun shines is true, metaphorically, for this sort of farming life – you have to have the freedom to do the farming work when it needs to be done, rather than when you can find the time

"The Farmer" by Michael Kluckner

to do it, and the patience and flexibility to do other things when the weather is awful or when nobody needs any attention. Every day is a little bit different from the previous one, but generally you only need to find a few minutes here and there for the different groups of animals, the fences, the fields, and the garden. In this scale of farming, there is usually enough time to sit back and smell the roses and, indeed, to earn some of the city money that everyone needs nowadays. After all, you don't have to watch the animals eat. But there is always the temptation to try something new … hmm, everything's working smoothly now, so maybe we should get some new animals. Where could we put a pig? How about llamas? Maybe a couple of dozen bronze turkeys?

Moving to a farm was the right decision for us, because we can no longer imagine living anywhere else. This sort of thing is presumed to be a retirement project – an alternative to the golf course or Winnebago – and perhaps is just that for those people with enough money to get the heavy work done by others, or to buy a place that's all set up. Maybe when we're older we'll feel differently, and we'll sell to someone young who can enjoy the fruits of our folly, as Cato put it. But we're glad we didn't wait. After all, retirement is too important to leave for old age.

Adapted from The Pullet Surprise *and reprinted with permission of Raincoast Books.*

Mount Iago,
Garibaldi Provincial Park
(Othello)

Mount Juliet, Vancouver Island
(Romeo & Juliet)

Mount Lady Macbeth
(Macbeth)

Mount Macbeth,
Garibaldi Provincial Park
(Macbeth)

Mount Macduff
(Macbeth)

Mount Romeo,
Vancouver Island
(Romeo & Juliet)

Ophelia Creek
(Hamlet)

Othello
(Othello)

In 1886, Oikawa Jinsaburo, a middle-aged entrepreneur from Towa-cho, Miyagi Prefecture, heard through the letters of a friend's son that Canadian fishing companies threw away salmon roe. He was so intrigued that he left his family and silk-reeling factory to visit Canada and see if he could set up a business exporting this valuable delicacy to Japan. On arrival in Canada, Oikawa saw many opportunities but determined that there was too much for one man to do alone; he would need fellow villagers to help realize his ambitions. He slowly built up a colony of fellow villagers and like-minded Japanese immigrants on two islands in the Fraser River: Lion and Don Islands (Oikawa-jima and Sato-jima) that he and his partner Sato Souemon had leased. He tried for many years to entice more people to Canada but the barriers of family ties and fear of the unknown were too great.

However, by 1906, years of bad weather and war with Russia had convinced many people that going to Canada was one of the few options left. Oikawa chartered a ship (the Sui-an-maru) and smuggled around eighty villagers out of Japan in the dead of night – the threat of continuation of the war with Russia had prompted the Meiji Government to forbid young men from leaving Japan. After a perilous journey and a secret deal with the Immigration Office and the CPR, these "phantom immigrants" finally arrived in Vancouver.

Part of the deal to admit entry was a year of labour on the CPR, but when this was finished, many returned to the Islands and became part of the colony. At its peak, the islands had several hundred residents who fished, exported roe and salted dog-salmon, brewed sake, milled rice, and took part in many other activities.

Jinsaburo eventually returned to Japan after a tragic accident, and the colonists gradually drifted away from the islands and assimilated into Canadian society or returned to Japan before World War II. As a matter of fact, there are many descendants of those colonists who still live in Canada.

David Sulz
Shawnigan Lake

In 1977, to commemorate the 100th anniversary of Japanese immigrants to Canada, a mountain in the region of Rivers Inlet was named after the first Japanese settler, Manzo Nagano. The mountain, which is nearly 2,000 metres high, is in the Coast Mountain range northwest of Vancouver, and it looks out over Owikeno Lake.

Francois Lake Outpit

*Once a day, or so, I visit the outpit. There's no "house,"
no roof, not even a seat. Just me and my bare bum,
squatting under the sky amongst the trees; two 2x4s
over a hole, and a rope to hang on to for the faint of
heart. It's one of the most peaceful places I know.*

*There's no magazine rack or spot for books, so I'm
forced to look either outwards or inwards. There's no
box hemming me in – I'm open to the world.*

*In summer, the sun gleams on the lake, sending
diamonds winking through the branches. In fall, breezes
surround me with showers of golden leaves. In winter, all
is white, still, and muffled until the lake cracks, gulping
and booming. In spring, birds sing and greens grow.*

*I've watched grouse drumming and dancing on a fallen
log – a perfect stage. I've heard loons wail, swans cronk,
and wolves howl. I've surprised a deer ambling past.*

An outhouse, not an outpit.

*Squirrels come to visit and birds fill the trees – chickadees
and nuthatches in winter; the whole panoply in summer. Our tame fox often stops by to leave
his mark. I saw my first three-toed woodpecker from our pit.*

*Our pipes never freeze. One hole lasts five years. No maintenance or cleaning necessary
(apart from the occasional pail of ashes before guests arrive). Open to the air, there's no smell.*

*Yes, there are challenges. In summer, there are bugs. The meditation changes from quiet
awareness to an active mind-vs-body match. Winter is generally easier – the bum is well-
insulated and not richly endowed with vessels. Being pregnant and constipated at -30ºC,
however, can be difficult, though an excellent practice for labour: squat, relax, push.*

*In days busy with work and a toddler, a trip to the outpit can bring inspiration and aware-
ness, enforced time to think and to be. I'd rather squat there than sit on the poshest of thrones.*

Karen Price

Burns Lake

TOP 10 PLACES IN THE WORLD
Caryl Dolinko

Caryl Dolinko is a travel writer and the author of Globetrotters Guide. *Her website is www.globetrottersguide.com.*

Whenever travel writer Caryl Dolinko steps into our studio she triggers a severe case of wanderlust, and our well-travelled listeners always respond to her advice on budget travel, not to mention her contagious enthusiasm for exploration. Caryl has travelled on her own to over sixty countries and teaches travel courses for women wanting to journey solo. We asked her to select her ten favourite desinations on earth. This is what she said:

"It's not about guided tours, tightly planned itineraries, and five-star hotels. It is about finding your way from the airport to the hotel, changing money, locating affordable restaurants with palatable food, seeing the sights, and protecting your valuables. It's standing in line to buy a bus ticket with your bowels in a knot and then sitting on a cliff (because your bus has stalled

Cultural Identity: Who Am I Now?

My cultural identity is a charming ratatouille, created from the passion of my parents and the geographies that we happened upon. My mother Kirsten, from Denmark, born of Anna Buchert in 1934, and my father Nirmal, from Bengal (India), born of Radha Rani Roy in 1927 or so, met in Manchester, England and there I came to be. Hence my British passport. My technical British identity is not my ethnic connection, but I do feel something. I felt something when I went back to those ugly row houses slated for demolition in the working class district and thought: "I was there." Perhaps because my first breath in this life was British oxygen, I feel something.

Then there's India. You see, I cry when I think of India. I grew up there. India formed me. There I am, sitting on a boat in the Ganges river during the ceremonial return of Durga to her beloved place deep in the waters of Ma Ganga. I am dreaming of eternity as three-year-olds do. My uncle took me to a baby beauty contest, and I won because my skin colour was lighter than the others. This was a premium asset. Sitting high up in a rickshaw, well shielded from the crowded street in Kanpur, I asked my mother whether they believed in Jesus and if they didn't, would they go to hell? The good sisters at the German Catholic St Mary's School for Girls had already explained it all to me, along with the English education they had promised my parents. Bengali was my tongue, the sweet smell of incense as my Takuma (my grandmother) prayed and all the thousands of colours and sounds were mine. The rice and dahl eaten with my hands as I sat on the cement floor, with monkeys in the trees and the hot afternoon sun, will always be mine. It cuts my heart deeply when as an adult I am told that I am not really Indian. Who are you to say what I am?

In Denmark, that sweet little patch of green, where I spent happy years playing in the meadows and backyard pear trees, I was always the darkie. In 1963, the kids at school didn't know I wasn't a nigger. They didn't know what that was, just that the word was an insult to someone who wasn't blond. I knew better. Niggers were negroes, and they lived in

Africa. It hurt, but I learned the language and got tougher. New table manners were acquired, to pass the potatoes, and to not raise your voice. My Mormor's (grandmother's) genteel table settings are with me still today, complete with candles and tablecloths. Standing proudly with my classmates, I sang songs of patriotism and fatherland. My fluent Bengali was eclipsed by fluent Danish. They are both in my heart.

Montreal becomes my new home suddenly when I am ten years old. I now know there are three ways of belonging. Learn to adapt. Quickly, quietly, learn to take care of yourself. What skin shall I wear today? Ah, they speak English here. Like my birth country, like the sisters in the convent, like the Danish people's second language. I know now that it is an art to slide in and out of body languages. People take stock. You speak this way, you eat that way, eat those things, you want to belong. I want to belong. Who am I now? Now I am an allophone, a person whose mother tongue is neither English nor French. I guess I'm

Denman Island

Canadian now. Gypsies make sense to me now, their wailings and longings and refusal to stay. For twenty-five years Montreal is my home, where I become a woman, learn to live in French and speak English with a vengeance. Who am I now? The whole world is mine. Some people think I am an "exotic" teenager. Good grief.

I've never been to Iran, but thirteen years of hearing the soft sounds of Persian and hearing about Iran through the one I love, leaves a mark on me. I identify with this culture. It is now in me as well as all that is English, Danish, Bengali, Hindi, and French. When the radio alludes to their primitive ways, I feel hurt, as if to defend my own. Who are my own? I feel a kinship to all that speaks and eats and dances.

In British Columbia I am again an outsider. From Quebec. Neither here nor there. A happy ratatouille in one more pit stop on the journey of my life. But how I love my children! I am linked to all the world as a mother. We laugh and take our place at the banquet of life.

Anita Roy

out) overlooking a valley of rice paddies, watching the tropical sun set, never feeling more at peace in all your life."

1. Nepal: Trekking in the highest, grandest, and most admired mountains on the world's rooftop is breathtaking even for the most jaded traveller.

2. Fiji: If you imagine tropical islands, with clear, warm, turquoise-coloured waters and swaying palm trees, you have Fiji.

3. Israel: With wandering tribes in the desert, seas that have parted, and pillars that have turned to salt, we are reminded that the cradle of the world's religions is nestled in this tiny, yet passionate Middle Eastern country.

4. Turkey: An incredibly diverse region stretching across continents, with hospitable people, flavourful food, and over 30,000 ancient ruins.

5. Morocco: The high Atlas mountains, the nomadic "blue people," and the prayers that sing from the Mosques hidden in the labyrinth of the market mayhem, remind you that Allah is everywhere in this country.

6. Tanzania: Mt Kilimanjaro overlooks the spectacular scenery of Africa's wildlife in the Serengeti and Ngorogoro Crater, and nearby, the origins of *Homo sapiens* rest soundly in Olduvai Gorge.

7. Bolivia: Being at such a high altitude, Bolivia boasts the highest freshwater lake, Lake Titicaca, the highest ski mountain, and the highest capital city in the world, La Paz.

8. Burma/Myanmar: The land of temples, shrines, and spiritual enlightenment reaches out to all who visit.

9. Guatemala: The sweltering jungle heat that suffocates hidden Mayan ruins, the colourful indigenous clothing, and the festive local music excites the senses.

10. Thailand: Boasting fabulous cuisine, accessible eco-friendly adventures, magnificent temples, and tropical islands (not to mention the great shopping), this country has it all.

In Search of BC
David Griffiths

David Griffiths, diver and maritime history nut, is one of BC Almanac's *"In Search of BC" columnists.*

I was twelve years old when I saw my first shipwreck.

It was the 1891 wreck of the barque *Bay Panama*. Her crew had frozen to death in the rigging, mere yards from shore and safety. As I swam along her crumbling hull and out across her fallen masts I could see those dead men; winter ghosts, haunting the half-light.

I think my life's course was set then and there, bound up with tales of the sea, sunken ships, and lost sailors.

Shipwrecks conjure up everything that is good and great, petty and indifferent, humourous and tragic, in the human experience. From Barkley Sound to the Baltic, from the High Arctic to the Bahama Banks, from the coast of Labrador to Vancouver Island, I've had the chance to reach out, to touch and know the past and the people who lived it.

Since moving to British Columbia in the early 1970s, I've been chasing down the yarns and the rumours, the clues and accounts, of a rich, diverse and totally unique coastal history.

On a rare, almost calm day off the West Coast Trail my pal Rod Palm and I slip down the anchor line of the old *Wreckchecker*. Thirty feet below, laid out on the bright sand bottom, lies the tangled skeleton of the steamer *Valencia*. At this spot, back in the winter of 1906, horror and dread screamed in across a black sea.

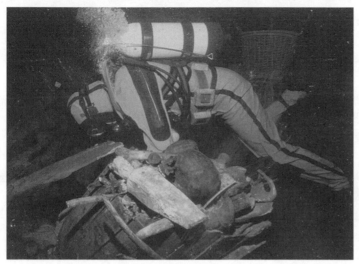

Stranded on the rocks thirty yards from shore, the iron ship was pulled to pieces in a matter of days. Most of her 160 passengers and crew, many of them women and children, perished beneath the cliffs of Vancouver Island. Just before the end, helpless, would-be rescuers on shore heard the women singing that old hymn "Nearer My God To Thee" above the cries of dying children. Then there was only the sound of the sea.

The *Valencia's* bow still stands remarkably intact. The anchor chains snake off across the sand towards the open ocean and the safety she would never see. Rod and I feel the swell increase on the bottom and head back up to the boat. On the surface the wind is picking up, it plays tricks in the caves and gullies along shore, sounds like children crying.

On an unnamed island in Kyuquot Sound, a few steps up from the beach and through the bush a little ways, in the green gloom a dugout war-canoe lies amongst the cedars. Her crew are with her still. Their flesh has been replaced by moss, their eyes are the hollows of unwritten history, their spirits are asleep in the forest, with the sounds of waves to soothe them. Every time I look out on the ocean or slip beneath it I wonder what faces I will see, what voices I will hear, what small adventures await me in British Columbia's emerald sea.

No More Razor Blades

Long gone are the days of lugging cassette tape recorders around town. These days CBC staff use palm-sized mini-disc recorders (at least until another technology muscles them out of the way). Interviews are recorded digitally on mini-disc; back at the station we download interviews into computers, then edit them at our desks. This is a far cry from how we operated just a couple of years ago; editing was done by hand with a grease pencil and razor blade on quarter inch tape. Today, just point and click.

BRIAN MINTER'S SPRING GARDENING TIPS: APRIL

Taking care of your lawn
Wait until late April before you seed a new lawn. There are specially formulated lawn seeds for a variety of purposes. Always use a high phosphorus, non-burning fertilizer when you seed. For overseeding lawns, use something like a perennial rye grass.

Time to plant your roses
New roses can now safely be planted for a sensational showing this year. Remember, new plants need to be pruned back hard, planted in well-drained, organically rich soil. They need a sunny location, too! Keep the bud union just below ground and make sure they are well-watered until the roots take off. Established roses can still be pruned back, top dressed with compost or manures, and fed. As the leaves appear, spray with anti-fungal agents alternately at ten-day intervals to keep mildew and black spots away.

Vancouver, From Behind the Wheel
Tom Sandborn

Tom Sandborn is a writer and driver for TransLink.

My favourite Vancouver place, perversely enough for someone who is a committed anti-car environmentalist, is behind the steering wheel of the mini-bus I drive as part of the city's Handidart special transit service. My passengers are unable to use the city buses or drive themselves for various reasons tied to the ills all flesh is heir to, and we move them around the city to doctor, church, job, and relatives.

The job has twin pleasures. On one hand, my passengers, many of whom are now in their eighties and nineties, provide me with a complex voice-over narration to our travels across the city, braided stories from their own personal journeys and Vancouver's urban past that make each day an adventure in found poetry and oral history. On the other, out the windshield, every day there are moments of heart-stopping beauty and poignancy.

Let me tell you about a typical day last week. I picked up Mr H, a regular passenger, at his doctor's office on Broadway. As we negotiated the lethal mid-day traffic across town to the east end home he's lived in for more than sixty years, he started telling stories, as usual.

"Look over there," he said, gesturing toward the rail yard in the flatlands east of Main. "When I was growing up that was all still water. False Creek ran up to where Knight Street is now. When cars got broken down, nobody took them to the wreckers. They just towed them to the water and pushed them in. By the time those flats were filled in for the railroad, most of the fill was old Cadillacs and Fords. Damn shame to fill in the Creek. A guy I went to school with – his father fished at the foot of Main Street – got paid three cents a salmon, and got rich doing it, they were so thick in the water."

By the time we got to that memory of abundance, and the image of the automobile graveyard beneath the flatland fill, we were at Mr H's stucco cottage. I helped him to the door and got back in the bus, richer with two images that will always stay with me.

Vancouver's Lost Streams & Shoreline

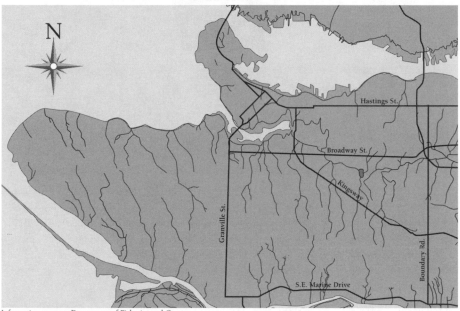

Information courtesy Department of Fisheries and Oceans.

But the day's treasures weren't exhausted yet. On another trip I had to drive north on Knight from 41st Avenue, which meant climbing a ridge line that divides the city and, on cresting it, rediscovering one of my all-time favourite views. From the top, you see the North Shore mountains gleaming, and beneath them the city and the harbour. Postcard-perfect and jewel-like in its radiant beauty, this take on the city is enough to make me forgive its many grimes and squalors. When, later in the day, I caught a glimpse of two randy crows mounting each other on a traffic divider in a celebration of spring and eros, the joys of the day were complete.

Vancouver isn't a perfect city, and my daily pilgrimages across its ragged grid of roads reveal evidence of that – the crack addicts dying on the downtown eastside street corners, the homeless pushing their grocery carts in back alleys, the auto-generated haze that fills the air and clogs all our lungs. With these imperfections come all the challenges of citizenship, the work of democracy, and ecological healing yet undone. Still, that would be true in any city, any job. I'm just glad I get to face the grim bits together with the pleasures of life behind the wheel.

Vegetable garden

The old vegetable garden should just about be ready for compost or manure and a dressing of lime. Remember: no lime in the potato patch. This year, try to make your rows of vegetables wider and your pathways more narrow for greater efficiency. If you raise or burm your seed beds, the soil will be between 8 and 13°F warmer, and you will have better drainage. Add gypsum and bark mulch to your soil if you are having trouble breaking up the clay. Freeze all your seed for forty-eight hours before sowing and keep the leftover seed in your freezer. Plant your seeds in raised burms and seed them shallow – it is cold and wet way down in the mud!

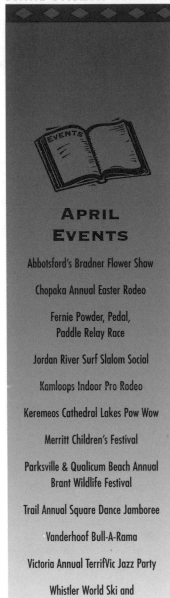

Lost in the Woods

Nine-year-old Dwight Lee took a Father's Day fishing trip he won't soon forget. On the way back from a fishing excursion to Petgill Lake near Murrin Provincial Park, Dwight became separated from his dad and older brother. Dwight curled up under a tree while Squamish RCMP, search and rescue volunteers, and three helicopters scoured the wilderness. The next morning, Dwight followed some green markers along a creek bed, and walked out of the woods that afternoon under his own steam. *BC Almanac* spoke with the young survivor the next morning.

Mark: What's it feel like to spend a night in your own bed?

Dwight: Hmmm. It feels good.

Mark: Take us back to when you were coming back from the lake; what happened?

Dwight: My dad said, "I wonder if we're coming close to this old logging road." And I said, "I'll speed up and check." I sped up, I checked, and I went in the wrong direction. My dad had a sprained ankle, he was kind of slow, and I just couldn't help myself.

Mark: How soon did you realize you were lost?

Dwight: When I yelled back and couldn't hear my dad. It started getting dark, so I saw these two pieces of wood and I went in between them so I couldn't fall down the hill.

Mark: What were you thinking during that night sleeping in the woods?

Dwight: I was thinking about cougars and stuff. I was kind of getting worried.

Mark: Did you see any wildlife at all?

Dwight: No, I just saw some chipmunks.

Mark: They're not too intimidating….

Dwight: No, but they make these beeping sounds.

Mark: What did you eat?

Dwight: On the way up I had a cookie, but at night I kept on searching and I found these strawberry bushes … uh, mulberries, actually.

Mark: How did you stay warm at night?

Dwight: I covered my shirt over my head and put my baseball cap on and rolled up in a ball.

Mark: Were you cold?

Dwight: Not really, my whole body was covered by my shirt and pants and stuff.

Mark: What was the terrain like you had to travel over the next morning?

Dwight: It was really rough, and I got all these scrapes from it.

Mark: How did you know what direction to go to find the road again?

Dwight: When I went down to the creek, I saw a sunny area and I heard a car, and that's why I went in the direction of the creek.

Mark: How worried were you that you might not be able to find your way out?

Dwight: Really worried.

Mark: What kept you going?

Dwight: Well I have a birthday tomorrow and I really wanted to get to that.

Mark: Did you have any idea that people were looking for you?

Dwight: When I went to eat some berries, that's when I saw a helicopter. It was yellow and red. I waved my fishing rod in the air but I don't think they saw me.

Mark: What did you think your parents might be going through as you're out there and everybody's looking for you?

Dwight: They'd probably be very sad. They were.

Mark: Is there a lesson here for other young people?

Dwight: Stay with their parents. I was just ten feet away from my dad and I got lost. Can I thank some people? I'd like to thank all the searchers that helped find me, all the police crews, and all the guys in the helicopter and everything.

Mark: They were sure happy when you came out of the woods, Dwight.

Dwight: Yeah.

Mark: Are you going to go back fishing?

Dwight: I might.

Mark: Did you catch anything?

Dwight: Nope.

Mark: Better luck next time.

BC'S WORST FLOOD OF THE CENTURY
MAY - JUNE, 1948

BC's Fraser River overflowed, drowning ten, inundating 22,200 hectares, destroying 2,300 homes and forcing 16,000 to flee. Row boats were the only means of transportation in much of the Fraser Valley, and for three weeks, Vancouver had no rail connection with the rest of Canada. In 1999, people prepared for the worst, but a slow melt limited flooding.

Information courtesy Environment Canada.

CHAOS IN THE CONTROL ROOM

Elizabeth Hoath

Elizabeth Hoath is Associate Producer with BC Almanac.

My job is to sit on the other side of the studio glass from Mark and make sure everything runs perfectly smoothly. Get guests on the phone line, shuttle others in and out of the studio, pick music, write last-minute scripts. And most days it's perfectly calm. But there are days when it's not. Take for instance the days when the show is about to begin and I still don't have the first script. The theme for the show starts, Mark's promoting a story I haven't even seen yet. Suddenly the researcher comes tearing into the control room with the number. I immediately reach for the phone and start dialing. Mark's talking to the weather office. Great, I have two minutes. The first number doesn't work, I'm getting voice mail. I hit zero for the receptionist. It rings and rings and rings. Meanwhile another line starts to ring, I think

Cariboo Gold

Mother's Day will always mean sunflowers to me. Not the nodding, dinner-plate-sized plants the rest of the world knows as sunflowers, but Cariboo sunflowers. They aren't really sunflowers at all, but a plant with an unpronounceable proper Latin name which has been shortened to balsam root or arrow leaf balsam root. But to those of us who live in the interior of BC's Cariboo region, their technical name doesn't matter; they are known simply as sunflowers and they bloom in May, filling the hillsides with colour.

The flowers are yellow, rather like a large daisy in shape and size, and they never reach the height of true sunflowers. On sunny slopes they seem to spring up overnight, nodding on their thick hollow stems, head bowed in the spring breeze, cradled by many pale green, slightly fuzzy leaves.

It began before we had children, my association of sunflowers with Mother's Day. Sunday drives in May ended with us struggling for footholds on steep roadside embankments as we picked armfulls of the flowers.

Later, when we had children, those trips to find the sunflowers became a tradition. The first springtime picnic, wonderful not only for being the first but for being the only picnic all season that would be mosquito-free, would always be on Mother's Day.

On the way home, we would pull to the side of the road and I would watch nervously as dirt-smudged, hot-dog-stuffed children scrambled up the hillsides and returned, smiling and proud, with armloads of yellow sunflowers. "For you, Mum. We picked them just for you."

For days after Mother's Day, those flowers filled the houses – in jars, bottles, jugs, and on tables, desks, counters. They gave off only a faint scent of dusty vanilla, but after the long winter months they were a heady perfume for the eyes. Spring is here. Rejoice.

Later in the child-raising years, the Mothers' Day picnic became, in itself, my gift from my husband. He would pack the hamper, fill the containers with juice, find and re-outfit the first aid kit, and unearth the rubber boots.

Then he would take the children on a picnic, leaving me with a gift beyond price – a whole day for myself. I remember treasured hours spent luxuriating in a bath, a new book read, an afternoon nap.

When they returned, my husband weary, the children smeared with toasted marshmallow, the dog thick with last summer's burrs, they brought me armloads of yellow sunflowers. "For you, Mum."

The first year that there were no children in our home, I picked my own sunflowers. I set them in nearly every room of the house, but they didn't look the same, not until the phone rang. "Yes," I said. "The sunflowers are blooming. Yes, I miss you, too." Then I cried.

The strange thing about Cariboo sunflowers is that although they cover the hillsides in the early spring, by July there is not a trace of them. Their thick leaves vanish shortly after the blooms themselves are finished, slipping back into the earth as if they had never left it. You can tramp the open fields for hours, and never come across the slightest remnant of the plants.

In the heat of summer or the icy grip of winter, it is hard to believe that the sunflowers ever existed, harder yet to believe that they will return. But they do.

And so do the children.

Ann Walsh

maybe the guest was told to phone in! One phone on each ear, I answer it. "Hello," says the voice on the other end. "I heard something, I think it was on radio two, maybe four or five months ago…" My heart sinks and I have to cut them off, I know I sound frantic possibly rude, but he's wrapping up the weather and there's still no guest! Mark raises his eyebrows slightly, wondering what to do. I shake my head frantically, two phones to my ears and unhelpfully gasp: "Fill." He carries on, calmly asking more questions of the weather office. Meanwhile the receptionist offers a cell number. My hands are shaky as I concentrate on the numbers. Finally, success, the guest answers the cell phone. Wait, the line is cracking up, going in and out of range. Darn cell phones. Another raise of the eyebrows from the studio, he can see I'm talking to somebody. Finally I spit out the studio numbers, the guest promises to call right back, which of course seems to take forever. Meanwhile Mark's talking about what's coming up later on the "Open Line", and then what's on *As It Happens*, and *Ideas*…. Finally the guest is there ready to go. Mark launches into the interview like he meant to fill the past two minutes with idle chatter. Listening, even if you were watching him, you'd never know there was a problem. Meanwhile, it's five minutes into the show and I'm already exhausted.

GRILLED POTATOES WITH AÏOLI

18 small potatoes
2 tbsp olive oil
1 tbsp fresh mint (or basil, sage, dill, or lovage), coarsely chopped

Aïoli:
4 to 8 garlic cloves, mashed
2 egg yolks
1 ¼ cups light olive oil
Salt to taste
Juice of 1 lemon

To make the aïoli, put yolks in a bowl and add the garlic and a big pinch of salt. Whisk until well blended and slightly sticky. Then add the oil, first a few drops at a time until the sauce begins to thicken, and then in a thin, steady stream, whisking constantly. The sauce will become very thick, and this is as it should be: traditionally, good aïoli is almost solid. Add the lemon juice at the end. Serve piled up in a small, attractive bowl.

Spring Grilling
Brad Ovenell-Carter

Brad Ovenell-Carter is a chef and writer who lives on Bowen Island.

Perfect Steak

You've noticed, right, how the steaks you barbecue bear little resemblance to those mouth-watering slices of beef, charred black on the outside and deep-red medium rare on the inside, seen in the ads for grills and steak sauce? It's not your fault, really. While really good grilling is a matter of experience and a little divination, bad grilling is the result of those half-inch-thick steaks and chops offered in jumbo packs in supermarkets.

It's impossible to cook anything decent with them. They are so thin that even a fast cooking leaves them tough and fairly tasteless. Meats are never any better than when cooked in large pieces, then allowed to rest so the juices are reabsorbed, which is what makes a baron of beef such a lordly cut. Luckily, you can follow the same principles for cooking entire joints of meat when preparing smaller ones.

You have, then, set your fire on the patio or deck where everyone can catch the aromas that will soon drive them into a frenzy of anticipation. They are enjoying a Caesar salad or perhaps some good bread and some vegetables, grilled earlier and drizzled with oil, garnished with a few shavings of Parmesan and served at room temperature. The flame burns high and hot. You have at hand a beautiful piece of marbled beef, trimmed with a forgiving blade by your butcher; a monstrous porterhouse no less than three inches thick.

And you have the dressing you prepared by gently warming herbs you tied together – perhaps sprigs of thyme and rosemary – in green olive oil to which is added a couple cloves of garlic crushed to the consistency of cream, salt, and a little pepper, just enough.

The beef, which has been patted very dry and anointed ever so lightly with this dressing is placed over a blue flame to sear briefly. A light and translucent smoke brings you the scent of an ancient fire lit at the very beginnings of cookery…. Move now to a less hot part of the grill to finish cooking at a slower pace, perhaps half an hour.

When it is done, which may be judged by poking the meat and seeing that it feels like the firm flesh between the thumb and forefinger of an outstretched hand, it is brought to table and left to rest a few minutes before you carve it into slices that look, to your guests' astonishment, just like the ads. Serve with a little spoonful of your dressing, not steak sauce, please.

Grilled Potatoes with Aïoli

Several times every day, food offers each of us the promise of brief happiness. As a source of satisfaction, joy, and renewal, few daily rituals have such extraordinary potential as the act of preparing and sharing a good meal. It's one of the best human acts of generosity and love.

The key word, of course, is good – and good cooking is no accident. But neither is it impossibly difficult. Typical dinner party menus, with their many extravagant dishes and parading wines, may elicit applause and ovation, but I could quite happily pass up that hubbub for a bowl of hot, new potatoes cooked in their skins. Dressed with salt, pepper, and butter or – best of all, aïoli, the thick, garlicky mayonnaise of the Provençal farmhouse – potatoes fill the stomach and soul with a satisfaction not too easy to attain.

You could contrive to serve just about anything with aïoli, as the French do in aïoli garni, a Friday dish which besides potatoes includes boiled salt cod, beets, sweet peppers either raw or cooked, carrots, boiled bream or mullet, hard-boiled eggs, sometimes a little octopus, French beans, artichokes, even little snails, and perhaps a salad of chickpeas.

But potatoes are enough provided they and the olive oil, garlic, and eggs are fresh and of the very best quality; free range, corn-fed chickens lay eggs with the rich orange yolks that give the aïoli the required shining golden colour. Grocery stores also occasionally bring in wonderful organic red potatoes that turn bronze when grilled and taste so deliciously sweet and creamy you would think you'd discovered a brand new vegetable.

Served with a plain salad of bitter greens – rocket, escarole, parsley leaves, and red lettuce dressed lightly and simply with olive oil, wine vinegar, salt, and pepper – and a thirst-quenching wine such as a Provence rosé, or Frascati, or Portuguese vinho verde, grilled potatoes and aïoli is an excellent dish for a family or a small dinner party of intimate friends.

To cook the potatoes, wash them, then steam or microwave them in their skins until they are just done. This takes 10 to 15 minutes, but be careful not to overcook them. They should feel soft when pierced with a fork, but not fall apart. Place the potatoes in a bowl and toss them with olive oil. Set over hot coals and grill until their skins are crisp and lightly charred. Return to the same bowl, add the chopped mint, and toss. Turn out onto a platter and serve with the aïoli.

35

TED REYNOLD'S GREATEST MOMENTS IN BC SPORTS

1891: Canada's first alpine ski club was formed in Revelstoke.

1908: The New Westminster Salmon Bellies win the Minto Cup in lacrosse. Thus begins the greatest Canadian team sports legacy as they won every year – except one – for the next 16 years.

1911: The first artificial ice rinks are built in Vancouver and Victoria.

1915: Frank Patrick's Vancouver Millionaires win the Stanley Cup.

1925: Lester Patrick's Victoria Cougars win the Stanely Cup.

1928: BC's greatest sports achievement: Percy Williams wins two Olympic gold medals in the 100 and 200 metre running events in Amsterdam.

1937: Kimberley Dynamiters claim the World Hockey Championship.

1939: Trail Smoke Eaters win the World Hockey Championship.

The Sporting Life
Ted Reynolds

Ted Reynolds is a retired CBC Sports broadcaster and journalist.
He also contributes to BC Almanac's *"In Search of BC" series.*

The "Roaring Twenties" were also known as the "Golden Age" of sport. Babe Ruth, Jack Dempsey, Gene Tunney, Bill Tilden, Fred Perry, and, of course, BC had its Golden Boy, the incomparable Percy Williams.

I began my lifelong love affair with sports in the last years of that decade. From the time I was four until I was nine we lived at Christina Lake. No running water, no electricity, and my sister and I went to a one-room, eight-grade school. My first rink was a patch of ice cleared on the frozen lake right in front of our house and I learned to swim and paddle a canoe by the time I was four.

The love of sport, all sports, came from my father. Remote as we were, we knew what was going on. We subscribed to the *Vancouver Sun*, which arrived a day late, and the *Nelson News*, which came the day it was published. We always had a radio, battery powered, of course. The first radio was a crystal set, with earphones. I remember hearing the Dempsey-Tunney fight.

Foster Hewitt, the voice of the Maple Leafs, was a regular Saturday night visitor, though our team was the Canadians. We followed the exploits of the Kimberley Dynamiters and the Trail Smoke Eaters. When we moved "uptown" to Grand Forks in 1934, we followed the Comets, the intermediate hockey team that played in a three-team league with Greenwood and Dentonio Mine. As midgets, the juveniles, we played in a town league and against Greenwood at times. Vancouver was in a professional hockey league with Spokane, Seattle, and Portland in the thirties.

BC's most famous teams were the Victoria Dominoes (basketball) and the New Westminster Salmonbellies (lacrosse). Rugby was a huge game on the coast and every town with over nine men had a baseball team. Golf was still mostly something played only at the coast, though Kettle Valley and Grand Forks had hard-packed, nine-hole layouts with sand greens.

Those are my youthful memories. It was after the war in 1945 when I started in broadcasting, that my sports reporting and broadcasting days began and professional sports started to take over as the biggest events.

Hockey and baseball were the biggest, but lacrosse, basketball, and rugby all continued to flourish in BC. Sometimes I think the old days were better, and I'm glad I was there.

1945: Ted Reynolds started his broadcasting career at CFJC in Kamloops.

1948: Frenchie D'Amour from Trail wins BC's first McDonald Brier Curling championship.

1954: The British Empire Games in Vancouver features the Miracle Mile. Roger Bannister beats John Landy.

1954: BC Lions play first game in the CFL.

1955: Penticton Vees win the World Hockey Championship.

1964: BC Lions win their first Grey Cup – defeating Hamilton at Toronto's CNE stadium.

1968: BC's second greatest international achievement: Nancy Greene wins a gold (Giant Slalom) and silver (Slalom) in the Olympics at Grenoble, France.

1979: The Vancouver Whitecaps win the North American Soccer League Championship.

1983: BC Place Stadium – the country's first domed stadium – opens.

Finn Slough

Part of what makes a place special to many people is its rarity, and perhaps the thought that it might not be around for very long. Finn Slough is this kind of special place: unique and vulnerable.

Looking west while the tide is in, you can see a small collection of little old cabins, fish boats, and scow houses – the remains of a traditional fishing village – all clustered around the banks near the mouth of the Fraser River. Looking east you see lush grasses and shrubs, water, and the swallows that live here, swooping for insects. You might smell the wild roses, viburnum, crab apples, and saxifrage. You'd see muskrats swimming and kingfishers hunting. And if you were very quiet, you might see the cedar waxwings who are courting, coyly passing salmon berries back and forth.

But there is also a lively human community. You might chat with the people who live here as they cross the footbridge, watch a boat putting up the slough to the net shed, listen to fishermen tuning their boat motors. Finn slough is still a fishing village, as it has been since before 1900, and it combines people and their activities in nature. Those who live at Finn Slough work ordinary jobs and participate in the twenty-first century, but cannot drive their cars to their door. They happily spend part of their lives in another era.

Finn Slough is special and it is threatened. We must protect such anomalous places and spaces. There are alternatives.

Nadeane Trowse

EXTINCT

Three of the five British Columbia species that have become extinct are fish. Each one was confined to a single lake. They include the Dragon Lake Whitefish, which lived in Dragon Lake, near Quesnel, and was eradicated in 1956 when the lake was poisoned to remove unwanted fish before introducing trout for sport fishing, and the Hadley Lake Limnetic Stickleback and the Hadley Lake Benthic Stickleback (a "species pair": two distinct but related species living side-by-side), from Lasqueti Island, which were lost in the early 1990s when non-native catfish, which eat stickleback eggs, were introduced to the waters.

Pentax Army Hunts Grays
Now Makah Indians Are Moving in for the Kill

and in the tropics tremble they
with love
and roll with massive, strong
desire, like gods.
– D.H. Lawrence, "Whales Weep Not"

As you read this, a gray whale is breaching off the BC coast, heading north, midway through a migration of Moby Dick proportions. The grays will leave Arctic waters in the fall to again complete the longest migration of any mammal, off to warm lagoons near Baja California for mating. Obviously a higher intelligence is at work....

For now, hundreds will linger off the west side of Vancouver Island, including one that researchers call Elvis.

In *Gray Whales: Wandering Giants* (Orca), Robert Busch explains, "Elvis has flippers that are shredded (likely by the teeth of killer whales), giving him the appearance of Elvis Presley in one of his tackier fringed Las Vegas outfits."

This migration is awe inspiring, and since it's so close to shore each year thousands of humans form a Pentax army, squeeze into survival suits, and jump aboard Zodiacs to glimpse this ancient creature.

"Part of the attraction is the sheer size of the whales, their almost unique ability to make us feel very small and very humble," says Busch.

"...or perhaps it is something deeper locked within the Freudian mysteries that slosh around inside our heads. Our own bodies are sixty-five percent water, and so it might be that whales symbolize in a very big way our own watery makeup and origins, for eons ago we too sprang from the sea."

On a busy spring day, whales can be surrounded by dozens of boats, sometimes even bumping into the grays. Some people worry the whales are being loved to death, and a Tofino artist recently burned his paintings to protest too many humans and not enough room for the grays to just be.

ENDANGERED

White sturgeon, resident in the Fraser and Columbia watersheds only, are threatened by over-fishing, dam and drainage projects, and declining water quality as human populations increase.

- in the Kootenay drainage, sturgeon have not reproduced since about 1974

- reaching six metres in length, 635 kg in weight, and over 100 years in age, the white sturgeon is the largest freshwater fish in Canada

- the white sturgeon has no scales. It has protective bony plates, or *scutes*, which give it a prehistoric look

- in 1994 commercial and sport harvest of the sturgeon became illegal in British Columbia

Information courtesy BC Ministry of Environment, Lands, and Parks.

BRIAN MINTER'S SPRING GARDENING TIPS: MAY

Cool loving annuals
Rely on cool-loving annuals until the latter part of May: fragrant stocks, snaps, mimulas, marguerites, petunias, lobelias, alyssums, violas, pansies, and dahlias.

Warm loving annuals
Hold off on planting impatiens, New Guinea impatiens, geraniums, begonias, celosia, and zinnias until it really warms up.

Given that man harpooned the gray to extinction in the Atlantic Ocean, and almost achieved similar results in Pacific waters, it is remarkable these whales routinely allow humans to physically touch them in the wild.

My one and only sighting of a gray came totally by surprise with a Tofino-based whale watching operation. The paying customers were eager to search out killer whales spotted nearby, but unsuccessful in actually locating a pod.

Suddenly, while rounding a point into a bay, the guide brought the craft to a dead stop. Then came a snort and blast of air, a misty veil shot skyward and a barnacle encrusted back arced across the surface in slow motion. Our reaction was total silence.

The creature slapped its fluke on the water, and headed for the bottom to sift lunch through baleen filters (grays don't have teeth). We forgot all about the killer whales, and stayed to watch the gray surface with a repeat performance.

* * *

This BC book on whales takes us beyond postcard sentiments to investigate natural history, native mythology, and current management issues.

The grays continue to be the source of many mysteries, not the least of which are grunts, moans, bubble sounds, and clicks thought to be a form of communication that can travel 600 kilometres underwater. They're also master cat-nappers, sleeping for half-hour stretches six or seven times a day. They can be playful, too, sometimes engaging in a cetacean form of shooting hoops. Young whales have been observed pulling kelp bulbs down, then releasing them to watch the bulb shoot to the surface.

The Makah Indians of Washington State began a sustenance hunt on grays in Neah Bay in 1998 – the first since 1928 when grays were commercially harvested to the edge of extinction. Their numbers bounced back and the International Whaling Commission approved a limited hunt by the Makah of four grays each year.

Enraged animal rights activists threatened to disrupt the hunt. The decision was controversial, too; some elders say the cultural and ceremonial justifications for the hunt are inappropriate today. Now Vancouver Island's Nuu-chah-nulth tribe wants to revive a hunt, too.

Perhaps more significant are threats to grays by tons of toxins spewed into the ocean. As a bottom-feeding creature, the gray is among the first in the oceanic food chain to suffer the consequences of pollution.

Gray Whales, illustrated with eighty colour photographs, has well-selected quotes. "I can only hope," says Robert Busch, "that one day we will look back at the nineties and say with pride that that was when humans and animals finally learned how to share the earth."

Currently, whale meat in Japan sells for forty-five dollars per pound.

Originally published in BC Bookworld, Summer 1998.

Vegetable gardening
Mid-season brassicas should be planted now: cauliflower, broccoli, cabbage, and Asian vegetables. Hold off on the late varieties, especially Brussel sprouts. Cool crops can still be planted in succession as each crop finishes: lettuce, radishes, peas, and early corn.

Watch for insects. A variety of organic substances and predator insects, such as nematodes, can be used. Covering your rows with Remay cloth will really help prevent most insect problems.

Moricetown Falls

MAY EVENTS

Campbell River Daiwa Fishing Derby

Chilliwack Dixieland Jazz Festival

Cloverdale Rodeo

Columbia Valley Wings Over
the Rockies Bird Festival

Creston Valley Blossom Festival

Duncan Cowichan Tribes Canoe Races

Falkland Stampede

Golden Wildlife Festival of
Birds and Bears

Hope Seabird Island Indian Festival

Kamloops Air Show

For the first time in thirty years, I sit on the bank of this river. A strange feeling of timelessness passes through me as I look into the same swirls and eddies, see the same sky reflected in the surface. I remember the shock of plunging into the frigid water and the pull of its current. We didn't have any running water that first year we lived alongside the Dean River – we filled buckets at the muddy banks. We carried the water to our house and filled pots, pans, and tubs. Water for heating things, water for cooling things. Water for washing, cooking, drinking, bathing. Water in troughs, basins, rain barrels. We made use of the water several times if we could because when it was gone, when we had thrown it out the back door from the basins, the buckets had to be filled and carried again, filled and carried.

I still think, when I look at the Big Dipper in the night sky, of the dippers we had in the vessels of river water in our kitchen. Dip. A pleasant little sound, like one of the many sounds down at the bank. Lift, then pour, clear and clean into my cup, or onto a facecloth, or over my dirty hands.

Now here I am decades later, dipping into memories as I look into the river that runs through the ranch my family lived on all those years ago. I feel hypnotized, taken back in time. The river seems to be travelling forward, but its motion moves me back and the concept of linear time softens. Though I am here, now, I am also there, then.

I notice many changes. My father dug a well and built a log house right over it. That way we didn't have to melt snow when the river froze, and we could keep our new pipes from freezing, too. But even after we had water running out of taps in the house, I went to the river with buckets to fill, to carry, to pour into other things, to dip, to drink. I would crouch and listen to the river's song, gentle and steady. I craved the feeling of the water on my body, and would jump in, feet first, holding my nose, then come up gasping and tingling from the cold.

In the early winter, before too much snow collected on the surface, we would find our way to a wider part of the river a mile or two upstream. We would lace up our skates and glide for miles on the highway of its solid surface, sometimes seeing a lynx or ermine searching for food along the banks. We would build goal nets for hockey games and play until we were exhausted.

The house my father built is gone; it burned down eight years after we moved away. Barns are gone, new ones erected. The log fences have sunken closer to the ground, shrunken and grey-black with age. Roads have changed; they've been made more direct and wider. There are few trees left, just a thin remnant of the forests in which I ran and hid, the forests I loved and feared.

I am no longer a twelve-year-old leaping into icy currents, satisfied and fascinated with a dipperful of water. There are many changes.

But the mountains and the sky and the river, they are there as ever they were. Thirty years is a sweet little sigh in their tune. I watch the surface swirl and glimmer and hear the water gurgle as it pirouettes along the banks. In the deep green places at the bottom I see the darker, shawdowy shapes of small fish darting between shards of light. They were there then, too, in the river.

Julie Andrés
Bowen Island

Luxton Rodeo

Okanagan Valley Annual
Spring Wine Festival

Prince George Canadian Northern
Children's Festival

Trail Silver City Days

Vancouver International Marathon

Victoria Harbour Festival

Victoria's Manulife Financial
Literary Arts Festival

Victoria Swiftsure Sailing Race

Whistler Summer
Street Entertainment

SALISH CHIEF, SIYAM

In the darkest hour of the night
when no one looked
death, that thief and coward
silently took your breath

drums in the big house
fall silent
red paints, black paints
spirit dancers weep

pink spring blossoms
softly grace the east sun
rising
seeking new life

in the Salish sky
high above
an eagle gently lifts higher
bearing messages to the Creator

above
Seagull
the protector
watches with careful eyes

Chief Joe Mathias

A sacred ceremony was held in March 2000 to honour the sudden passing of Squamish Nation Chief Joe Mathias. The hereditary chief and political leader touched many British Columbians with his dignified and firm approach to resolving long-standing issues between First Peoples and Canada. Ed John, Grand Chief of the First Nations Summit, was a pall bearer at the traditional Coast Salish service; we asked him to describe what Joe Mathias meant to him:

* * *

Chief Joe Mathias made an incredible contribution not only to aboriginal people, but to the people of British Columbia and Canada. It was a contribution that goes straight to the heart of one of the most fundamental struggles of society; the struggle for basic human rights.

As a hereditary chief and elected leader of the Squamish Nation, Joe Mathias dedicated his life to the fight for a just, secure, and prosperous future for his people. To all whose lives he touched, he was a person of great personal strength and awesome vision. Yet he always referred to himself simply as that bow-legged Indian from the other side of the tracks. But the Squamish Nation also had to share his great leadership as the battle for our lands, titles, rights, and governments gained momentum on the national stage. Chief Joe Mathias played a integral role in aboriginal constitutional conferences, the founding of the First Nations Summit and the BC treaty negotiation process. "Always, always, Joe was there and his particular style dominated many of these historic times," spoke Wendy John to the 2,000 people who filled the Squamish Nation Recreation Centre upon his passing. "Side by side with aboriginal leaders across the country, he argued, debated, cajoled, and persuaded," she said. To make things better for our people was never enough for Joe. He would settle for nothing less than a change in our relationship with non-aboriginal Canadians. Recognition, respect, and reconciliation through negotiation were the goals he pursued and the results he demanded.

Chief Mathias, *t ecuxanam siyam* was his Squamish name, led us through many difficult times. He sat across the table from international leaders, prime ministers, premiers, ministers, and leaders from many communities, forging many deep and enduring friendships along the way. But he never wavered from his commitment to honour the dreams, aspirations, and teachings of his ancestors. His deep spirituality was embodied in his strong attachment to the great gift of the language, words, and culture of all those who came before us. Those words, he said, can never be silenced. They echo through the universe for all time. Miles Richardson, a former leader of the Haida Nation and now Chief Commissioner of the BC Treaty Commission, spoke of being with Joe on a crisp, clear December evening in 1993. It was a historic day, the opening of the Treaty Commission office, another important landmark on the long path of achieving modern treaties. "Joe and I stood on the street talking for a long time about the significance of that moment. I know Joe slept really well that night. He knew there were many difficult days ahead but that we needed to celebrate the progress and the steps along the way." Chief Mathias' words, his dreams, and his powerful spirit lives on in all of us. As we look back on his rich life and the many gifts he has given us, we have an opportunity to look forward as well, to the day when his vision of social and economic justice for our people is realized.

bow-legged kid
from the other side of the track
your words soar
dancing, echoing through
the great halls of
time

a million points of light
touch the recesses
of dark corners in the universe
messages true & clear, the living tree

SIYAM, Salish Chief
forest, not a street
brilliant light passing
look the thief, coward in the eye

be in peace
your mortality before us
we hold you up
on wings of song and prayer

Rejoice, SIYAM
with the quiet ones
the Ancestors
on the other side —

Akile ch oh (Edward John)

LIAR, LIAR

British Columbians' keen interest in environmental issues usually sparks an immediate and passionate response from listeners and guests. When activists threatened to boycott BC old-growth lumber products, we invited the two sides to debate the matter on the "Open Line". The discussion began in civil fashion, but the forest industry rep rather quickly became agitated. It wasn't until I glanced at the environmental activist's t-shirt that things became clear: it proclaimed the guest sitting across the table from him was "a liar." Neither mentioned it, but the t-shirt tactic found its mark. It's the only time we've considered bringing in a dress code.

A Love of Boats

I love tugboats. I love the look of them, their structure, their lines. I particularly love wooden boats, especially old ones. So I thought I would like to work on a boat. At the age of twenty-two, I strolled the docks of the False Creek commercial fishing community, eventually finding a suitable wooden troller: a thirty-four-foot boat, with a young skipper that wasn't as emotionally challenging as some of the other skippers I had introduced myself to.

This new job began in the month of March, 1979. By June of the same year, there was a fishing area open in the waters around Campbell River. We had been tied up in Bull Harbour (the northern tip of Vancouver Island) and had a long travel ahead of us. From Queen Charlotte Strait, down to the Strait of Georgia, we made the opening!

"Whale Watching," by Susan Pearson

It was a long run. My skipper had been on the wheel the whole way, so after we had gotten the trolling poles down and all the lines in the water, my skipper took a nap. Alone in the stern of the boat, I proudly worked the gears. Nothing had bitten yet and the waters were calm.

From a passing troller, a voice called out through a megaphone, "Your pigs are under water!" "Pig" is a word used to name a rectangular piece of dense foam board which holds the trolling lines up and out of the way of the boat and propeller. What had happened was I had hooked the ocean floor, better known in the area as Mitlenatch Island. I hadn't been paying attention to the depth sounder. All the gear was caught up in the rocks and had caused the "pigs" to go under. Next, the port side trolling pole began to bend and we listed way over. Then the forty-foot aluminum trolling pole snapped in half and we bobbed back and forth while cables and wires came crashing down and crisscrossed the entire deck! I panicked. My skipper had awakened and came up from down below. With sleepy eyes he viewed the situation, then looked at me and said, "I guess it's time for lunch."

I went on to enjoy an eleven-year career in commercial fishing.

Susan Pearson

GEOGRAPHICAL TRIVIA

Most westerly point in Canada:

Mount St. Elias and Demarcation Point, the south and north (respectively) points of the border between the Yukon and Alaska, which is along the 141° longitude.

BC BIG TREES

Sitka Spruce (*Picea sitchensis*)
Windy Bay, Lyell Island, Haida Gwaii
Healthy, broken top
Circumference: 13.6 metres
Height: 52.9 metres
Average crown spread: 15.5 metres

Information and image courtesy BC Conservation Data Centre's Big Tree Register: www.elp.gov.bc.ca/rib/wis/cdc.

Water from the Clouds

In the Spring of 1909, Sam and Lem Chin – who could speak Carrier and Tsimshian – came up from Bella Coola through Chilcotin territory, and on their way through Barkerville met my great-grandfather Mah Bon Quen. They told Great-Grandfather they were headed for Prince Rupert, on Kaien Island, near the mouth of the Skeena River. At that time, the Grand Trunk Pacific Railway was at the height of construction, and Prince Rupert was a thriving boomtown and a magnet drawing people from all over the world. Great-grandfather, who was working as a labourer at a mining operation, decided to join the brothers on their journey north.

The three men travelled from Barkerville to Quesnel, then walked along the Collins Overland Telegraph trail to Fraser Lake. From there they travelled eastwards, along a series of lakes, and north up the Bulkley River, to the confluence of the Bulkley and Skeena Rivers. At Kitwanga – an ancient Gitksan village just west of Hazelton – they joined a native trading party headed down the Skeena in dugout canoes, loaded with furs, to trade for seafood on the coast.

The Skeena is called "water from clouds" by the Tsimshian people. From Hazelton to the sea, a distance of 180 miles, there is an 800-foot drop in elevation and the Skeena is marked by swift currents, turbulent rapids, canyons, and sharp bends. It is considered one of the most difficult rivers to navigate in North America.

About mid-summer, Great-Grandfather and the Chin brothers arrived at the river's mouth. Prince Rupert harbour had been the site of Tsimshian winter villages for thousands of years. But the town was restricted to Asians and First Nations people. In 1910, Great-Grandfather became the first Chinese merchant to start a business in Prince Rupert. He did so by arguing that trade concessions exacted from China, following the third Opium War, gave Chinese merchants the right to work overseas. In 1911, he paid the $500 head tax three times over to bring his two wives and son from China. Ten of his eleven children are among the very first Chinese born in Canada.

Skeena River near Prince Rupert

Great-Grandfather became a prosperous merchant and grocer. In the early 1900s, Chinoiserie was in vogue and he imported silk clothing, porcelain, carved teak, and other goods from China. In 1921, he and his eldest son started the Sunrise Grocery Store, serving Prince Rupert and small communities in the Pacific northwest. Great-Grandfather also traded with native people in the region; tea, coffee, tobacco, flour, and sugar for abalone, seafood, and potatoes as far away as Haida Gwaii, Hazelton, and into the Bulkley Valley.

According to the Prince Rupert-based historian and writer, Bruce Wishart, in his trading relationships with the Haida, Tsimshian, and Gitksan people, Great-Grandfather essentially became a coastal Tsimshian trader, following trade routes used by Native people for thousands of years. Great-Grandfather and the Chin brothers would also have followed interior native trade routes, along overland trails and navigable waterways, on their way north to Prince Rupert.

In retelling this story, I am deeply indebted to Cedric Mah, the family historian.

Anne Ying Der
Vancouver

49

TEN GREAT BC SCIENTIFIC ACHIEVEMENTS

1. Site-directed mutagenesis. 1993 Nobel Prize winner Michael Smith of Vancouver discovered this process, which allows genetic engineers to create a mutation in a gene exactly where they wish. Before this, mutations were caused by chance by exposing creatures or genes to harsh things like radiation or chemicals. Now we have precise control over the mutation process.

2. Development of computerized weather forecasting systems now used worldwide. Roger Daley, who grew up in West Vancouver, developed the systems in Montreal in the 1970s. Few know that most world forecasts are based on Canadian technology. Daley is currently employed by the US Navy in Monterey, California, working on shipboard forecasting systems.

3. Development of the Ricker curve. Again few realize that this mathematical theory is used worldwide to determine sustainable fisheries catches. William Ricker, of Nanaimo, developed the formula in the 1950s.

In Search of BC Science and Innovation

Barry Shell

Barry Shell is Research Communications Manager at Simon Fraser University's Centre for Systems Science and the author of Great Canadian Scientists. *He's a frequent contributor to* BC Almanac. *His website is www.science.ca.*

As a BC science writer, I always enjoy learning new things and new ideas about how nature works. But to me, the scientists themselves are always at least as interesting as the discoveries they make, and in BC we've got some very exciting ones. It's fun interviewing scientists, engineers, and doctors. While I chat to these people, even over the phone, I have their full attention as they talk about what they love – science. A lot of the people I interview are also great teachers at BC's universities and I always come away amazed by something new I've learned.

The other day I was interviewing a kinesiologist at Simon Fraser University, someone who studies how the body works. She showed me an incredible electric wand that she waved around her head. It could send a magnetic pulse into your brain and make your arm jerk. I didn't want to try it, but she was using it to figure out how nerves control muscles.

The greatest enjoyment in my work has come from moments like that while researching or interviewing a scientist when I find myself saying, "That's amazing!" or, "So that's how it works!"

The thing I like about science is the way you can just add A to B and get C in a predictable way – at least most of the time. In a world so confusing, so unfair at times, and incomprehensible in so many ways, the predictability of science can be a comfort.

Science and technology dominate BC society in many ways. Wherever you live, almost everything you do, eat, wear, hear, or see is brought to you through scientific discoveries. Yet most British Columbians don't know very much about these modern-day wonders that rule their lives. I'm trying to change this.

People sometimes ask me, "Why does it matter? Why should I care about science? What practical value is there to it?" Using science is important, but many scientists I interview do not plan their experiments with a view to making something useful. They experiment mainly to satisfy their innate curiosity about the mysterious workings of Nature. For instance, the great Canadian cosmologist, Werner Israel, who lives in Victoria, once told me the biggest mystery in physics today is gravity – the basic force that keeps us all on Earth. Believe it or not, nobody really knows how or why gravity works. Israel, and others like him at UBC and SFU, have spent entire lifetimes deep in mathematical formulas trying to figure out this mystery. Asking one of these scientists, "What's it good for?" would be like asking a great artist the classic question about their masterpiece, "Will it match the sofa?" In a purely practical sense, great science, like great art, isn't good for anything. But if you consider exploring the limits of human genius and creative expression a good thing, or if you value pushing forth the boundaries of human understanding of the Natural world, then science matters. (And if they ever do figure out gravity, maybe you will be able to "beam" yourself to work instead of getting stuck in rush hour traffic. Who knows?)

At its best, science also teaches you to be critical. It encourages you to question the world around you and to examine everything you know over and over again. Scientists I interview for *BC Almanac* frequently tell me how important it is to question science itself. Perhaps this built-in quality of science – the ongoing questioning and criticizing – is what attracted me as a child and remains with me as an adult. By asking questions, never taking anything for granted, and always reviewing your assumptions, you can improve your knowledge and understanding of yourself, others, and everything around you. To me that is the essence of science.

4. Pagers. The world leader in telephone paging systems is Glenayre of Burnaby. The principal inventor was Glen Fawcett, in the 1980s.

5. Michaelis-Menten equation for enzyme kinetics. Maud Menten, born in Harrison Hot Springs, conceived the process in Germany in the 1930s. Every first-year biology student learns about this famous equation that explains much about the processes of life itself. Few realize that it was a feisty woman from BC who came up with this fundamental of modern biology.

6. Photodynamic drugs. Developed in the 1980s by Vancouver's Julia Levy and her company, QLT Phototherapeutics, a fast growing giant in the Canadian pharmaceutical industry. Their drugs for cancer and blindness are in a class by themselves, and in some cases offer the only cure.

7. Federal Express' mobile electronic terminal. The device carried by FedEx couriers which catapulted FedEx to world dominance was invented in Richmond by Mobile Data International. It was developed around 1980 by Danny Gelbart, now with CREO/Scitex.

8. Top computer games like NHL 2000 from EA Sports in Burnaby. BC's Electronic Arts outsells Sony, Nintendo, and Microsoft in the computer game market. Don Mattrick started the company in the 1980s.

9. ATM telephone switch. Asynchronous Transfer Mode switches are used by all the major world phone companies and were invented at the Pacific Microelectronic Centre on Burnaby Mountain in the 1980s. The principals, including Greg Aasen, have gone on to form PMC-Sierra, BCs biggest company and a world leader in communications chips.

10. Generation II knee brace. Worn by Shaquille O'Neal and Pavel Bure, this is the world's best-selling knee brace. It comes from Richmond's Dean Taylor, who developed it in the 1970s.

Not to mention: Ballard Power and their fuel cell, International Submarine Engineering, PMC-Sierra and the telecom chipset, and MacDonald Dettwiler's MDA-Remote Sensing, satellite mapping system.

Forest Products Rescue Anglers

Float tubing is the slowest mode of transport yet devised by man. The average flyfisher propels his craft at less than 0.5 knots – quite adequate for our favourite lakes. But for those of us on the wrong side of fifty, hull speeds and fin propulsion become very significant.

There you are, in the middle of Fawn Lake, on a bright spring morning. Knowing it would be chilly, you had a hearty breakfast, swilling it down with mugs of steaming coffee. The trout have been co-operative. But deep inside those neoprene waders, you become conscious of a problem. You have been vaguely aware of the problem for about an hour now, but several Rainbows in the sixteen- to twenty-inch range somehow distract you. Now that they have gone quiet, you are suddenly faced with reality – you have to relieve yourself.

Entertaining as our tales of woe may be, we have a problem. And it gets worse as we get older. We need a solution. Mercifully, the forest industry has perfected one. It is the Incontinent Brief. The Incontinent Brief Module, or ICBM, dear anglers, has a proven track record. It is used throughout North America to keep all manner of people comfortable day and night, despite the many disorders that affect bladder control. This remarkable apparel allows fluids to pass through a filter, and then gel in a secret wood product. Even used, they offer comfort, such that patients refuse to have them replaced. The competition among producers is fierce. But as far as I can tell, they have not realized the potential and growing clientele out there on floating tubes.

As a service to anglers everywhere, I field-tested an ICBM. My wife happens to be Canada's foremost authority on this matter, having logged thirteen years fitting and evaluating ICBMs for a leading company. She fitted me with a new module, over which I wore my usual capilene tights and neoprene waders. I had two cups of coffee, downed two glasses of water for good measure, grabbed a home brew for back-up, and headed for

Prospect Lake. The beer was a mistake. However, I can report that, in addition to three nice cutthroat, the four-hour test was a qualified success. Without getting into unnecessary details, here is my conclusion: incontinent briefs can provide protection for tubers, but they should be used only as a last resort. If called into service, they must be used with restraint. This is not a bucket, but a pad of wood fiber that absorbs fluids slowly. Nevertheless, its capacity is surprising. And remember, you have to dispose of the used brief. This could be a problem at the camp or lodge, so be prepared. And don't drink beer out there.

Doug Pollard
Victoria

Wilderness in the City in the Byrne Woods, South Burnaby

Hot Springs Island

I used to walk my dog daily in Byrne Woods in South Burnaby. The entrance to the woods leads off busy SE Marine Drive, where now a new connector road is being built. I worry that this development will destroy a place I love, but so far, just a few steps beyond the madness of bulldozers and tarmac, lies wilderness.

The forest smells are loud and shout of all life's stages. Always, there are the bright green spikes of new shoots forcing their way out from under layers of decaying needles, leaves, and crumbling bark. Fallen logs are rotting back into the earth. They look as if they're growing there or as if the ground is gradually coming up to swallow them. The moss on the bark is always damp and feels both smooth and textured at the same time. Ferns

BC WEATHER EXTREMES

Longest wet spell
33 days
from Apr. 19, 1986
Victoria

29 days
from Jan. 6, 1953
Vancouver

15 days
from May 25, 1980
Kamloops

Most days with fog in 1 year
254
1964
Old Glory Mountain

Compiled by Jamie McDuff and Anne McCarthy, of Victoria's Environment Canada weather office.

photo: courtesy Xá:ytem Longhouse
Interpretive Centre

The Xá:ytem Longhouse Interpretive Centre — also known as the Hatzic Rock site — near Mission, is one of the oldest human occupation sites in North America. It was saved from subdivision development in 1991. This "transformer rock" is sacred to the Sto:lo people, representing three chiefs or Si:yams who were turned to stone by Xá:ls the Creator, for not sharing the written language with people. Linnea Battel, director of the Interpretive Centre, says 11,000 students visit each year to experience Sto:lo culture, history, archaeology, and spirituality dating back more than 9,000 years on this National Historic site.

are everywhere, forming the dense bottom strata of this habitat for an incredible variety of wildlife, from creepy-crawlies under the logs to the twice-a-year visit from the pyliated woodpecker that bashes away at the tops of the oldest trees.

It was a Sunday a few years ago, when we were there as a family, that I first realized in this one verdant and vibrant stretch of woodland each of us had planted our own version of the sort of place it was.

My son Tom was then only eleven, and saw his challenge in the creek that runs through the middle of the ravine. He loved to find a long stick to be his staff and to jump, hopscotch, from rock to rock, searching for hidden caves along the banks where I'm sure he expected to find a wizard or at least some buried treasure. Wet feet never dampened his enthusiasm.

Rosa, my daughter, was just a toddler. Closest to the earth, she stooped to collect all the bits of magical playthings the wind and the rain had left for her. Twigs and cones, catkins and "helicopters" from the trees, all became trinkets to be sorted and stored back at home. She ran along the trail shrieking with delight through a kaleidoscope of falling shadows flickering through the leaves.

Her father Stu walked steadily, pacing his thoughts. He stopped to study the path itself, watched it ahead and behind and talked of the eternal fascination with destiny. The path is symbolic of the place we have left and the way we still have to tread.

As for me, I went back to the ancient forest's first breath: trees as saplings, undergrowth full of the energy of new life. Knowing that plants found a place to grow and have renewed themselves again and again for thousands of years put me in a place which connects with the essence of life itself.

That Sunday, as we walked our different paths through the woods, we noticed that someone before us had built a small sculpture of three stones. I considered the different meanings we each might attach to this cairn.

For Tom, maybe it was a secret sign of the wizard. For Stu it was, perhaps, a marker, suggesting a direction in which to go. For me, it told of rituals performed on moonlit nights deep in forests, of spirits dancing. Rosa toddled toward the answer, took the smallest stone and tossed it into the water!

Pam Galloway
Vancouver

Preserving the Bounty
Barbara Lindstrom

Barbara Lindstrom is a home economist who tells us how to can up BC's goodness.

Home canning is a satisfying pastime for a growing number of British Columbians. Home gardens are brimming with fresh produce and many people are choosing to preserve their harvest. Rows of mason jars filled with brightly coloured food evokes sweet memories of Grandma's kitchen and hold the promise of summertime pleasures to be enjoyed all winter long. However, preserving techniques have changed a bit since Grandma's days in the kitchen and companies like Bernardin have updated their recipes to reflect current home canning recommendations. Mason jar closures have changed from rubber rings and glass lids to two-piece metal "snap" lids. Application techniques for these closures have changed too. Current two-piece "snap" lids are boiled five minutes to soften the sealing compound. Screw bands are applied "fingertip tight" only in order to allow air in the head space to vent during processing. This will ensure a strong vacuum seal so it is not necessary to retighten lids after processing.

Fraser Valley Blueberries, Fort Langley

Processing methods are changing, too. Current home canning recommendations indicate that all jams, jellies, chutneys, and relishes must be sealed with two-piece metal "snap" lids and heat processed in a boiling water bath canner. This will prevent spoilage by micro-organisms and ensure a tight vacuum seal. Sealing jars with paraffin wax or by the open kettle method of canning (without heat processing) is no longer recommended.

ABORIGINAL LANGUAGE FAMILIES

BC is home to more than thirty of Canada's fifty aboriginal languages and represents eight of the eleven distinct language families.

Tlingit

Haida

Tsimshian: Gitxsan, Nisga'a, Smalgyax, Southern Tsimshian

Wakashan: Ditidaht, Haisla, Heiltsuk, Kwakw'ala, Nuu-chah-nulth, Oweekeno

Salish (Coast): Comox, Cowichan, Halq'emeylem, Nuxalk, Semiahmoo, Sishiatl, Songish, Squamish

Salish (Interior): Nle'kepmx, Nsilx, Secwepemc, St'at'imc

Athapaskan: Carrier, Dunne-za, Kaska, Sekani, Slavey, Tahltan, Tsilhqot'in, Wet'suwe'ten

Ktunaxa

Algonquin: Cree

CHINOOK JARGON

Virtually a lost British Columbian language, what remains of Chinook is mostly confined to maps and colloquialisms. Chinook began as a trade language between Europeans and First Nations, borrowing from English, French, and Aboriginal languages. It thrived as part of everyday life — as many as a quarter million people spoke it a hundred years ago. The story of Chinook is told in *A Voice Great Within Us* by the late historian and writer Charles Lillard with editor Terry Glavin. Here are examples of Chinook, some of which will have a familiar ring.

bit - shilling; dime

Boston - American

canim - canoe

Chinook Cove - fish in the cove

chuck - water

cultus - worthless

glease - grease

hyack - quick; fast; hurry

iskum - to receive; take

kalakala - bird

klootchman - female; woman

kwahtah - quarter

lapome - apple

lope - rope

moosmoos - cattle; buffalo

Tips for jams and jellies

- Measure ingredients carefully.
- Do not add extra fruit or reduce sugar indicated as jam may not set properly.
- When jams are made with added fruit pectin, use fully ripe fruit. For recipes without added fruit pectin, use ¼ slightly under-ripe fruit and ¾ fully ripe fruit.
- Use a large, deep stainless steel saucepan to allow space for a full rolling boil (cannot be stirred down), and a long-handled wooden spoon.

Sterilizing jars

- Sterilize mason jars when foods have less than ten minutes processing time.
- Heat jars in a boiling water bath canner and boil for ten minutes.
- Do not sterilize in the oven or by pouring boiling water over the jars as both methods will cause the mason jars to break.
- Do not sterilize using the dishwasher as heating cycles vary and may not be sufficient for proper sterilization.

Spring Preserves
Strawberry Rhubarb Jam

½ cup fresh mint leaves & small stems, packed

¾ cup water

1¾ cups rhubarb, finely chopped

2 cups strawberries, crushed

1 tbsp lemon juice

7 cups sugar

1 pouch (85 ml) liquid pectin

In a large, deep, stainless steel saucepan, bring mint and water to a boil. Cover and let steep for 10 minutes. Discard mint leaves, reserving mint water. Add rhubarb to the mint water. Return mixture to a boil and simmer gently until rhubarb softens, about 2 minutes. Add strawberries, lemon juice, and sugar. Over high heat, bring fruit mixture to a full rolling boil and boil hard for 1 minute. Remove from heat. Immediately stir in liquid pectin, mixing well. Continue to stir 3 minutes to prevent floating fruit. Skim foam. Ladle jam into hot sterilized 250 ml mason jars, leaving ¼ inch (0.5 cm) head space. Wipe jar rims clean. Centre prepared canning lid and apply screw bands fingertip tight. Process filled jars in a boiling water bath canner for 5 minutes. Cool. Sealed lids curve downwards. Store in a cool, dry, dark place. Makes 7 250 ml jars.

Recipe courtesy Fraser Valley Strawberry Growers Association.

Spring Preserves
Cherry Raspberry Jam

3 cups cherries, pitted and chopped
2 cups raspberries, crushed
1 pkg (57 g) fruit pectin crystals
6 cups sugar

In a large, stainless steel saucepan, combine cherries, raspberries, and fruit pectin crystals. Stirring frequently, bring mixture to a boil over high heat. Add sugar. Stirring constantly, return mixture to a full rolling boil then boil hard for 1 minute. Remove jam from heat and skim foam. Ladle jam into hot sterilized 250 ml mason jars, leaving ¼ inch (0.5 cm) head space. Wipe jar rims clean. Centre prepared canning lids and apply screw bands fingertip tight. Process filled jars in a boiling water bath canner for 5 minutes. Cool. Sealed lids curve downwards. Store in cool, dry, dark place.

Recipe courtesy Kelowna Orchard Museum.

Pasaiooks - French; Frenchman

potlatch - to give

pusspuss - cat

shantie - to sing

skookumchuck - fast, dangerous waters

siwash - indian (from the French *sauvage* and considered to be derogatory)

tictic - a clock; a watch

tillicum - people; friends; relatives

tyee - chief

Wagh Creek - pour out, vomit

Other words from Salishan languages we use every day:
coho
sasquatch
sockeye

Thanks to Terry Glavin and linguist Bill Poser in Prince George. Information from A Great Voice Within Us: The Story of Chinook (New Star), by Charles Lillard with Terry Glavin.

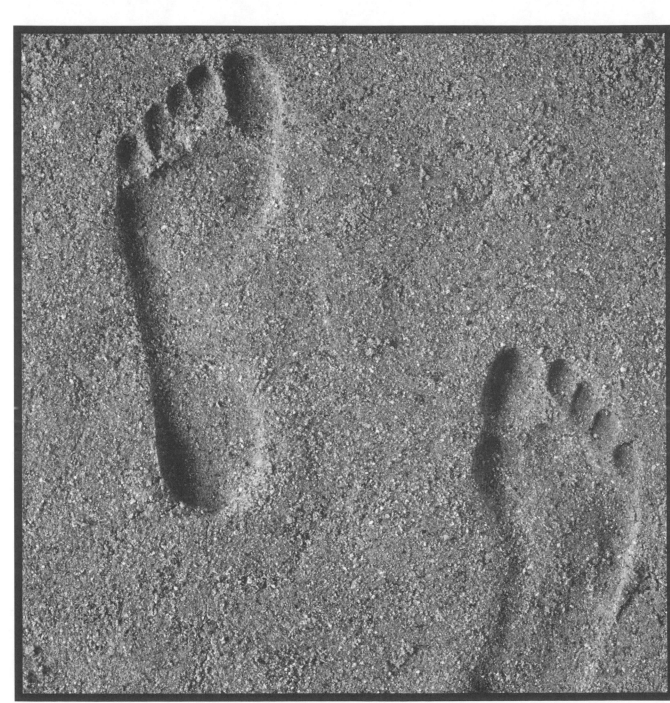

Galiano Island. Summer 1967. The tide, beginning its retreat to the other side of the world, has turned. Water slurps past barnacle-encrusted rocks and hisses through sand and seaweed. Purple starfish cling to rocks like bizarre hood ornaments and salty air mingles with a hint of sun-baked kelp. Tiny crabs scurry for cover in one of the hundreds of tidal pools. I'm twelve years old, experiencing the ocean for the first time. I'm hooked.

I had boarded a westbound passenger train two weeks earlier in Toronto with my mother, brother, and grandparents to attend an uncle's wedding in Vancouver. My idea of British Columbia was pretty much limited to stereotypes of lumberjacks and what I'd gleaned from a multicoloured wall map of Canada. Shaded wrinkles hinted at mountains, the veins flowing from them were rivers, and the blue Pacific appeared to go on forever. Little did I know how much forest, rock, and prairie occupied the middle.

St. Mary's Lake, Saltspring

Our train jerked and squealed to a stop near Mount Robson; the conductor said although it was summer, all that snow and ice near the summit was 500 feet deep. I wasn't sure if I should believe him or not – this was the same man who solemnly pronounced that CNR rules didn't permit gambling, even if it was for pennies with my grandfather (a glint in his eye gave him away). In the Fraser Canyon we heard that salmon propelled themselves through the churning rapids to later spawn hundreds of miles up river. Everything about the place seemed grand and glorious – even the maple leaves made their Ontario cousins look puny. A week later on that Galiano shoreline, my heart was swept out on the summer tide. I knew I'd be back.

There are countless stories like this from others who've landed here from another

Summer

WE ALL LIKE TO TALK ABOUT THE WEATHER

If you're in Bella Coola, there's no one that knows more about it than Joyce Mikkelson.

In April of 2000, she marked forty years of taking weather readings. Here's what she told us on the day that Enviroment Canada visited her backyard weather station to recognize her service.

"The original weather station was just along the road. A lady there had been doing it since 1939, and someone in her family had probably been doing it before that. And they were going to be away for the winter and asked me if I would take over. So her son came over, brought the equipment, dug it in, and I've been doing it ever since and enjoyed it thoroughly. The weather is always fascinating, isn't it? It's always interesting. And it's very simple to do.

province or country. Skip Rowland sailed the world and finally fixed a line to Ucluelet where he operates a B&B with his wife. Angela MacKenzie was an "immigrant twice over to Vancouver" – first from Korea, then from Toronto. Of course there are the BC born and bred who you might think take all this splendour for granted. Think again. Eric Mogensen calls Burnaby Mountain "a green oasis in the middle of a bleak suburban web," where he and his young son "explore the trails, watch the coyotes, and play in the rainwater."

British Columbians are noted for tackling summer with gusto – out come the kayaks and canoes, up go the sails and tents; paragliders soar from Grouse Mountain, river rafters leap Thompson River rapids, and rock climbers scale Stawamus Chief. Outdoors enthusiasts Jack Christie and Jayne Seagrave pinpoint invigorating hikes and prime camping spots, astronomer David Dodge looks with awe to summer night skies. A siting of the mythical Ogopogo can't be far behind. Summer isn't complete until chef David Veljacic tosses a BC salmon on the grill and our listeners offer up some favourite micro-brewed beers for lawn chair sipping. Ah, sweet summer. Grab it before it's gone.

Burnaby Mountain

In a land dominated by mountains, Burnaby Mountain barely rates mention. Its steep northern slope rises just 300 metres above Burrard Inlet, summits with Simon Fraser University, and then transitions to its lazy southern expanse, marked by streams that drain into Burnaby Lake. That most natural aspects of the Mountain have remained intact is an anomaly in our apparent desire to clearcut the suburbs. Sure, there are townhouses and an oil tank farm hidden in the trees to the south, and a four-lane highway bisects the forest, and there are plans to add another 10,000 people to the crown of the mountain. But in spite of all this, it's still a place of quiet, natural beauty, a green oasis in the middle of a bleak suburban web.

Growing up in West Coquitlam, the glowing red aircraft marker lights on the mountain-top water tower served as distant sentinels over my earliest memories. The obscuring cloud canopy of autumn and winter would rise and fall, and the impossibly clear, pink twilight of summer nights would last past bedtime, but the mountain's beacons were a constant. In later years, the bumpy concrete of Gagliardi Way would become the location of choice for testing the top speed of ten-speed bikes. Later still, the parking lot at Centennial Park would serve as the perfect spot to sit in a leaky sports car on wet November mornings, smoking cigarettes and killing time during a spare period in grade eleven. On a hot summer night in July of that same year it would serve as the top-down site of a clumsy experience with too much gin and a far more experienced girl.

The slopes of Centennial Park fall away to forest on the west side, but before the eyes reach its dark green boundary, they can't help but drink in the view of the Lions Gate Bridge, downtown, Stanley Park, and the outer harbour. Burnaby, Richmond, and Delta spread out flat to the south and slip into Boundary Bay. The Gulf Islands and Vancouver Island lurk on the horizon like a pod of killer whales. At night the view pulses with a million streetlights, punctuated by Morse code patterns of car headlights that seem so far away. So very far away.

Six years ago, my wife and I made the Mountain our home, in a townhouse on the southern flank. Today, my young son and I often explore the trails, watch the coyotes, and play in the rainwater descending gullies on its way to the Fraser River and the sea.

We will climb to the top of the mountain and eat our lunch in the shadow of the water tower and call home on the cell phone to tell Mum we made it safely. We will walk to a clearing in the trees that affords a view of Coquitlam and look down, over recognizable landmarks and streets. Through his six-year-old eyes the world spreads out at his feet, vast and full of things not yet learned; excitement and potential. I will turn to look at the water tower, then return to scanning the leafy fringes of the old neighbourhood and reflect on all those places I have been to reach this moment.

Eric Mogensen
Burnaby

All I do is go out twice a day and it just takes me a couple of minutes and I send down the report to Victoria at the end of the month, it doesn't take very long and I would miss it now if I didn't do it.

"I started out in 1959 getting twenty-five dollars every three months. Or was it fifteen? About five dollars a month. But then there were cutbacks a while ago and they phoned me and said they were sorry but they were going to have to discontinue, they didn't have the funding. But they asked if I would like to do it on a volunteer basis? And I said certainly, it's no problem! So, now I do it on a volunteer basis, they just send me the equipment, that's all."

BARBECUING DOS AND DON'TS

DO

Always clean your barbecue after using.

At the beginning of each barbecue season, prepare your barbecue by servicing all gas connections, and having your propane tank checked at your local refill station.

Always shut off the source of gas to your barbecue before turning off the temperature dials. This will empty the lines of any gases.

For kabobs, use two skewers parallel to each other and about one-quarter to one-half inch apart to stop vegetables, fruits, and some meats from spinning.

Season meats at least half an hour before you barbecue.

Just like your oven, always preheat your barbecue before cooking.

Always barbecue with the lid closed.

Coat the grid with a non-stick spray before you begin to cook.

Where There's Smoke There's Barbecue

About ten years ago, *Afternoon Show* host Patrick Munro dragged a gas barbecue onto the CBC Plaza. Once a week he'd invite different guests to pull on an apron and show their stuff. (Once when I was filling in for Patrick the guest put rattlesnake on the grill, and yes, it did taste like chicken – sort of.) One listener known as "Vinny the Manifold Chef" actually cooked a salmon while driving his car from the Tsawwassen ferry terminal to downtown Vancouver. After wrapping the fish in tin foil, he strapped it to a platter hugged up against the muffler. Under the hood he cooked mushroom caps in garlic butter!

photo: Stephen Mitchell

Patrick inspired *BC Almanac* to also grab the tongs; among the cooks we love to have back is the Fire Chef David Veljacic. A captain with the Vancouver Fire Department, David tested recipes on fire hall crews, family, and friends for thirty years. He's also a competitor on the barbecue and chili circuit; serious business for cook-off devotees around North America. From grilled halibut to barbecue pork shoulder, his prowess is legendary. Whenever he appears on *BC Almanac*, the phone lines light up as backyard enthusiasts quiz him for advice.

Here's the Fire Chef's recipe for Peppered Sweet and Sour BC salmon (he's a fan of wild salmon and never uses tin foil. David argues flavour is always best when grilled over open flame.)

Peppered Sweet & Sour Salmon

For most salmon recipes I use either coho or spring salmon. They have more oil than most breeds, and have a solid flesh.

1 cup demerara brown sugar
½ cup pickling salt
2 cups water
1 2 lb salmon fillet, deboned
½ cup black pepper, cracked
¼ cup demerara brown sugar
2 tbsp butter, melted
2 large limes

Combine the 1 cup of sugar, pickling spice, and water in a saucepan. Bring to a boil, then simmer and stir until the sugar is dissolved. Remove from the heat and allow to cool to at least room temperature. Place the fillet, skin side down, in a glass dish that is just large enough for the fillet. Pour the sugar mixture over top, cover with food wrap, and refrigerate for twenty-four hours. During this time, if the fillet is not covered with the brine, spoon some over the fish several times. Remove the fish and rinse well under cold water. Pat dry with paper towel and set aside. In a glass bowl, combine the black pepper, the ¼ cup of brown sugar, butter, and the juice of the two limes, and make a paste. Pat the paste over top of the entire fillet. Place the fillet on the grill, on the unfired side. Close the lid and barbecue at about 200°F for about half an hour, when the sugar is beginning to melt. Turn the flame on directly under the fillet and grill for another eight minutes to crisp the skin. Slip two spatulas between the skin and the flesh and gently remove the fillet to a serving platter. You then have a boneless, skinless fillet of salmon to enjoy. Makes 4 servings.

More recipes can be found in David Veljacic's The Fire Chef.

DON'T

Never thaw meats, poultry, or seafood in the microwave.

Chicken and turkey should be thawed in your refrigerator.

Never line the bottom of the grill with aluminum foil. It can hinder proper air flow and doesn't reflect heat.

Keep small children away from the barbecue. The outside is always hot, and stays hot for some time after using.

Never light the barbecue with the lid partially closed. It should be open fully.

Big Bar Lake Park and the surrounding country provide a beautiful setting for a summer holiday.

The park comprises approximately 330 hectares of rolling landscape situated on the shore of a large lake, and scattered with small lakes and ponds. It is couched in Cariboo ranching country on the southern edge of the Fraser Plateau, which stretches north beyond Lac La Hache, and was formed from lava flows some five to ten million years ago. The park was established in 1969, and is a very popular destination for family camping vacations. It features twenty-five new lakeside campsites in addition to a large day-use area offering beachside picnic sites.

The park's setting is typical of the southern Cariboo. Set against a mountainous backdrop, the lake is surrounded by lodgepole pine

photo: Jeff Juthans

Finny

Mount Finlayson has been the proverbial rock for my large and extended family for the past thirty years. Father first introduced us to the after-church Sunday hike when I was twelve. He, mom, and their nine kids set out on what he promised would be a "cake walk." My eldest brother helped me over some sections, while I would do the same with my less surefooted siblings who were as young as five. My mother made her way slowly, enjoying the cool shade of the pines, all the while encouraging her brood. Father set the pace, allowing for rests after difficult sections were conquered. Our eyes looked up to the next outcrop, assured that when reaching the top of that section, we would be at the top. Of course, we were wrong.

"Finny" has stood as a silent witness to many of our individual rites of passage. In our teen years the climb became the acid test for a future partner. When my brothers needed a new fitness challenge they started running up the 1365 foot mountain.

Finny has lent its support to us. It was the site of at least one first kiss, an engagement, and is the final resting place for my infant niece. We initiate our newborns to the hike at a tender age, often stopping at the mountain on the way home from the hospital.

Mount Finlayson sets us free and allows us to return to our lives refreshed, renewed, and content.

Maria Lyne
Prince George

Jayne Seagrave's
Best Camping Spots

Jayne Seagrave's books include British Columbia's Best Camping Adventures: Southwestern BC and Vancouver Island; British Columbia's Best Camping Adventures: Northern, Central and Southeastern BC; Provincial and National Park Campgrounds in British Columbia: A Complete Guide *(Third Edition coming early 2001).*

Jayne Seagrave caught the camping bug early. She pitched her first tent beneath her grandmother's dining room table at age five. Most weekends you'll find her exploring a new BC park with her family, and possibly writing another book. Jane's published three so far covering everything from BC's best beach campgrounds to best campgrounds to hike or kiss. She's appeared on our "Open Line" a number of times, and listeners always rise to the challenge of adding another gem to the list. We asked for Jayne's Top Ten List – a formidable task for someone who's slept under the stars in every corner of the province.

1. Liard River Hotsprings: The most northerly of BC's provincial parks on the Alaska Highway has the most amazing hot springs consisting of two pools which campers walk to along a beautiful boardwalk. These pools can be accessed twenty hours a day. One pool is circular and can be swam in, the other has a number of benches positioned in the water where it's great to sit and chat to fellow campers and travellers. And, the vegetation is stunning.

and spruce. Visitors to Big Bar Lake Park often see wildlife on the four kilometre hiking trail surrounding the scenic wetlands, and enjoy angling for rainbow trout in the three-mile-long lake. The area is an extremely popular fishing destination, and is also widely used by other recreationists. Area attractions include several guest ranches, the towering Marble Range south of the park, and Gang Ranch country. Visitors can also travel along the Jesmond Loop, by continuing past Big Bar Lake Provincial Park, and eventually connecting with Highway 97 by way of the Jesmond and Kelly Lake Roads. This scenic drive passes by Little Big Bar Lake and the historic townsite of Jesmond, where the OK Corral – one of the oldest ranches in the area – is situated. The loop also accesses the Jesmond fire lookout by way of a narrow four-wheel drive road, from which visitors can enjoy panoramic views of the surrounding landscape, including Marble Range and Edge Hills Provincial Parks. Another option is to continue westward on Big Bar Road to the reaction ferry across the Fraser River.

Big Bar Lake Park is located approximately forty-two kilometres northwest of Clinton.

Information courtesy Kate Alexander, BC Parks.

OPEN LINE: BC'S PARTY LINE

Whether it's two-tiered health care, the ethics of genetic engineering or a favourite summer read, listeners are rarely at a loss for words. Opinions erupt left, right, and centre. The daily "Open Line" is something like the old telephone party line, except you don't feel guilty about listening in. Voices from rural Metchosin speak directly to downtown Vancouver or upcountry Fort Nelson. You never quite know who's on the other end of the line either. Valerie McLean of the Better Business Bureau was answering listener questions about unscrupulous home renovators when her son phoned to say hello. Party line indeed. Topics sure to jam the lines include: privatizing health care, forest practices and land use, gardening, native land claims, gun control, pets, fish farming, access to health services, politics, whale hunting, gay rights, alternative medicines, transit issues, and hockey violence. There really aren't enough days in the week.

2. Mount Robson: The largest provincial park in the Rockies has three campgrounds and excellent access to hiking routes. Mount Robson itself is the highest peak in the Rockies and there are many fantastic walks ranging from day hikes (the best being the valley of the thousand waterfalls) to week-long excursions. The park is quite developed with a shop and restaurant and over 150 camping spots. Breathtaking scenery.

Mount Robson

3. Kokanee Creek: My favourite town in BC is Nelson, and this idylic campground is just a brief twenty minute drive from this settlement which is one of the oldest in the province. Not only are the camping places here superb, with easy access to swimming, fishing, walking, wildlife viewing, and sunbathing activities within the park itself, Ainsworth Hot Springs and the lovely community of Kaslo are just up the road. There are myriad things to do if you decide to pitch your tent or RV here. An ideal family campground.

4. Newcastle Island: This provincial park cannot be accessed by car, but is just a stone's throw from Nanaimo on Vancouver Island. There are only about twenty designated camping spots, but large grassy fields provide ample space for the

overflow. You reach the island by a small ferry and once there can hike the numerous trails, swim, beachcomb, mountain bike, picnic, and watch the deer. The island is rich in history and BC Parks have done a great job detailing this. In the summer, a concession stand operates and even serves dinner with wine on its veranda in the evening. A delightful alternative camping spot.

5. Gordon Bay: This campground has a superb beach and is close to the town of Lake Cowichan on Vancouver Island. It is a great family campground and boasts some of the hottest temperatures in BC, so it's the place for families to hang out in the summer if all you need is sun, sand, and swimming. The fishing and boating is also very good. Its proximity to civilization is also an added bonus in case you've forgotten anything.

Saltspring Island

6. Montague Harbour: This campground is on my favourite Gulf Island, Galiano. I adore this campground as it is adjacent to the harbour and throughout the summer the local Hummingbird Pub operates a free shuttle service to and from the harbour. I have very pleasant, although a little hazy, memories of my first stay here.... It is a relatively small, forty-space campground with a number of

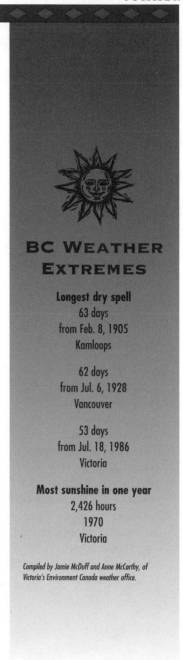

BC WEATHER EXTREMES

Longest dry spell
63 days
from Feb. 8, 1905
Kamloops

62 days
from Jul. 6, 1928
Vancouver

53 days
from Jul. 18, 1986
Victoria

Most sunshine in one year
2,426 hours
1970
Victoria

Compiled by Jamie McDuff and Anne McCarthy, of Victoria's Environment Canada weather office.

BRIAN MINTER'S SUMMER GARDENING TIPS: JUNE

Rhododendron care

Now that the blossoms have finished on most varieties, you should pinch back the blossom stems and at the same time pinch out lanky growth. The winter frost has played havoc with many plants and created some foliage damage. Mulch your rhododendrons with bark mulch or peat moss to preserve the moisture and prevent stress in hot weather. Feed them and if they are under the eaves of your home, make sure they have adequate moisture. They can also be pruned back now.

spaces being walk-ins. There is a calm sandy beach and easy walking trails. Kayaks can be rented from the harbour as can bicycles. Galiano itself is a wonderful place to cycle around.

7. Birkenhead Lake: A four-hour drive north of Vancouver, this campground is positioned on a remote glacier-fed lake, surrounded by snow-capped mountains. I like travelling to this campground (on the wonderful Sea to Sky Highway which I never tire of) and love the camping spaces, which are large and secluded; a number have a small stream running through them. There are a couple of hiking trails and you can rent canoes here, but its real beauty is that it provides an ideal weekend retreat from the city.

8. Premier Lake: I regard this provincial park as very adult-oriented as it seems to be patronized primarily by those in their golden years. Situated in the Rocky Mountains forty-five kilometres from Kimberley, it contains six lakes, a number of hiking trails, a boat launch, a fish hatchery, and numerous wildlife viewing opportunities. It also has solar-heated showers. This is not a well-known park, but it is a real hidden gem.

9. Naikoon: Situated on the Queen Charlotte Islands, this large provincial park has miles of wonderful coastline, but unfortunately a high annual rainfall, so even if you plan to visit in August go prepared. There are over 100 kilometres of beaches to wander, boat wrecks to explore, and wonderful walks through rainforests to experience. Two campgrounds, one on the beach and one more sheltered inland, are available. Even at the height of summer few visitors access this wonderland, so if you want to get away from it all, this is the place.

10. Wells Gray: Known as the waterfall park – and the fourth largest in the province – this provincial park is great for those who love hiking, fishing, canoeing, and boating. However, it is not one oriented towards those who have children to entertain. One of the real joys of the park is the range of scenery it displays: alpine meadows, forests, rugged peaks, glaciers, rivers, lakes, and, of course, the waterfalls for which it is renowned. While some of these wonders are not easily accessible, the famous waterfalls are. There are over 150 camping spots in four locations in the park.

Tin Fishing

In 1977-78, I was working in Port Hardy on the Federal Fisheries patrol vessel Seal Rock. It was about a sixty-foot, two-crewmember ship, with me working as engineer/deckhand/cook/bottle washer, and a wonderful skipper, Harry Cartwright.

One sunny day we left port for a patrol of the local waters. Once out in the middle of Johnstone Strait, I spotted something gold glittering in the water a mile or so away. We went to investigate and found a four-foot-square plywood pallet with a little pile of thirty-one tin cans sitting precariously in the middle of it. I hooked it with the pike pole, pulled it in, and tossed the cans on board. Opening a tin, we discovered they were full of delicious sockeye salmon. In short order we found two more floating pallets carrying twenty-nine and thirty tins of salmon. It turned out that a salmon cannery in Port Simpson was shipping out a fresh load of its production by barge when a storm damaged one barge and it dumped its load of pallets of canned salmon into the chuck. Most of the cans went to the bottom except for a few which miraculously stayed on some of the pallets, which we then "caught."

I dare say that there are few fishermen who can say that they caught their salmon already cooked and canned! The salmon was a very welcome gift from the sea, especially as I was making very low wages. I enjoyed salmon sandwiches and casseroles for several months.

Kevin Neish

Tomatoes
Use tomato rings and stakes to keep all your plants up off the damp and slug-infested ground. I am also convinced that "tomato bags" are the way to keep your tomatoes blight free.

Early blooming perennials
Choose a cool, wet day to divide or prune back your primulas and other early blooming perennials. Use methoxychlor to control weevil problems. Start looking for perennial seeds now, and get them planted this month, especially wallflowers. Delphinium, columbine, gaillardia, lupines, coreopsis, and dianthus are a few of my favourites that will bloom next June.

Vegetable gardening
Side dress all your vegetable rows with a vegetable fertilizer. You can still plant vegetables the whole month of June.

JACK CHRISTIE'S TOP FIVE FAVOURITE TRAILS

Cycling Trail: Greater Victoria's Galloping Goose Trail. The Capital Regional District's Galloping Goose Trail Regional Park represents one of the most successful rail-to-trails initiatives in any Canadian city. At the moment the trail runs for approximately sixty kilometres from Sidney to Sooke.

Marine Trail: The Sunshine Coast's Sechelt Inlets Provincial Marine Recreation Area. There are eight marine park wilderness campsites located on both sides of Sechelt Inlet and along Narrows Inlet in Sechelt Inlets Provincial Marine Recreation Area. Most sites are located within two to three kilometres of each other and provide a welcome resting place, particularly when strong winds funnel through the inlets on summer days.

Hiking Trail: Northeastern BC's Stone Mountain Provincial Park. Beginning at kilometre 645 (mile 400) on the Alaska Highway, the seventy-kilometre loop through the headwaters of MacDonald Creek and the adjacent Wokkpash Recreation Area can take from one to two weeks to complete. Much of the route

How I learned To Hit the Road and Love It
Jack Christie

Outdoors columnist Jack Christie's "Beyond the Backyard" is heard on BC Almanac. The author of five regional recreation guides, Jack welcomes inquisitive guests to visit his website to learn more: www.jackchristie.com.

photo: Louise Christie

I filed my first outdoors travel story with the CBC almost twenty years ago. I didn't plan it that way. After I'd spent several years contributing items on the world of drinks and drinking trends, two producers approached me with the idea of submitting summer travel reports. Ray Charles' "Hit the Road Jack" came to mind as a theme. It was a perfect fit. I was all but born on a train (near Toronto) and have been on the move ever since.

Not surprisingly, it was a train that first brought me to British Columbia. In 1958, I rode the Burlington Northern Railroad to Crescent Beach near White Rock. At the time, our family was living in northern Alberta. While my parents and younger brother explored Vancouver, I stayed with friends at a cabin on the shores of Boundary Bay. To my prairie mind, that exotically-charged locale epitomized the West Coast. Homemade surfboards stood by the sunporch. As the tide rose over the shallow, sandy-bottomed bay, we'd paddle out on them. Most days only a modest swell rippled the broad surface. Sets of breakers were a rarity, but that hardly mattered. Our imaginations filled in the blanks as we lay on those smooth plywood boards, flapping our arms in the ocean to build up speed. Salt water seeped through my pores. I knew then that I wanted to spend the rest of my life beside the ocean and the mountains.

It took a while, but by the mid-1970s I had made BC my home for good. Not that

I still don't journey elsewhere. However, the more I explore BC, the more I realize one thing: there are lifetimes of adventures for the taking. Right here. Right now. What a staggering concept. As someone who makes a living acquainting others with the outdoors, I find BC to be a gold mine that never peters out. With almost twelve percent of the land base set aside as provincial park – double the amount of a decade ago – there are some truly epic tracks of wilderness to explore. Here's one example: Northeastern Rockies Provincial Park, created in 1997, is as large as Nova Scotia. Or Switzerland. Small wonder the world is beating a path to our patch of paradise.

Classifying BC as a paradise is not far off the mark. The origin of the word is Persian, meaning "a walled garden." In a sense, that's BC in a nutshell. Our landscape is walled in by the Pacific Ocean to the west and boxed in by mountains on the other three sides. And what an astonishing expanse. It always astounds folks from south of the border when I point out to them that BC is larger than Washington, Oregon, and California rolled into one. Even when you live here, the sheer size of the place can, at times, weigh heavy on the traveller. For one backcountry trip north of Fort Nelson, I drove for almost three days from my home in Vancouver – just to reach the trailhead in Stone Mountain Provincial Park. That's a lot of hours, and I still hadn't covered the length of the province.

These days as I make my way around BC, I notice the changes that have occurred since those early "Hit the Road" days. The food is fresher and better prepared, so is the local beer and wine. German is now firmly established as the unofficial second language, at least north of the Trans-Canada Highway. Lodges and guest ranches promote wildlife viewing as much as they once did hunting and fishing. Everywhere, roof racks are adorned with kayaks and bikes. One thing that hasn't changed is the bugs. Maybe they're a blessing in disguise. At least in summer they keep the crowds down.

follows well-trodden game trails laid down by cariboo but adhered to by all, as attested to by the wide variety of scat encountered along the way.

Historic Trail: Sea to Sky Corridor's Pemberton Trail. The Pemberton Trail was once an active Indian trading route, part of a vast network that linked Squamish with villages in the interior. Extant sections are easiest walked in the Paradise Valley north of Squamish and beside the Cheakamus River in Brandywine Provincial Park near Whistler.

Scenic Driving Trail: Northwestern BC's Trail of the Totems. One of the most unique scenic drives in the province leads around a well-marked circuit in the Hazelton Valley called the Trail of the Totems Tour. From the ceremonial poles in the village of Kitwanga, through Kitwancool, Kitseguelca, Kispiox, to the 'Ksan Historical Village and Museum in Hazelton, this trail was once a part of the coastal "grease trail" along which highly valued fish grease obtained from oolichan was transported from the coast to the Interior.

"The Totem Poles at 'Ksan," by Carl Chaplin

Aldergrove Festival Days

Armstrong Funtastic Summer Festival

Cowichan Bay Boat Festival

Cranbrook's Sam Steele Days

Dawson Creek's Doe River Rodeo

Enderby Funtastic Summer Festival

Gold River Loggers' Sports

Kitimat Hill Climb & Car Show

Langley Days

Lumby Days

Lumby Funtastic Summer Festival

Mill Bay Country Music Jamboree

Nelson's Heritage City Half Marathon

Wheel Power

My husband and I have hiked and backpacked through incredibly beautiful territory in BC: the West Coast Trail, Kokanee Glacier Park, and Cathedral Lake Park, to name a few. When multiple sclerosis surfaced in my life, we had to find creative ways to access and enjoy the outdoors.

In 1989, we helicoptered into Mount Assiniboine Provincial Park where two of our good friends were rangers. After it took me an hour to walk a kilometre, due to poor leg strength, the guys said they would take me anywhere in a wheelbarrow.

With a big grin I rode the alpine paths in a wheelbarrow, thoughtfully draped with a shock-absorbing pad. I was only ejected once, when the tire of the barrow hit a root on the path. I was most pleased as I landed on my feet, avoiding a face plant, something that, for me with my poor balance, was a miracle.

Silver Lake

For some unknown reason, and to my disappointment, the guys wouldn't take me to the higher ridges.

Now I have discovered the "scooter," which gets me in the bush and is more comfortable than a wheelbarrow. I have bounced over the Cariboo turf dodging cow pies, picked huckleberries at a subalpine lake below Kokanee Glacier, and watched the surf, seals, gulls, and eagles play at Long Beach, Rathtrevor, and Newcastle Island Parks.

Freedom to enjoy outdoor adventures is mine again!

Nancy Chamberlayne
Parksville

Ghostrider: Spirit of Home

When I look back on my childhood and reflect on the influences and events that formed the sense of who I am, one specific place stands out as a cornerstone of my person: my grandfather's farm. It is there that I truly felt a sense of "home" and developed a feeling of belonging to a place.

My grandfather had a large farm about six miles east of where we lived in Fernie, at the base of Mt Hosmer, in southeastern BC. It may not have been mine in a physical sense, but on a spiritual level it was as much a part of me as the wheat that grew in the fields was a part of the dark, rich soil, fused and rooted together, only to be separated by being cut off or torn out of the ground and shaken apart.

All of my uncles, aunts, and cousins would spend many long hours working the land, only stopping to give way to their grumbling stomachs and the long shadows thrown down from the Rocky Mountains. My grandfather's house would then be filled with the sounds of life, the sounds of family, the sounds of love.

When school was out for the summer, I would go and spend a few weeks on the farm. My Uncle Dave lived across the road from Grandpa and Grandma's house, and I would stay with his family. I loved the times when everyone was at the farm and we worked the land together and shared our lives, but it was my time there alone that I loved best.

There is one very special thing about the family farm that stays with me to this day. It had no shape, no physical feature; it was intangible but very real. It was in the tall, flowing sea of grass, gently waving. It was in the wind and its quiet touch to my face, turned up to a warm, sweet-smelling summer sky.

In the midst of all this is the Ghostrider. On certain evenings when the sun is setting on Mt Hosmer, a shadowed image is cast on the mountain's face: a person on a horse being led by another person. There are many legends of who they are but whatever story one believes, the Ghostrider and its companion are special to me. When I first saw them, it seemed that they were watching over the farm and many times since I have felt their

Port Alberni Harbour Days

Prince George Annual Rodeo

Prince Rupert Sea Fest and Indian Cultural Days

Prince Rupert Sea Level Drag Races

Smithers Midsummer Music Festival

Squamish Adventure Festival

Stewart International Rodeo

Vancouver's Dragon Boat Festival

Vancouver Storytelling Festival

Vernon Funtastic Summer Festival

Victoria Jazz Fest International

Williams Lake Annual Stampede

TRAIL USER'S CODE OF ETHICS

Hikers, mountain bikers, and horse-back riders are increasingly sharing the trails they travel. All recreationists who are aware of others and practice "treading lightly" will help reduce conflicts and environmental damage. Respect trail closures and use restrictions because sensitive environmental conditions or safety concerns may be the cause.

Trail Etiquette

Remember the "3 Cs":

Common sense: assess the situation and use common sense to determine who can get out of the way most easily. In ideal cases, cyclists yield to everyone and hikers yield to horses. Communication: a friendly word of greeting reassures horses and lets others know of your presence. Courtesy: treat other trail users with courtesy.

presence. Sitting on a knoll on moonlit nights, I would hug my legs to my chest and listen for them. Quietly resting in the beauty of the majestic mountains, looking up to the same stars above me, as they must have, to the same questions, the same sense of wonder.

It's been many years since I visited the farm, yet I continue to look to the mountain of my childhood and my life; watching the shadows of my past grow longer, deeper, richer.

Bob Hutchinson
Cranbrook

The Sleeping Beauty

photo: John Roders

The Skeena

The Skeena, BC's second largest river, 350 miles long, flows through the coastal mountains of northern British Columbia. Ikshean is the name given to this river by local natives. The word iksh means "out of" and shean means "clouds." It is a river of much beauty, with narrow canyons, powerful rapids, and shifting sand bars; it was considered by many riverboat captains to be the most treacherous river in North America. The Skeena River rarely gave up its dead.

The river was instrumental in opening up the frontiers of northern British Columbia and the Yukon. Miners, prospectors, fur traders, and missionaries would make the 130-mile journey up the river from Prince Rupert to Hazelton. Places with names like Hornet's Nest, Devil's Elbow, and the infamous

Kitselas Canyon with their narrow, rocky passages made river travel dangerous.

As I sit on a large rock beside the Skeena, I see to my right the old Skeena Bridge. It is a one-lane, wooden-decked structure that was built in the mid-1920s, one of the longest wooden bridges still in use today. Below the old bridge straddling Little Canyon, the water pushes and churns through a narrow gorge. I see men and women pulling in a net and filling large metal tubs with salmon, working quickly to empty the net and get it ready for the next run of fish. They are, however, not the only fishers on the river. Ospreys and eagles are flying overhead. They, too, have mouths to feed waiting back at the nest. It is not uncommon to see seals in the river as they follow the salmon, too.

On the rock before me is a large ring bolt. At this spot, river boats would tie up to take on wood for fuel before continuing upriver. The bolt is a link in the chain between the old and the new, the past and the present. My mind drifts back to the time of miners, prospectors, and fur traders; a time when local natives would gather berries, and cedar bark, and hunt animals for food and clothing.

The train whistle blows and I am suddenly brought back to the present. Across the river I see the sparkle of sunlight on steel rails that carry passengers and freight trains between Prince Rupert and Prince George. This is the same railroad that the riverboat helped build and ultimately spelled its demise.

Terrace has been my home since emigrating to Canada from England in 1961. I come to the river often with my family. It is one of my favourite spots. My boys run up and down the sandy beach, climb on the river-worn rocks, and beg for a campfire while my wife and I sip our coffee waiting for the sun to set behind The Sleeping Beauty, a mountain named for the reclining face and figure of a lady that outlines the deepening blue of the sky. She has watched over Terrace since its conception. As the sun disappears, I feel the cold of the river seeping through my jacket. In these last few minutes of daylight, I sit waiting for that magic moment for a faint white shadow to appear in the form of a Kermode bear as it makes its way down to the river bank.

John Roders
Terrace

Hikers

The backpacker's motto, "Take nothing but photos, leave nothing but footprints," can be adopted by all trail users.

When encountering horseback riders, a group of hikers should all step off to the same side of the trail, the lower side if possible. Allow two or three metres for horses to pass. Use existing trails as much as possible. If you're not on an established trail, spread out so as not to create a trail, especially in vulnerable areas.

Mountain Bikers

Be aware of other trail users. Always anticipate a horse or hiker around a blind curve and slow down. Yield to hikers and equestrians. Get off your bike and move to the lower side of the trail to let horses pass. Learn how to minimize damage to trails through proper riding techniques. Practice erosion-free cycling or soft cycling.

Horse Riders

When passing other recreationists, steady your horse and give the hiker or cyclist clear instructions on how you would like them to stand clear. Warn others of dangers on the trail.

Information courtesy Outdoor Recreation Council of BC.

Postcard from Mayne Island

BC BREWS

"He was a wise man who invented beer."
— Plato

Nothing beats the summer heat like a well-brewed beer, and these days British Columbians are sipping more suds from an expanding mico-brewery industry. When beer aficionados Tim Vandergrift and Stuart Derdeyn hit the airwaves to discuss their favourite BC brews (thankfully they bring samples), listeners also pitch in with theirs.

Mayne is a southern gulf island surrounded on three sides by Galiano, Pender, and Saturna. As young children my sister and I were brought here for two weeks every summer by our parents. We stayed in a cabin called Sleepy Hollow on my great-uncle's property.

This was surely the happiest time of the year for all of us. We left the city behind and had the field leading down to the beach. It was the ultimate freedom to run through the long, dry grass and over the short bank into the sand.

I was obsessed with the island's mysterious and beautiful deer, and was astonished one morning to see my uncle chasing a graceful buck out of his orchard. It ran across the field in full view of our cabin and leapt easily over the fence, disappearing into the forest that still covers the point.

We lost both our parents when I was seven, and I was in high school before I revisited Mayne Island. Auntie Elsie was gone, and Uncle Bill, a wizard with his divining wires and the author of Science of a Witch's Brew, *succumbed to a heart attack. Several years later, my partner and I were enjoying the view at the end of the point when we saw the "For Sale" sign.*

You can imagine my joy when the provincial government bought the land and turned it into a park. It is strange to see people in the woods that were always so private and quiet for us, but I believe Uncle Bill would have been happy to share such a wonderful place. His house is now the home of the park's caretaker and Sleepy Hollow is gone, but the field is still there, and the sight of it still makes me cry.

Christine Lowther
Tofino

Another Fish Story

On a warm summer day (about 110°F) in Lytton, in 1932, my dad was summoned by his Indian friends. They had "a big one on!" Dad and his friends climbed into his Model A Ford and drove down to the Fraser River, across the ferry, and up toward the Stein River. Below the Stein was about an one-quarter mile back-eddy, where the Indians had a sturgeon on the line! When he arrived, they had a four-horse team starting to drag the huge sturgeon onto the shore. A discussion ensued and it was decided that this 1,300-pound denizen of the deep should be "walked" down the river to the junction of the Thompson and Fraser Rivers. They tied it to the old gold dredge with steel clothesline, where it stayed in the clear water of the Thompson. I'll spare you the gory details, but suffice to say that lots of folks in Lytton had fresh sturgeon for at least a month!

Neal Hallisey
Kelowna

**BC Micro-brews
(in no particular order)**

Mt Begbie High Country Kolsch

Mt Begbie Tall Timber Traditional Ale

Nelson Blackheart Oatmeal Stout

Nelson Paddywhack India Pale Ale

Okanagan Spring Pale Ale

R&B Brewing Raven Cream Ale
(Silver Medal Winning Beer, 1998
World Beer cup in Rio Di Janeiro!)

Shaftesbury Cream Ale

Tin Whistle Rattlesnake ESB

Vancouver Island Hermann's
Dark Barvarian Lager

Other Canadian beers they enjoyed:
Big Rock Traditional Ale, Warthog
Unibroue La Fin Du Monde, Maudite

OUR DAILY
BREAD

Whenever chef Karen Neilson arrives at Studio 31 loaded down with baskets of bread, we're swarmed. Staff are drawn by the aroma like bees to honey. Her multi-grain, buttermilk sourdough, and pumpkin cheddar bread recipes also elicit a huge listener response: hundreds ask for copies (check our website for examples at www.vancouver.cbc.ca)

Here's a BC Flatbread recipe she whipped up for kayakers, campers, and outdoor cooks everywhere.

Griddle Fried Flatbread
Karen Neilson

This basic bread recipe contains a little oil, making it easier to handle. This is important for when I make this recipe while camping. While I work the bread into a disc before cooking, I also lightly oil my hands and the dough. This prevents the dough from sticking to me, and then the dough is already oiled so I don't need to add any to the pan. Serve it with stews, soups, and curries for dinner, or stir grated apples, a little sugar, and cinnamon into the batter for breakfast bread.

1 tsp yeast	2 tbsp olive oil
1½ cups warm water	Salt to taste
1 tsp honey	Pepper to taste
3 - 3½ cups flour	

In a bowl, combine the yeast, warm water, honey, and 1½ cups of flour. Beat the batter for 5 minutes to develop the gluten. Allow to proof for an hour and a half.

Stir in the olive oil and 1½ cups flour. Work the dough with a wooden spoon, as it should be a little sticky. Using the remaining ½ cup flour, sprinkle a smooth work surface with some of the flour and turn the dough out on to the floured surface. Knead the dough, using small amounts of the remaining flour, until the dough is smooth and springs back to the touch. Place in a clean bowl, cover and let rise for an hour.

Punch the dough down. Divide the dough into 4 or 6 pieces, depending on how large you want your flatbreads. Flour your hands lightly, then pull and press the dough into a rough disc. Repeat with remaining dough.

Preheat a cast iron frying pan (or a pan that can be heated empty without damaging it) to medium high. Oil the pan lightly, and cook the flatbread about 3 or 4 minutes a side. Remove to a wire rack to cool and repeat with remaining breads. Sprinkle the still warm bread with salt and freshly cracked pepper. Serve warm.

It is easy to play with this bread by stirring seasonings into the batter stage (after it's been proofed). A teaspoon of toasted cumin seeds and 2 tablespoons of minced sundried tomatoes, or a ¼ cup of caramelized onions tastes great, while grated apple with fresh sage would be wonderful with roast pork.

Summer Preserves

Peach Honey Jam

4 cups peaches, crushed
1 pkg (57 g) fruit pectin crystals
2 cups liquid honey
2 tbsp bottled lemon juice

In a large, stainless steel saucepan, combine the crushed peaches and fruit pectin crystals. Bring to a full rolling boil over medium-high heat. Boil hard for 1 minute, stirring constantly. Add the honey and lemon juice. Return to a full rolling boil. Boil hard for 5 minutes, stirring constantly. Remove from heat and skim foam. Ladle jam into hot sterilized 250 ml mason jars, leaving ¼ inch (0.5 cm) head space. Wipe rims. Centre prepared canning lids and apply screw bands fingertip tight. Process filled jars in a boiling water bath canner for 5 minutes. Cool. Sealed lids curve downwards. Store in a cool, dry, dark place.

Recipe courtesy Kelowna Orchard Museum.

Ride to the Rainforests

In 1992, five of us rode our bicycles from Vancouver to Walbran Valley on Vancouver Island. We called the trip, "Ride to the Rainforests."

As far as humans were concerned, we were completely alone at our riverside campsite. We spent days picking berries and walking along the river to some small pools in between waterfalls. The river was just warm enough for us to jump in naked, then jump out shivering to warm ourselves on sun-baked boulders. This was the furthest from civilization, and the closest to nature, that I have ever felt.

I'll never forget that week, ceremoniously capped with pizza and beer, at the first town we encountered on our way home. I've since moved to Vancouver Island, where my children can be close to nature, as remotely as they choose.

Andy Telfer
Qualicum Beach

BC BIG TREES

Western Larch (*Larix occidentalis*)
south of Cranbrook,
west of Plumbob Mountain
healthy, dead top
Circumference: 4.54 metres
Height: 52.1 metres
Average crown spread: 8.2 metres

Information and image courtesy BC Conservation Data Centre's Big Tree Register: www.elp.gov.bc.ca/rib/wis/cdc.

BC's MOST REMOTE LOCATION

BC's land mass is mind boggling in its diversity. Rainforest. Desert. Grasslands. But where do you go to really get away from it all — the most remote place in the province?

Don Mortimer in Rossland had this to say: "My work in forest fire suppression takes me into some pretty remote places. A lot of time the only way we can get into these areas quickly is by rappeling out of helicopters or parachuting out of fixed wing aircraft. You get a very strong sense of being a long way from anywhere — especially when you think the only reason you're in that spot is because lightning struck the ground there a few hours or days earlier. These lightning fires are usually up high on steep and rugged slopes. It's not very hard to believe you are probably the first human to ever set foot on that ground. It feels, and is, very special. Certainly changes the way you watch a lightning storm."

Oar & Sail

Fresh out of Aberdeen University, Kenneth Macrae Leighton arrived at Alert Bay to begin a distinguished medical career in 1952. Smitten by the BC coastline, he resolved to one day explore it under his own steam, slowly.

Some thirty-nine years later his wife Nancy saw him off from Jericho Beach in the *Morag Anne*, a hand-built cedar rowboat that was named for a daughter who never arrived. In the summer of 1991, Leighton rowed north to Cape Caution; across from Port Hardy, and rowed back home again; in the summer of 1993, he rowed from Port Hardy to Port Rupert.

From the launch of his boat to the launch of Leighton's book took most of the decade. *Oar & Sail* (Creekstone) is Leighton's account of his 850-kilometre adventure averaging two knots per hour. He stayed out of shipping lanes, bucked wind and tides, and mainly ate Japanese noodles, biscuits, and Cream of Wheat.

"It's a long way to Alert Bay and twice as far to Prince Rupert," says Leighton, "but time and distance are not worth thinking about. The sun is coming out. I have no deadlines. It's great to be alive."

Oar & Sail includes eleven hand-drawn maps by Anne McLean and sixteeen scratchboard illustrations by the author's son, Dr. Roderick Leighton, a former art student who provides graceful images of the *Morag Anne*, his father at the oars, and shimmering seascapes.

Other mariners weren't sure what to make of the lone figure bent over the oars. Typically a cabin cruiser would pull up to make sure Leighton wasn't having a heart attack, then speed away again.

Full days of rowing left him "knackered" but in good spirits. He could always dig into his "emergency only" parcel supplied by a friend. It contained his favourite Royal Navy chocolate, sardines, and, "joy upon joy, a bottle of Glenlivet malt whiskey no less, which has been known to raise the dead on more than one occasion, or so I have been told."

Leighton points out landmarks and provides historical notes behind the place names such as Broughton, Johnstone, and Chatam. In Surge Narrows the good doctor gets the scare of his life, becoming trapped in a whirlpool for five frightening hours. This teaches him to scrutinize his charts and tide tables with extra rigour.

Sometimes during his first voyage, our not-so-ancient mariner pushed himself too hard, always in the grip of determination to reach the next beckoning island. "I have few regrets … but, as I write, I can see a constant error threading its way throughout. The goal appears to have been everything. This is foolish and very short-sighted … I must live with my mistake."

Leighton heeded his own counsel on the second journey and took more time for new friendships on the water, accepting a tow when badly needed or a bag of freshly baked oatmeal cookies. With calloused hands and Gaelic wit, he propelled the *Morag Anne* all the way to Prince Rupert's harbour.

The former head of anaesthesia at UBC Hospital, Ken Leighton died suddenly in June, 1998, of complications related to hepatitis C; his lyrical narrative was published in November of 1999. Three months later it was reprinted.

Originally published in BC Bookworld, Spring 2000.

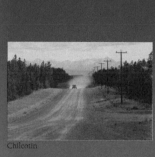
Chilcotin

And there was this from an ex-urbanite: "My family and I moved up from the Lower Mainland to Smithers five years ago and that seemed remote enough. We were always fascinated by some of the empty parts of the map found in northern BC — if you look at the circle formed by the Alaska Highway and the Cassiar Highway there's a big empty spot in the middle. One day we took a long roundabout way to Prince George and headed north on back roads ending up at Germansen Landing on the Omenica River. We were surprised to learn there was a gold rush there about 100 years ago. We were made to feel very much at home when we got a flat tire and got some help — the family were Quakers and the girls were wearing long dresses. It felt very much like a place out of time."

And there was this from a Vancouver listener: "I and my teenage sons and husband had the glory of doing the Tatsensini River. It starts in the Yukon and dips down into British Columbia before it turns into Alaska. I have on my wall the most astounding picture of a land that looks like it was untouched for the last millennium. In the picture you can see snow geese flying over and a pair of beautiful bald eagles on the edge of the river. It was a memorable trip and one I wish upon every British Columbian because it really does teach you what this province is really about."

Johnstone Strait

Yuquot: The Place of Winds

Our Great Escape destination in the summer of 1991 was Friendly Cove in Nootka Sound on the west coast of Vancouver Island. We must have looked like a circus: inching down the Muchalat Inlet in our old wooden dory which my father had modernized by adding a one-and-a-half-horsepower outboard motor. The old dory was laden to the gunwales with tarp-covered mounds of supplies, our golden retriever sitting atop as both lookout and figurehead. Our dinghy trailed astern, carrying as much as possible while still remaining seaworthy. Even at full power, the little motor struggled to propel her heavy charge; so to promote forward progress my father rowed one long oar. I perched on the aft corner of the dory, steering the caravan, with cotton stuffed in my ears to keep out the motor's incessant drone. All that could be seen of my brother was the top of his head as he pumped the bilges, while my mother tried to lift rain-dampened spirits with liberal rations of GORP (good old raisins and peanuts). In this fashion we set out from Gold River under overcast skies and drizzle, ready to brave the Muchalat Inlet, renowned for its heavy inflow winds that often prompt small craft warnings.

Amenable hot and sunny weather greeted us the next day, but the infamous inflow winds forced us to wait ashore in Mooyah Bay. We took a walk along a dusty logging road to stretch our legs, the dog sniffing road-side salal bushes with interest. All at once, she stopped and uttered a low, throaty growl. To our great alarm, the bushes growled back! We didn't stop to investigate, but returned to the boats post-haste. Judging from the berry-filled droppings on the road, we narrowly avoided an intimate encounter with a bear.

Our journey continued early the next morning in a heavy mist. All we could see was a limited circle of water immediately around us. In the muffled silence, time seemed to become as fluid as the misty air. I almost expected to see Maquinna's people in one of their elegant cedar canoes glide out of the mist in search of the oolichan. Or to come upon Captain Cook's ship tethered in Resolution Cove with seamen scurrying about to refit her for her homeward voyage. But soon the sun burned away the mist and we found ourselves within sight of the Nootka light-station, though still a fair haul from Friendly Cove. As the inflow winds were beginning to blow, we decided to put into Burdwood Bay and camp on shore. It was not until we were near the foot of the deep bay that the sound of breakers caught our ears. We were going to have to contend with surf if we intended to go ashore. The landing was rough and wet. No sooner had we beached the boat than we realized we'd have to fight surf all night long with an incoming tide. Although we were loath to venture out in the dreaded inflow winds, battling surf was worse. So we set out for Friendly Cove, our soaked motor sputtering feebly – powered by about half of her one-and-a-half horses.

Large Pacific swells rocked the boats mercilessly, frequently lifting the little motor out of the water. After hours of struggle we finally rounded the headlands past the Nootka lighthouse. Friendly Cove lived up to its name and we welcomed the peaceful waters with grateful relief after the stormy crossing. To this day, when I lie still in the sunshine, I find myself transported back to the sunny, flower-studded meadow where we relaxed by the cove after our memorable ordeal. I can smell again the fragrance of sun-warmed grass in salty air and feel the fresh breezes of Yuquot – the place of winds.

Kelly Marshall

ON THE ROAD

Radio's portability takes us just about anywhere — and we do like to get around. *BC Almanac* has broadcast live from a Campbell River restaurant patio, a Burnaby high school music room, a snow encrusted sundeck at Rossland's Red Mountain, the shrubs and flowers at Chilliwack's Minter Gardens, an Okanagan Vineyard, and other spots around the province. A couple of years ago when Salmon Arm forests were ablaze and half the town was wondering when they could return home, we attempted to get as close to the scene as we could. With just a few hours warning, technician Bert Cervo connected our equipment to a motel fax line and set us up for broadcast outside in the parking lot. From this vantage point we watched water bombers battle the fire, and were easily accessible for emergency officials who updated people during the broadcast. Blind faith and a good technician can take you just about anywhere.

BC Almanac listeners are voracious readers. Here's a summer reading list of soft cover favourites for the beach, campground or backyard hammock.

**Listeners' Beach
Blanket Favourites:**

The Alienist Caleb Carr

Boy: Tales of Childhood Roald Dahl

The Boys Life Robert R McCammon

Bridget Jones' Diary Helen Fielding

Broken Wings John Douglas

The Burning Secret Stefan Zweig

City of Ice John Farraw

The Concubine's Children: Portrait of a Family Divided Denise Chong

The Curve of Time
Muriel Wylie Blanchet

The End of the Affair Graham Greene

A Fine Balance Rohinton Mistry

The Garden of Eden Sharon Butala

Hannibal Thomas Harris

The Hot Zone Richard Preston

In a Sunburned Country Bill Bryson

Pizza with Salad
Brad Ovenell-Carter

Generally speaking, there are two kinds of pizza: thin-crust Neapolitan and deep-dish Chicago. The latter has its merits, when you are young and palate-blind; full of appetite and empty of taste. Italians, masters of style, take a less-is-more approach: unlike a cheese-laden Chicago pie, a pizza from a wood-fired oven in Naples has no more than a scattering of toppings, say chopped fresh tomato and basil, some artichokes and anchovy.

I will often take a third tack: pizza with salad topping. A rich pile of greens, a little red onion thinly sliced, and shavings of Parmesan are a heinous crime to the Naples Pizza Authority (the organization really exists) and deeply suspicious to Chicagoans. But they are deeply satisfying and refreshing to me on hot summer night when I feel lazy.

You can do this in the oven, but a gas barbecue and a pizza stone take the cooking outdoors. The barbecue also burns hotter than any domestic oven and will, therefore, give you a better crust.

1¾ tsp dry yeast or 12 g fresh yeast	Olive oil
pinch of sugar	Few slices of mozzarella cheese
1⅓ cups warm water	¼ cup red onions, thinly sliced
¼ cup olive oil	Balsamic vinegar
3¾ cups unbleached flour	Handful of mesclun or mixed greens
1½ tsp salt	Shavings of Parmesan cheese

Proof the yeast with the sugar in a third of the water. Stir in the oil. Add the salt and flour and mix until the dough comes together. Knead for about 8 minutes or, in a mixer, about 3 minutes. The dough should be soft and smooth.

First rise. Place dough in a lightly oiled bowl, cover tightly and let rise until almost fully doubled – about an hour.

Shaping and second rise. Cut dough into 2 to 4 pieces. Shape each onto a ball and let rest about 5 minutes. Shape into disks by hand or with a rolling pin. Cover and let rise no longer than 30 minutes.

Baking. Set a pizza stone on the grill and preheat the barbecue to 550°F. Brush the pizza dough with olive oil and top with a thin layer of mozzarella. Bake about 5 minutes, depending on the size of the pizza.

Toss thinly sliced red onions with balsamic vinegar, a small amount of olive oil, and a pinch of sugar. Let marinate briefly while the pizza is baking.

The pizza is done when the crust is golden and lightly blistered. Remove from the barbecue and immediately brush the rim with oil. Toss a handful of mesclun with the onions and arrange on top of the pizza. Garnish with shaved Parmesan.

Makes 2 medium-sized pizzas.

Into Thin Air John Krakauer

Phoenix Island Charlotte Paul

The Prodigal Spy Joseph Cannon

The Reader Bernhard Schlink

Red China Blues Jan Wong

Reflections of a Siamese Twin
John Raulston Saul

The Remorseful Day Colin Dexter

Small Death in Lisbon Robert Wilson

Stones from the River Ursula Hegi

That Nice Miss Smith Nigel Moreland

Under the Dragon's Tail
Maureen Jennings

Wild Swans Jung Chang

The Wings of Fire Charles Todd

The Woman in White Wilkie Collins

Summer's Night Sky
David Dodge

David Dodge is an astronomer with the H.R. MacMillan Space Centre.

When medical columnist Dr Jane Hailey pays *BC Almanac* her weekly visit, it's often after a late night delivering babies. Dr Jane's energy level is amazing – she just keeps on ticking. We asked her for some tips on staying healthy in a hectic world.

Have breakfast on Granville Island – and "go mad" buying summer fruit.

Walk around the seawall on a warm, sunny day – but don't forget to wear sunblock.

Try the occasional vegetarian dinner – such as "Chickpeas with Cumin and Ginger" from the *Vancouver Sun's* cookbook *Six O'Clock Solutions.*

Attend a Bard on the Beach performance – to enjoy summer, relax, and stimulate your mind.

Try kale (a great winter vegetable that grows everywhere). Vancouver's James Barber has several great recipes in his cookbook *Peasant's Alphabet.*

Oh, you fortunate folk who live in the country! The summer's night sky is truly the finest of all the skies and can only really be appreciated well away from the intrusions of street lights.

photo: Jack Newton
M-8, Lagoon Nebula

The star chart is set up for all dates in the summer once the sky is totally dark.

As twilight falls, the first thing you will see will be the brightest stars. Two will vie for your attention: Vega and Arcturus. Vega will be the one almost directly overhead while Arcturus will be to the west.

Canadian summer twilights last forever, or so it seems, but your patience will be rewarded. Over in the northwest you will soon spot the Big Dipper, which is part of a much larger group of stars called Ursa Major, the Big Bear. The two end stars of the dipper, called the pointers, will assist you in finding the Polaris, the North Star, while the handle of the dipper can be used to find Arcturus.

Overhead, Vega, shining sparkling white, is one of three bright stars making up the Summer Triangle. The other stars are Deneb and Altair. Deneb is the brightest star in the constellation of Cygnus, the Swan, and Altair is the brightest star in Aquila, the Eagle.

By now you should be able to make out the Milky Way, the name we have given our own galaxy. The Milky Way consists of a hundred billion or more stars. Those that are close to us we see as individual

photo: Jack Newton
M-31, Andromeda Galaxy

stars, those that are farther away from us we see as the fuzzy path of light, but train a pair of binoculars on the Milky Way and you will see those other stars and more.

Low in the south lies the constellation Sagittarius. A glance at the sky chart will show that Sagittarius is imbedded in the thickest and brightest part of the Milky Way. Indeed, when we look at Sagittarius we are looking to the heart of our galaxy. Classically, Sagittarius is the archer, but most astronomers recognize the constellation as a teapot and visualize the Milky Way as the steam coming out of its spout. A pair of binoculars trained on the Milky Way will reveal a number of "lumps" in the sky. These are nebulae, Latin for cloud or fog. These nebulae are places in our galaxy in which stars are evolving from interstellar gas and dust. Starting from the tip of Sagittarius' spout, move your binoculars up and the first lump of sky you will trip over will be the Lagoon Nebula. Indeed, a pair of binoculars, once trained on the Lagoon, will likely also have the Trifid and Swan nebulae in the same field of view.

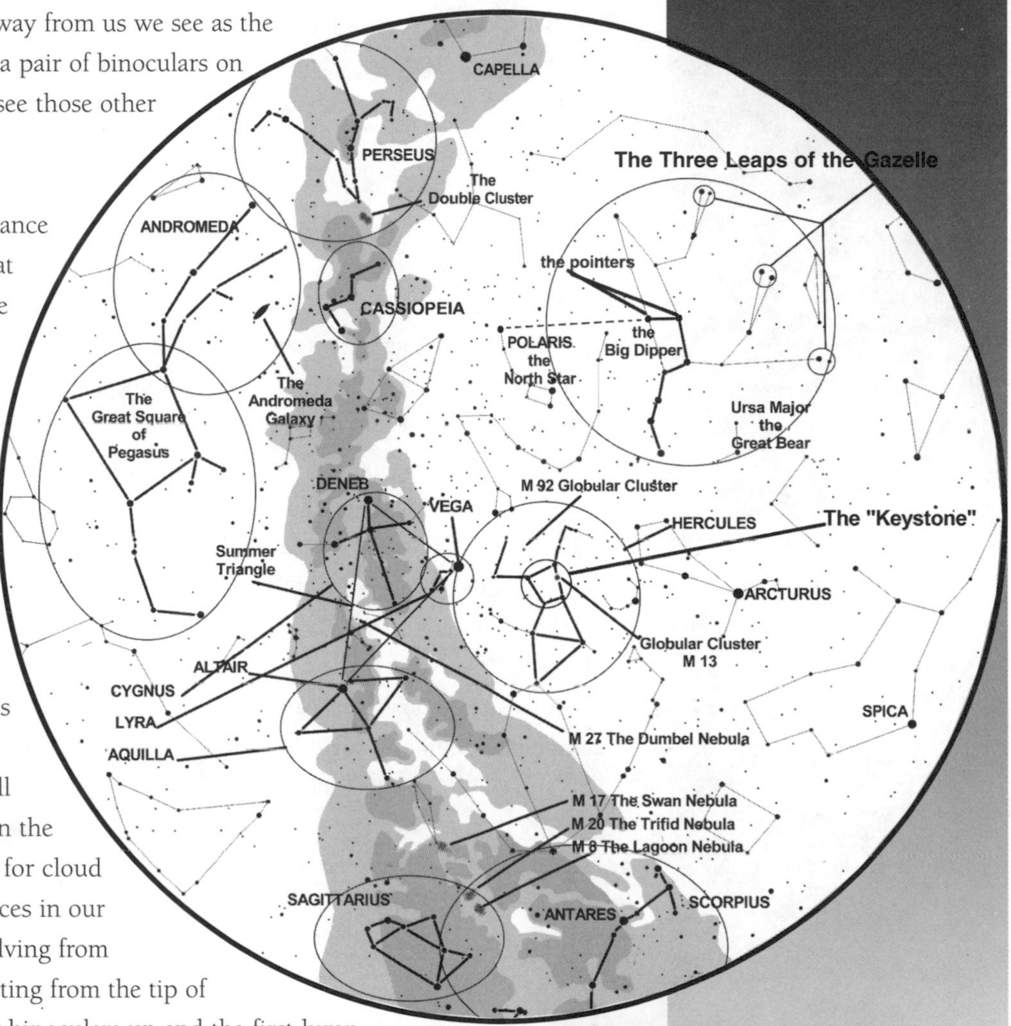

Following the Milky Way we, once again, trip over Vega. To the west of Vega is the constellation of Hercules. Most of Hercules is composed of rather faint stars, but there are four that are easily seen to make up the shape of a

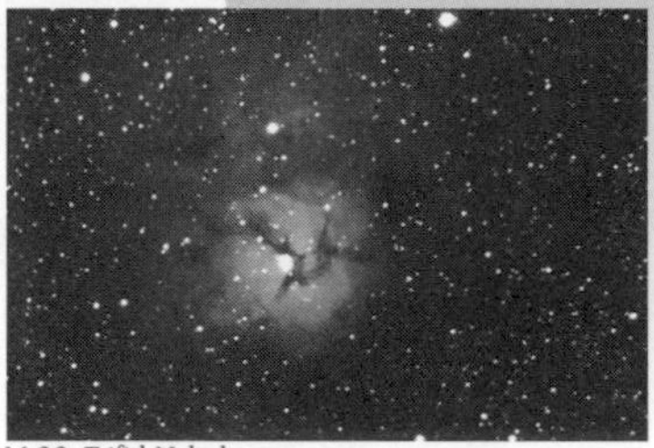

M-20, Trifid Nebula

photo: Jack Newton

keystone. Train your binoculars on the upper right star of the keystone and then slowly draw them down to the lower right star. As the former star reaches the edge of the field of view, you should easily spot a large-ish fuzzy star. This is M-13, a globular cluster laying at the edge of our galaxy some 20,000 light years distant.

Rising in the east is the constellation of Cassiopeia, which looks for all the world like a giant letter "W." Cassiopeia can easily be found by extending the line between the pointer stars in the Big Dipper beyond the North Star. That line will point almost exactly at Cassiopeia. Just off the western most point of the W of Cassiopeia you will spot a large fuzzy object. This is the Andromeda Galaxy, one of the nearest galaxies to our own. When you spot the Andromeda Galaxy, you are looking at an object about three million light years away. In other words, the light you see from the Andromeda Galaxy left over three million years ago. Looking at it with a pair of binoculars will reveal an elliptical form that may just, depending on the binoculars, fit in the field of view. The Andromeda Galaxy spans an area equal to the size of four full moons placed next to each other.

Closer to the northern horizon but next to Cassiopeia is the constellation of Perseus. Train your binoculars towards this indistinct phalanx of stars and you will spot two fuzzy objects close to each other. This is the Double Cluster, two open clusters containing some 400 and 800 stars each about 8,000 light years away. The location of the double cluster is approximately the radiant point for the annual Perseid Meteor shower.

Every August, the earth glides through a veil of dust left behind by the passage of the comet Swift-Tuttle. The best way to observe these meteors is to choose a dark site well away from city lights, lay back, and look up. Bring along some food and warm drink. The meteors will fly across the sky emanating from the double cluster but visible all over.

diagrams: David Dodge

Out of Suburbia

Mount Hays, Prince Rupert

Grade ten: the year I got chicken pox marked the first time I saw a starry sky, unpolluted by city lights. I'd learned about constellations, but because I'd never been far from an urban centre, I imagined that such visions were of the ancient past or for a few astronomers with expensive equipment. Furthermore, though I'd been a Girl Guide, my camping experiences were limited to cabins with indoor plumbing.

It was an identity crisis that led me to the Harrison-Lillooet trail. My sojourn with a starry night sky and trees that put Hong Kong skyscrapers to shame had more to do with teenage angst than a love for green landscapes. During a time when most kids smoked outside school, drank in parking lots, or hit the bong in damp
basements, *I could have sold my urine samples to Olympic hopefuls. I was neither a smoker, drinker, or pothead. Nor was I a jock or beauty queen. Who was I? I suffered a suburban existence. I was bored. I needed to escape. I wanted adventure, a beautiful moment. I looked to Wordsworth's drug of choice: nature.*

I decided I was a hiker. I scaled the Grouse Grind before it became a yuppie status symbol. I'm afraid of heights, so the first time I did the Grind, I was on my hands and knees on steep stretches, trying not to cry. I reached the top in record (slow) time. A woman wearing strappy heels passed me on the way to the summit, saying, "I'm wearing the perfect shoes for the occasion." Despite this humiliation, I continued to hike.

The wilderness beckoned a few months later. My favourite teacher, Marlena Morgan, organized an annual five-day trip to Harrison. I signed up. During the trip countdown, the chicken pox swept through my neighbourhood; both my brother and my hiking partner succumbed to it. I had never had the itchy red spots, so there was a possibility I'd miss the hike. But when the time came, I received a clean bill of health. I headed to Harrison. I was

Nanaimo Great International World
Championship Bathtub Race

Nanaimo Marine Festival

Nelson's Canada Day in the Park

North Vancouver's Annual Clam
Chowder Cook-off

North Vancouver's Caribbean Days

Port Alberni Folkfest Celebrations

Quesnel's Billy Barker Days

Vancouver's Symphony of Fire

Vancouver's Festival Vancouver

Vancouver Folk Music Festival

Williams Lake Children's Festival

Williams Lake Stampede

sluggish and had trouble breathing the first day. I couldn't keep up with the other hikers. I was relieved to reach camp. That night, the clouds obscured the stars as we told stories around the campfire. The next morning, I didn't want to get up. It was still cloudy. I was the last person ready to go. When I finally joined the group, the nurse took me aside: "You have chicken pox." Instead of hiking, I rode the infirmary van.

I stayed one more night. Unable to sleep due to thirst and the itch, I journeyed to the river while everyone slumbered. I drank greedily, putting my face in the cool water. When I looked up, I was greeted by thousands of stars in the clear, vast sky. In the face of such cosmic beauty, I forgot about my chicken pox, my teenage problems. It was the sublime moment I'd been waiting for.

Doretta Lau

"Sunray Cabin," by Anne Adams

Sunray Cabin

In 1974, we purchased a share in Wesquarry Retreats on Quarry Bay on Nelson Island. We tented with four kids on open bedrock the first year, and then built a platform for the tent the next year. In 1978, we built a "cabin." It looked like a glorified garage. Since then we've built a roomy and comfortable cottage.

We didn't set eyes on Sunray until 1979, when we had built up our courage enough to set out into the open Malaspina Strait from Quarry Bay in a small aluminum boat, and travel the three miles to Cape Cockburn. Now, of course, we are much more confident in our seafaring skills and go there many times each summer, usually in our twelve-foot aluminum boat which we can pull up on the pebble beach at the cape.

Every day we visit Sunray, we salute Harry Roberts, who lived in

BRIAN MINTER'S SUMMER GARDENING TIPS: JULY

Repotting your house plants
Now is an ideal time to repot your indoor plants. Houseplants should only be repotted if they are really rootbound. Be sure to use a pot only two inches larger in diameter than their present container, and use only quality potting soils. The important thing to remember is: do your repotting soon so your plants have plenty of time to become established before poor winter growing conditions arrive.

the wilderness of Nelson Island. He was, however, somewhat curmudgeonly and he did not leave Sunray to his children, Yolana, Lee, and Zoe, for whom he had named three small lakes near Cape Cockburn. After Harry's death, Sunray and much of the land around Cape Cockburn was sold to BC Hydro for right-of-way for the Cheekeye-Dunsmuir 500,000-volt transmission line which goes into the saltchuck at Cape Cockburn, crosses over the spine of Texada Island, and then crosses underwater again to Vancouver Island. Sunray continued to deteriorate after Hydro purchased it; boaters, kayakers, backpackers, and other passers-by camped there and built fires on the pebble beach, but no one was responsible for maintaining the place.

During the late 1980s, Barry and Marge Pearson from Sechelt sought to purchase the Sunray site from Hydro. Hydro decided not to sell it, but allowed the Pearsons to establish summer residence there as caretakers. They did much to halt the degradation and clean up the site, and they have been staying there every summer since. A few years ago, our son Andrew met Lee Roberts while visiting the Pearsons. Lee had recently taken out the few remaining "sunray windows" (from which the house derived its name) in order that they not be destroyed as other ones had.

The Sunray site itself has several fruit trees that were planted by Harry. Every summer and fall we pick apples and plums there to enjoy at our cottage and even take home for pies and apple sauce.

When the Pearsons leave at the end of each summer, they put up a sign at the entrance saying:

> Please respect Harry's memory.
> Leave no garbage.
> Light no fires.
> Enjoy the peace and quiet.
> Take only pictures.

I respected this sign and took only pictures. (And some apples and plums!)

Anne Adams

Healthy summer lawns
If we have a great deal of rain in the spring, our lawns get really leached of nutrients. Now is the ideal time to bring back that colour with an appropriate fertilizer. It will strengthen your grasses and help them to better withstand the summer heat. Use liquid weed killers to take care of unsightly clover. Cut your grass between one and two inches in length this time of year, and mow in different directions each time to prevent thatch.

ENDANGERED

Restricted to southwestern British Columbia, the Garry oak ecosystems are among the rarest in the province, largely due to agricultural and urban developments.

- fire suppression has allowed Douglas fir to invade areas once dominated by Garry oak

- the Garry oak landscape includes a mosaic of woodlands, meadows, grasslands, and open rocky areas

- Garry oak ecosystems have been identified as a "hot spot" of biological diversity

- two Ecological Reserves that have a primary focus on Garry oak ecosystems are the Mount Tzuhalem E.R. near Duncan, and the Mount Maxwell E.R. on Saltspring Island

Information courtesy BC Ministry of Environment, Lands, and Parks.

For the Love of Bears

Simon Jackson

photo: Clive Jackson

West Vancouver's Simon Jackson is one of Time Magazine's *Heroes of the Planet. Seventeen-year-old Simon is campaigning to preserve habitat for BC's Kermode bear, also called the Spirit bear.*

For as long as I can remember, I've had a passion for bears and the wilderness they call home. When I was seven, my family took me to Yellowstone National Park where I caught my first glimpse of a bear and at the same time, I came to the realization humans had an option – the power to destroy or preserve these magnificent monarchs of the wilderness.

When I was in grade two, I learned from the evening news that plans were being drawn up to develop the home of the Kodiak bear in Alaska. I immediately wrote letters to Prime Minister Brian Mulroney and President George Bush requesting their help in saving the Kodiak bear. My neighbour and I raised sixty dollars at our lemonade stand which we sent to the World Wildlife Fund. A few months later, Kodiak Island was made a National Wildlife Refuge, protecting the Kodiak bear. Although I know our letters and money had little impact on the decision to protect Kodiak Island, it indirectly taught me one of the most important lessons of my life – one person can make a difference.

In 1995, while photographing a grizzly bear in Yellowstone National Park, a young couple approached my family's car after noticing our BC license plate. After they briefly described an almost mystical and seemingly unreal creature, I promised to write a letter to the Premier of British Columbia asking for the Spirit bear's protection. When I returned home that summer, I found a package of information which included a video. There, captured on video, was a bear so striking in appearance, it took my breath away. In sharp contrast to the backdrop of its forest home was a white bear, the elusive Spirit bear.

photo: Simon Jackson

After visiting the home of the Spirit bear, I began presenting the issue to schools, conferences, and service clubs across the Lower Mainland and Vancouver Island. In 1999, I founded the Spirit Bear Youth Coalition, which today has over 300 members, backed by the likes of Jane Goodall and supported by Charlotte Church and Haley Joel Osment. The coalition's sole purpose is to set aside a large wilderness sanctuary for the Spirit bear in the last place they can call home. In the Earth Day 2000 global edition of *Time Magazine*, I was named as one of sixty Heroes for the Planet; one of three Canadians and one of six youth selected from around the world. While this was a tremendous honour, it has helped raise awareness and support for the issue, as well as adding credibility to the campaign.

For only once in a world, once in lifetime, is there a chance to preserve such a vast tract of intact wilderness, with such beauty and ecological importance, as is the chance we now have to preserve the Spirit bear's last intact habitat in and around Princess Royal Island. It would be a lasting legacy for British Columbians and indeed, the world.

BC BIG TREES

Garry Oak (*Quercus garryana*)
Somenos Road, Duncan
Healthy
Circumference: 4.5 metres
Height: 30.6 metres
Average crown spread: 26.6 metres

Information and image courtesy BC Conservation Data Centre's Big Tree Register: www.elp.gov.bc.ca/rib/wis/cdc.

CAMPING CODE OF ETHICS

BC's wilderness areas are popular destinations. However, over-use and improper travelling and camping practices have led to damage to the natural environment and unfulfilled wilderness recreation experiences. To retain the high quality of the BC wilderness, we must all accept responsibility for minimizing our impact.

Choose a suitable campsite. This is probably the most critical choice you will make. Choose a site that will be least damaged by your stay, and won't affect the experience of others. Generally the site should be at least sixty metres away from water, well away from the trail, durable enough to withstand the impacts of camping, and away from other campers.

The best places to camp are high-use sites that are so damaged that further use will result in little additional deterioration, or pristine sites that are durable and show no signs of previous use.

The wildest thing that happened to me in BC comes back to me from my childhood.

My father has an adventurous streak in him that makes him almost completely incapable of driving on paved highways between two known points. His habit of going to the Queen's Printer and acquiring the highest resolution geological survey map to find the tiniest and most obscure route between two towns, comes, I'm sure, from his uncle who was chair of the geology department at Trinity College in Oxford.

But dear dad is a psychiatrist, and unless I'm mistaken, geography is not a required discipline for medical training.

On this particular day, we were on our way from Kamloops to Boston Bar in our venerable and reliable 1951 Pontiac Star Chief. Dad, with his map carefully folded beside him, had chosen a faint mark on the map as our route.

We had been on a very twisty and windy and muddy road for what seemed like hours. We rounded the last bend in the trail and below us the valley of Boston Bar was laid out like a perfect postcard. We stopped the car and at the base of the hill we were on we could see a corral. Crowded around it on three sides was a colourful assortment of local cowboys and cowgirls enjoying a rodeo. On the upper, valley side of the corral, a fence had just given out and three or four cowpokes were in hot pursuit of a pair of bullocks at full gallop. The dust and yelps of joy rising from the audience as we stood transfixed by the – until now only imagined – scene, still rings in my mind.

We had only been residents in BC for a few years, having arrived from England. To this day that event was the wildest site in BC.

Roy Kerwood
Vancouver

Great Camping Story

A decade ago a girlfriend and I visited the Queen Charlotte Islands for the first time. We hiked obscure trails, climbed Tow Hill, went crabbing at North Beach (another story in itself), and hiked six miles along East Beach to view the wreck of the Pezuta, a shipwreck from earlier in the century. We even had the chance to paddle the Haida war canoe, Loo Taas, around Skidegate Inlet. We decided to end our perfect fairytale holiday with an overnight camping trip to Gray Bay on Moresby Island.

Sitting around a roaring campfire that evening, listening to the rolling surf pound against the sandy beach, we suddenly became aware of a loud huffing sound from the bush behind our campsite. We froze. A sign at the entrance to the campsites had warned that the Charlottes are home to the largest black bears in North America. A couple of heartbeats later, we

Port Clements, Queen Charlotte Islands

heard a strangled sneeze, then a stealthy slipping, sliding sound. I looked at Diana. Diana looked at me. We both had the same thought: this was no bear, this was an axe murderer who preyed on lone female campers!

We bolted for the camper and locked ourselves in. Since we couldn't come up with a workable plan to break into the cab of the truck, we took stock of our weapons — a hammer and a flashlight. We did have a perfectly good axe, but in our panicked flight, we'd left it leaning against the tailgate, and neither of us was willing to open the door and rescue it. So we settled instead for a heated discussion on how we would defend ourselves with the flashlight and hammer. It was a very long and scary night. At any moment we expected a crazed killer to begin ripping the camper apart, probably with our own axe.

Early the next morning we crept out of the camper. Everything looked exactly as we had left it the previous night. Even the axe was still in the same place. Thinking maybe

Under no circumstances should trees be cut to provide firewood, furniture, or boughs for beds.

Use a camp stove.

Protect water quality. To help prevent the spread of Giardia and other infections, never urinate or defecate directly into water, either in camp or when travelling.

All water should be considered to be contaminated, and should always be treated before drinking it. Three common methods are boiling, water filters, and adding iodine.

If you pack it in, you can pack it out. Never bury your garbage or scatter food waste as animals will find it and dig it up.

Respect wildlife. Remember that you are entering the animals' home and you want to respect their needs and minimize the intrusion on their lives. Don't do anything that will cause animals to lose their wildness. Watch animals from a distance. If they are watching you, you are too close.

Leave pets at home.

Information ccourtesy Outdoor Recreation Council of BC.

CATTLE DRIVE COWPOKES

Events around the province take *BC Almanac* out on the road fairly regularly. Take Cattle Drive 2000, for instance. That's where greenhorns ride across ranchland around Kamloops for a week, learning about the western way of life. But it's not always a smooth ride, as city-slicker Denise Schreyer found out. Here's part of what she told us on our show from the Sugarloaf Ranch, about riding through country that was the scene of a forest fire a couple of years ago:

This is not funny (laughter in the background). I'm geographically dyslexic. I was told to go around the corner to go to the washroom but of course me, I'm used to just taking off. Anyways, I head up for the hills and in the burn, the trees are real skinny. Like, I'm not real skinny, and these trees are real skinny so you've gotta go real high to get a big tree and so I had to go quite a ways. Of course I wasn't even supposed to be going at this point.

the killer had decided to go off and find less neurotic prey, we hurriedly began packing our belongings. We'd almost finished when the sounds of the previous night echoed from the bush once again. A few seconds later a doe and her fawn sauntered through the campsite. Each wore an unmistakable smirk that pretty well summed us up – Greenhorns!

Eventually my husband and I moved to the Queen Charlotte Islands. And every time I see a deer I'm reminded of that long ago summer of July, 1989. But something in their eyes sometimes makes me wonder if perhaps Diana and I have become legends in the deer kingdom.

Harriett Fjaaajesund
Port Clements

Unlike most Canadians, I have never camped. A classic, west coast Canadian love story is the reason why.

My mother is from solid Fraser Valley Mennonite Brethren stock. In fleeing the Russian Revolution her father was more preoccupied with putting a roof over his family's heads than communing with nature; thus, Mom, as a girl, had never camped.

Leaving the valley as a young woman in the 1950s to make her fortune in the big city, she landed a great job at Woodward's in the employment department. One day she interviewed a handsome young Australian, fresh off the boat, who cheekily asked her out after his interview. She refused him that time, but eventually broke down when he offered to fly her up to Nanaimo in a float plane. Dad was chalking up flying hours to sign on with a then fairly new commercial carrier, Canadian Pacific Airlines.

They were married about a year later and Mom became pregnant with me.

Dad had camped a lot as a teenager in Brisbane, but the Queensland bush is a lot different than Cultus Lake, as he was about to find out.

My very pregnant mother was comforted by the thought of the modern rubber inflatable air mattresses Dad had scrounged up for the trip. They set out in beautiful sunshine and Dad picked an idyllic campsite on the side of the mountain overlooking the lake.

They settled down for the night. At about 2 am, the rain started. The tent poles and ropes slackened as the pegs released from the squishy earth. All of a sudden, the entire tent, air mattresses, and ground sheet began to slide down the mountain. Mom and Dad clung to each other as they gained speed.

When they reached the bottom they wasted no time in staggering back to the car. Wet, cold, and shaken, they drove back to Vancouver.

For years, my sister and I had no idea why our family never camped....

I must be the only person to be turned off camping in utero!

Colleen McLaughlin Barlow

From England with Prince Charles

At the beginning of July 1977, I was preparing, as a newly qualified physiotherapist, to head off on my adventure to a new job which I had just been offered in Golden. The British newspapers had announced that Prince Charles would be opening the upcoming Calgary Stampede and I jokingly announced to family and work colleagues, "When I go to Canada I'm going with Prince Charles!"

When I checked in at Heathrow for my flight to Calgary, I was told that I might be subject to some extra special security checks as an important passenger would be on board. Daringly I said, " Oh, you mean Prince Charles!" A horrified look spread across the face of the woman who was checking me in as she whispered, "How did you know?"

The flight to Canada passed uneventfully and as we landed Prince Charles emerged from the first-class section to chat to those who were sitting in the first few rows of second class. As we descended the plane, two or three minutes after Prince Charles and down the same red-carpeted steps, we were treated to a twenty-one-gun salute and were greeted by RCMP and native Indians dressed in their finest regalia!

What a wonderful welcome to Canada for a new immigrant who now resides here as a proud Canadian.

Judy Doyle
Golden

So I tied my horse up to this tree and this tree was covered with soot, it was just black! And as soon as my horse heard all the other horses leaving he got scared. He jumped up and was running around the tree. I was sort of in the middle of doing what I was supposed to be doing (laughter) and the rope got loose and I was sort of dragged, um, with my pants half down, and I was trying to be all lady-like about this but you don't really have a choice when you're being dragged through the brush with no pants on. So I finally got my horse under control, and I put my hands — I was wearing these gloves — on my face and said, "Oh, I'm so happy." And of course my hands were covered with soot, so I had a better beard and moustache than any of the wranglers. I looked great, just covered with soot from one end to the other. Next year, I don't care, I'm wearing Depends!

BC MYTHICAL CREATURES: OGOPOGO

Since at least the early 19th century, a mysterious creature known as Ogopogo has been spotted frequently in Okanagan Lake, Kelowna. The name Ogopogo comes from an early 20th-century music hall song, but the native people in the Okanagan area had already named it N'ha-a-itk, or Naitaka, which means "Devil of the Lake." They feared this monstrous creature which is reported to be anywhere from twelve to seventy feet long, two feet in diameter, black or dark green in colour, with a head

If I lay on my back in the lake and watch the trees rise to meet the sky, I can feel the lapping of the water and the swirling of the cedar skirts match the dance of the skidding clouds in a single song.

At the age of three, I was astonished that Cultus Lake looked just like the postcard that had enticed my mother to pack up her four daughters and start a new life. It was a three-day train ride. We sang Christmas carols in October because those were the only words I knew. We ate peanut butter sandwiches and cereal from little boxes that converted into bowls. It was a treat in every sense. We pretended that whole days passed as we charged through dark tunnels. "Is it morning already?" we'd chime as the sun emerged from the other end. These are my first memories.

We left behind innumerable relatives, the shadow of a father, and cold Ontario winters.

We were met by a kind uncle and his reluctant family who quickly helped us settle into a vast old house with wood floors and stained-glass windows. I guess it had been neglected, but it was the mansion of our adventures. The lake was outside our door and we paddled in the shallow waters or roamed the docks. We loved to walk along the shore to the post office and general store at Main Beach to buy everything from bread to a blue teapot.

When the summer homes were shut up, we would invent imaginary tenants. I can still pick out the homes of the Wicked Witch, the Three Little Pigs, and the Big Bad Wolf. Cross the street here.

I believed we lived in semi-wilderness. We were lumberjacks cutting down our tall tree sisters.

We still live near Cultus Lake and visit with our assortment of husbands and children. But we have to picnic in the fall or at least mid-week before the hoards of day-trippers stake their claims on public beaches and the reckless speed boats slice up the calm water and quiet air.

"The Lake" retains its grand serenity on working days.

Angie McDermid
Sardis

Riding the Rails on the Cariboo Prospector

"All aboard!" The conductor's cry is a final warning for passengers to board "BC-31," northbound to Prince George. Whistle blasts puncture the morning sky – two longs, a short, and a long. We creep out of North Vancouver station, picking up speed; as tons of metal lean into serpentine bends, wheels scrape and squeal in reply. The atmosphere on board is casual. Conductors joke with passengers, a steaming breakfast is delivered to our seats, and chatter is muffled in the sound of vintage Bud cars meeting steel track. A fourteen-hour journey on the "people's railway" has begun.

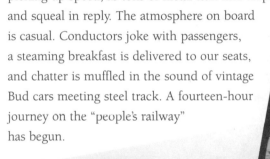

The train is now slowing to a crawl inside Cheakamus Canyon, where water released from winter's grip crashes through a narrow, rocky gorge. Boundless raw energy. Tourists are at the windows, cameras poised, pointing. "There's nothing like this in Oklahoma!" drawls a man beside me. A visitor from Israel is in awe: "I've never seen so many snow capped mountains in one day – in all my life." Seton and Anderson Lakes are ahead, where the track snakes beneath shear rock faces that

like a horse or sheep, and a body like a serpent. Whenever the natives went out on the lake they first searched the horizon for any signs of Naitaka and also made sure to bring along a small animal in order to prevent the creatures from attacking them. Cryptozoologists believe that these creatures may be remnants from the dinosaur age that somehow survived in the deep, cold waters of the lake. It has been spotted alone, or in groups of up to three at a time, though of late the number of sightings have decreased. Scientists suspect that the effects of increased human population are endangering the population. Because of this, in 1989, the Province of BC granted the Ogopogo protected wildlife status, making it illegal to harm, kill, capture, or disturb the creature.

plunge into emerald water. We are beyond where roads go.

BC Rail – born the Pacific Great Eastern – suffered its share of growing pains. Cost overruns, politics, and scandal delayed its arrival at Prince George by forty-one years. The publicly funded PGE proved an easy target for headline writers: "Province's Greatest Expense," "Please Go Easy," and, "Prince George Eventually." The vision to connect the interior to the coast was finally realized in 1956 when Premier W.A.C. Bennett cut the ceremonial ribbon. CBC Radio recorded the event – and his dream of a railway that would continue to Alaska, connecting to Asian markets. Optimistic, yes, but something crews still talk about. BC Rail's meat and potatoes is serving communities along the line. Tourists and goods come in, wood and coal go out. As a Lilloet resident tells me, "It's the lifeline of the interior of BC. We just regard it as our railroad. It does a good job." Besides, how many other railways still pick up ranchers at flag stops?

Kim from Squamish is on her way to visit friends at 100 Mile House; she tries to make this BC Rail trip at least twice a year. "We went through the eco-preserve

The Fraser River seen from the baggage car.

ORGANICALLY SPEAKING

Whenever agronomist and organic gardening expert Arzeena Hamir appears on the program, listeners eat up her organic solutions. Here are some of her most popular suggestions — that don't involve pesticides. Get more information, on-line, at Terra Viva Organics: *www.tvorganics.com*.

at Whistler when my son was six. We looked out the window and there were dead salmon everywhere, and thirty eagles sitting in the trees. His face just lit up – and his jaw fell open. He thought it was the most wonderful thing in the world. I would go on this trip any day."

As we climb high to the Cariboo Plateau, a crew member slides open the baggage car door so I can take a photograph out the side. It's 2,000 feet straight down. I grab the door frame to fight a surge of vertigo. The conductor still shakes his head in wonder over this engineering feat – one of the steepest railroad grades anywhere in the world. His grandfathers, uncles, and brothers also worked this line. "It just gets into your blood. No clocks to punch, you have to be trusted to do the job. There's no other life like it." I believe him when he says he never tires of this landscape.

In Cariboo country the track runs beside the old BX Stage route – the gold rush wagon road travelled by thousands seeking fortune. Today I come seeking another sort of nugget – interviews for my tape recorder. The string of lakes, marshes, and timber seems endless. Time slows. Click. Clack. Time to think. I remember my first train journey to BC as a twelve-year-old kid from Ontario – seduced by a train's magic and British Columbia's mystique. A few years later I crammed all my belongings into one blue trunk, boarded another train, and chanced a new life in the west. Now, twenty-five years later, I'm content to be back on the rails, riding into a long summer's night.

* * *

The Prospector runs daily between North Vancouver and Lillooet and to points further north on to Prince George three times a week.

ARZEENA'S TIPS

Ladybugs will control a variety of pests, especially aphids. Attract them in your garden by providing plants like dill, parsley, caraway, and fennel. You'll soon see their bright orange eggs all over your garden and once they've laid eggs in your garden, they'll be permanent residents there.

To repel many common insect pests, use members of the allium family such as chives, onions, scallions, and garlic as companion plants. Plant whole rows or slip in seedlings wherever you can fit them. The skins of onions and garlic make an excellent mulch around carrots to prevent carrot rust fly damage.

Powdery mildew thrives where high rates of nitrogen have been used. High nitrogen promotes tender leaf formation, causing dense stands that are more susceptible to infections. Adequately fertilize but avoid stimulating succulent growth. Organic fertilizers or slow-release formulations of lawn fertilizers are good choices

Here's a recipe to make your own powdery mildew control spray:
- 1 tbsp baking soda
- 1 quart water
- A few drops of liquid soap

Spray every couple of days to prevent the spread of the disease. Before treating your plants, test the spray on a few leaves to make sure they are not too sensitive.

Here's one way of controlling two pests at the same time. Quack grass damages the nerves that slugs use for feeding. Chop up the grass and use it as a mulch. Make a tea by cutting it up and soaking the leaves in one quart of warm water for twenty-four hours. Use the spray directly on the soil as a deterrent, but be careful not to spray plants.

Protect your seedlings with two-litre plastic soda bottles. Make sure no slugs are around the seedlings first. Cut the bottoms out of the bottles, sink them into the soil around the seedlings and remove the caps. Not only will this provide a barrier to the slugs, the mini-greenhouse will spur the growth of your seedlings.

My favourite river is precious to me only in memory. It no longer exists as it once was.

The banks of the Okanagan River that flows through the valley past Oliver were a favoured haunt when I was a young girl in the fifties. I grew up in Kelowna, but each summer, for two glorious weeks, I visited my grandparents at their Oliver fruit orchard and reveled in freedom from parental supervision and the demands of younger siblings. The river wound its looped and lethargic way below branches of land where peaches, apricots, and plums thrived in the blazing south Okanagan sun. Like a lazy brown snake it twisted through the valley, its coils pinching off chunks of land into near islands, ideal for exploring. I and my much-admired boy cousins from up the road spent blissful hours on expeditions in the thick stands of sumac and cottonwood that lined the banks, caught sun fish in bordering ponds, swam off sand bars silky smooth on bare feet, and built bullrush forts from the vast stands of upright brown spikes.

The river was, and remains, the life blood of the area. It supplies irrigation water that makes bounty of the land possible. Water for my grandparents' orchard was supplied from a pump house. The small building of bleached, unpainted boards was filled with a Rube Goldberg tangle of pipes and machinery. Granddad, an ex-army major, decreed it off-limits to us children, which only piqued our curiosity. He seemed to spend hours down there keeping the cranky contraption functioning so that sprinklers would continue to turn over his orchards and alfalfa fields.

The idyll ended the summer the bulldozers and earth movers came in and carved a dead straight channel down the valley, chewing through the wooden almost-islands, truncating the lazy bends that turned over time into stagnant ponds. Small dams referred to as drop structures were erected every few miles to hold back the now unimpeded water. These were comprised of a narrow foot bridge topping a series of openings where green water thundered through. The undertow and current they created made swimming a risky endeavour. The boy cousins who swam like fish made a game of swimming under the glassy curves of water, jumping from the foot bridge, or floating over the brink on black, patched inner tubes. I watched their antics with envy from a spot safely downstream where I stood teetering, knee deep, braced against the strong flow on the now rocky bottom, filled with regret for the soft sandbars and lazy rhythm of the old river.

From time to time I visit friends in Oliver who have a place on the river north of town. They've been there for fifteen years, think of themselves as old hands, think the river was always as it is now. This isn't surprising since, over the intervening years, the river has softened. Giant cottonwoods and shrubby undergrowth have blurred the hard lines. Weather has rounded off the high dykes, carved out pools and thrown up small islands. It is heartening to see the old river reasserting itself and looking once more like the river of my childhood.

Denise de Montreuil
Victoria

SETTLING IN

Skip Rowland

Skip Rowland is the BC Almanac community correspondent in Ucluelet.

Denise and I first saw the West Coast around Ucluelet in 1992 while on a visit to Vancouver to see my sister. After enough "relative talk" we grabbed a rental car and headed for the thin red lines on the map that take you to places small and often unknown. Such was Ucluelet.

We drove over the crest of the small hill outside town, looked down on the Canadian Princess complex with the small fishing boat harbour behind it, looked at each other and came to one of those rare, nearly instant, decisions that we could be real happy in such a place.

We are not strangers to decisions of heart or emotion. Fed up with the pace of California living, we sold everything we owned in 1984, had a yacht built in France, and for the next six years did some serious "drifting and blending," which means taking

103

a closer look at the world in slow motion, i.e., from the deck of a yacht averaging about five knots.

We raced many events, became nearly barley-soaked at a few yachtie get-togethers, and came to have a true respect for nature, the world we occupy, and the presence of God.

Serious illness struck Denise in Thailand (after nearly six years of cruising) so we sold the boat, settled there, and built Thailand's first genuine miniature golf complex, with two eighteen-hole courses, a restaurant, and, of course, a bar.

After several years of enjoyable operation, that once-in-a-lifetime opportunity came our way in the form of a Singaporean who "just had to own" our course. We made that possible.

We spent another year in Mainland China constructing another course, and we finally ended up coming to the incredible west coast of Vancouver Island in January of 1996.

We had blinders on for our approach and knew nothing of the forestry problems or the devastation of commercial fishing. Ucluelet was, literally, on its butt, and things were not looking cheery.

But we settled in anyway and started building A Snug Harbour Inn, the small luxury bed and breakfast that we still own and where we still get to meet so many wonderful people.

Summer Preserves
BC Bumbleberry Preserves

3 cups raspberries, whole

2 cups blackberries, whole

2 cups blueberries, whole

6½ cups sugar

2 tbsp + 1 cup water

1 pkg (57 g) fruit pectin crystals

In a large, stainless steel saucepan, combine the berries, sugar, and 2 tbsp of water. Stir gently. Let stand for 3 hours, stirring occasionally. Bring the fruit mixture to a full rolling boil over high heat, stirring constantly. Boil hard for 1 minute. Remove from heat.

In a separate saucepan, whisk together fruit pectin crystals and 1 cup (250 ml) water. Bring to a boil then boil hard 1 minute. Add to hot fruit mixture and stir 8 minutes. Skim foam. Ladle jelly into hot sterilized 250 ml mason jars, leaving ¼ inch (0.5 cm) head space. Wipe jar rims clean. Center prepared canning lids and apply screw bands fingertip tight. Process filled jars in a boiling water bath canner for 5 minutes. Cool. Sealed lids curve downwards. Store in a cool, dry, dark place. Makes about 8 250 ml jars.

Recipe courtesy Barb Lindstrom.

A Special Place

I grew up on the prairies. There, meadowlarks sing up the rising sun, Thunderpumpers call down the evening rain, and a summer gallop of perpetual wind tosses its gold and black barley mane. After moving to BC, my homesickness for those sights and sounds was laid to rest when I found a narrow, tree-lined nature trail at Salmon Arm's waterfront.

Grasshoppers, blurred wings snapping and flashing, go clickety-clacking ahead of us with every dust-filled stride we take. To the west, a hungry hawk slowly quarters the foreshore's undulating carpet of summer-crisped golden grasses and sage-green sedges. Sweeping ahead of him, the big bird's shadow panics some small creature, driving it out into the open. Hovering, the hunter hangs in the hazy blue of this hot August afternoon while below him, tiny, trickling streams mirror sunlight back to his slowly fanning wingtips. In a golden blur, he plummets earthward. Then, after a short feather-snapping scramble, mantles his kill.

To the east, cool fingers of smoky shadows caress the old boat bay. Three female mergansers, diving for fish, ripple the water's dull surface. Crested heads foremost, the ducks spear silently downwards and, with their reappearance, bring a palette of unsuspected colour back from the depths. Curving away from their sleek, ash-grey bodies, the stone-washed denim-blue wavelets show highlights of amethyst and lavender, with overtones of verdigris. Subtly subdued, birds and water offer the understated elegance of a masterful Oriental painting as they blend into a timeless pattern of serenity.

Accompanied by the kingfisher's rattle, we pass one downed and dying willow after another and realize that the beavers have returned to the bay. Although it is this method of coppicing that ensures succulent new growth for their future needs, the sight of their over-zealous harvesting is disconcerting.

A whistle of wings overhead diverts our attention from the carnage and brings a swirl of blackbirds sweeping past. Somewhere in the surrounding bushes a pair of magpies softly natter, while behind us a raucous parliament of crows is called to order by their speaker.

Over the last four years, the town has pulled together and worked diligently to improve its image to the world and help those in the resource sectors who were so economically hurt.

I like to think it's worked. The people of the west coast, and Ucluelet in particular, are both friendly and dedicated. This little community, sitting in one of nature's most breathtaking vistas, shows all the resolve and promise of being one of Canada's premiere intelligent growth areas during the next millennium.

Denise and I are delighted to be a part of it ... and I love sharing the stories, chuckles, and yarns of our Ucluelet as the community reporter for Mark and *BC Almanac*.

THE GIN AND TONIC SCALE

Anne McCarthy

Anne McCarthy is one of the two Environment Canada weather forecasters who appear on BC Almanac.

Every business develops its own jargon. Some is widespread and descriptive. You'll find pilots calling a thunderstorm a "tunderbumper" from coast to coast. Some jargon is quite local — one favourite is used, to the best of my knowledge, only in Victoria. This is the "Gin and Tonic" scale.

With so much water around Victoria, temperatures are moderated both in the winter and summer. During a normal summer's day, we get temperatures into the low or mid-twenties, but as soon as the sun gets lower in the sky, the nearby water brings the temperatures back down for the evening. So you may wear shorts in the day, but a long-sleeved shirt is very nice at night.

Perching at the pinnacle of an old wind-whipped cottonwood, she gleams steely blue on ebony black. Below her, on limb after limb, the tree presents ranks of the suddenly silent, funereal scavengers.

On the western flats, little brown birds zigzag as they stitch the mud with their darning needle beaks. In the distance, long-legged waders follow the same probing procedure in their search for aquatic sustenance. Far out on the lake, rafts of gulls ride the sparkling water. Occasionally rising to wheel over the light-washed waves, they mew and, climbing higher, straddle the wind until lost from view among gold-brushed cloud tatters.

Nearer the earth, another bit of gilt-edged fleece draws the eye. A sac of spider eggs comes undone and, like the fraying edge of a colour-drenched medieval tapestry, a shimmering skein of silk unravels in the breeze. Kiting away across the blue, autumn's first spiderling goes sailing, taking our hearts along for the ride, even as our feet turn reluctantly homeward.

Bonita K. Lingenfelter
Salmon Arm

Around Vancouver Island by Kayak

Writer Maria Coffey and her photographer/veterinarian husband Dag Goering have kayaked in Asia, Africa, and Europe. During the summer of 1999, they spent a wet and windy three months circumnavigating Vancouver Island. The couple dubbed it their "Visions of the Wild" tour, with plans to turn the experience into a book. *BC Almanac* traced their journey around the Island, and their return home to Protection Island near Nanaimo. Dag and Maria's book *Visions of the Wild* is planned for publication in the fall of 2001.

Occasionally this doesn't work. If there is a strong ridge of high pressure inland, with a low off shore, the low will continue to draw warm dry air out from the interior throughout the day and overnight. This pattern can last for a few days at a time but generally happens only a couple of times over a summer. The jargon short form for this pattern is outflow. Sometimes we like to detail the strength of the outflow more precisely.

That leads us back to the G&T scale, or more fully, the gin & tonic scale.

Gin & Tonic times one: it will be hot until about 4 pm

Gin & Tonic times two: still warm enough for another about 6 pm

Gin & Tonic times three: still warm enough for another about 8 pm

Gin & Tonic times four: still warm enough for another about 10 pm

A normal summer day in Victoria rates a G&T times one, or perhaps two rating. Which is perhaps best for me in the long run.

BRIAN MINTER'S SUMMER GARDENING TIPS: AUGUST

Protect your vegetables from insects and disease

This is a critical time for vegetable gardens. Most vegetables are in their final stages of maturity and lack of careful attention could result in crop loss due to insects or disease. Try to use organic pesticides whenever possible because you can use your vegetables within one day of harvest. Be sure to note the harvest limitations on the bottles of all insecticides.

Don't neglect your trees and shrubs

The trees under the eaves of your house need lots of water during the hot summer months, so please don't neglect them. If you are going to fertilize in late summer, use slow-release nitrogen for evergreens and shade trees, and a vegetable fertilizer for most fruit and flowering trees.

Mark: Dag, you're a photographer, what are the mental snapshots rolling around in your mind after such a journey?

Dag: I think it's the diversity of the Island that caught my eye, be it Nootka Sound, Brooks Peninsula, or Barclay Sound, and of course the Gulf Islands. They all have their own distinctiveness and beauty. Some of the images that really remain with me are the seas on the west coast. The swells, it's kind of hard to erase those from your memory.

Mark: Especially when it was a wild and wet day … it was hard work there for a while, wasn't it, Maria?

Maria: It certainly was. A long journey along such an exposed coastline. I think it was bigger and more demanding than we expected; I hadn't been out in seas that big, ever. We were sometimes in ten-foot swells offshore. That's pretty awe-inspiring.

Mark: What's it like, psychologically, to be battling the elements that way?

Dag: It's demanding in making a decision as to when to leave and go out there. Sometimes we were committing to passages where you can't go to shore for five, ten, even fifteen miles. So if you get caught out by the weather it can be a very serious situation. It's actually very stressful making those decisions, and of course when you're in the seas themselves in rough conditions it's another thing. I think Maria has a story.

Maria: Yeah, I went through a lot of psychological walls on this trip and I think the biggest one was when we were off the outside coast of Nootka Island. We made the decision to go way offshore to avoid the reefs; we had to go about two and a half miles offshore, and it got pretty gnarly out there. We were in eight- to ten-foot swells and they started to break. I went into one of those resistant fear modes: "I don't want to be here." That's a dangerous state of mind to be in because you are there and you've got to deal with it. Dag just said quite calmly from behind me, "Remember all your bracing skills." Bracing is when the wave starts to break over you and you lean into it, stick your paddle into the water to stabilize the boat. I just went through a moment when I thought, "Yes, I know how to brace and we're okay. If this huge wave breaks on us we'll work as a team, and we're going to survive." I went from this moment of abject terror to actually enjoying being out there.

Mark: Part of this journey was to experience your physical surroundings, but you were also meeting artists who've decided to live close to the water. Tell us about one.

Dag: We met quite a few artists on the inside coast in the Discovery Group, Cortes Island. We also met artists underway: a filmmaker, a jeweller, people either in boats or hiking out there. It was neat to meet them because we felt in a sense we were meeting people of our own tribe. We made a lot of friends out there.

Mark: Maria, how do you compare this to those other journeys? I remember talking to you on the Ganges River and from Africa a few years ago.

Maria: They're all equally demanding but in different ways. In places like India and Africa you have a lot of cultural challenges. We were in countries where we didn't speak very much – if any – of the language and we had to learn all the different cultural morés to be accepted. Of course, here it was much more of a physical and psychological challenge than journeys abroad. They're all challenging and therefore rewarding in their own way.

Flowering shrubs
The finest flowering shrubs this month are the Rose of Sharon, Buddleia or Butterfly Bush, and sensational Hydrangeas.

Healthy lawns
Our lawns will probably keep growing until late October. As the weather is often hot in August, be sure you mow your grass a little higher to protect the root system. When you water, water thoroughly to a depth of 1½ to 2 inches.

Weed control in your lawn
During hot weather, tackle your weed problems in the early morning or evening.

Back in the summer of 1979, I lucked into a job with the Department of Fisheries to patrol a remote section of British Columbia's coastline just north of Bella Bella. The work, which didn't feel at all like work to me, consisted mainly of walking up the creeks that flowed into Laredo Inlet on Princess Royal Island, avoiding bears, and counting the salmon that arrived there to spawn.

Sitting aboard my boat one evening, I heard wolves singing their hauntingly sad chorus far off in the distance. The next morning, having paddled my canoe across a tidal lake that drained into the inlet, I came upon a pair of half-grown wolf pups sitting near the shore, their heads cocked and staring curiously as I sang a little song for them. Not quite knowing what to make of me, the pups didn't run away in fear, nor did they wag their tails in greeting. I got the distinct impression that they had been told to stay put while the grown-up wolves went foraging for lunch. Just as I was preparing to walk up the salmon stream that fed into the lake, a pack of eight adult wolves came dashing along the beach straight toward me. They quickly herded the two youngsters away into the woods, then fanned out around where I stood with my back to the lake.

Stifling a strong urge to leap into my canoe and start paddling like an Olympic hopeful, I instead reached slowly into it and lifted out my shotgun. At this, the wolves stopped their advance and sat down, forming a perfect semi-circle around me. Although I felt the little hairs on the back of my neck sticking straight out, I wasn't really all that worried. I had just finished reading Farley Mowat's book, Never Cry Wolf, and clearly recalled the part where he insisted that there had never been an attack by wolves on humans in all of Canadian history. A strange calm descended over me, and I somehow knew that if I didn't act frightened or overly aggressive, all would be well. After all, these were Canadian wolves, weren't they?

After a minute or two of this silent standoff, the lead wolf, a huge black female, abruptly began to howl. The others soon joined in, and I wasn't sure if this was a pre-dinner social custom or their way of greeting me into the fold. I decided on the latter, and began to howl right along with them. If they were surprised at this, they were too polite to show it, and we stood there in the drizzle, howling together for a good twenty minutes. I then shouldered my gun and started walking slowly up the creek to count fish. The upstream wolves glided casually out of the way to let me pass, as if I had every right to be there. When I returned about an hour later, the whole pack was still on the beach near the canoe, with the puppies playing in full sight. I guess they had decided that anyone who could howl that well must be all right by their standards.

Jim "howls with wolves" Russell
Salt Spring Island

Nanaimo's Vancouver
Island Exhibition

Nelson Annual Boat Regatta

North Vancouver's Under the Volcano
Festival of Art and Social Change

Prince George's Dekah'l Pow-Wow

Prince George Exhibition

Smithers Fall Fair

Squamish Days Loggers
Sports Festival

Vancouver International
Comedy Festival

Vancouver's Pacific National
Exhibition (PNE)

Vancouver's Powell Street Festival

Vernon Cowboy Festival
& Wild West Show

Victoria's First Peoples Festival

Victoria Fringe Festival

Whistler's Classic Music Festival

Williams Lake Cariboo Fall Fair

My friend Bruce is coaxing his pickup truck into the Cascades on Highway 3; we're just beyond the Hope Slide where half a mountain fell away. Manning Park's sculpted bear sentry is just ahead. It's the annual apple run to Keremeos – a fall ritual Bruce's family has honoured for years. We'll load up on Macs, Jonagolds, and Royal Galas so fresh that a lapful will be consumed on the return journey. There should be more than enough to go around when we get home.

Fall whispers all around us, putting senses on high alert. A chilly mountain breeze whips up clouds of yellow cottonwood leaves. I'm wishing ethnobotanist Nancy Turner was along for the ride to make more sense of what we're seeing. The Skagit River zig-zags across our path; part of me wants to follow it to where the trout are rising, to cast a hand-tied fly sent by North Vancouver listener Vic Marchiel.

Al Hoag, orchardist, Creston

School's back, so for inspiration we talk to Nobel Prize-winning chemist Michael Smith. He reminds us that "really amazing things can come from an experiment which went wrong." Persistence. We'll need it to survive the onslaught of rains and wind cranking up in the Gulf of Alaska, not to mention the fall book season! An avalanche of new titles is about to let loose.

The salmon runs are tailing off now, but as Frank Hanuse at tiny Oweekeno on the Central Coast tells us, their numbers are down. Dangerously so. Janet May, our community correspondent in Powell River, will be topping up her wood pile, food guru Don Genova is eyeing the BC fall harvest, while East Vancouver's Eileen Mosca awaits the first grapes of the season. Weekend hikers are bound for quieter trails; and

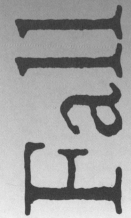

MICHAEL SMITH
BRAIN POWER TIPS

Hands down, Michael Smith is British Columbia's most celebrated scientist. In 1993 he was awarded the Nobel Prize in Chemistry for groundbreaking gene research that launched a whole new field of protein engineering. We asked the always amenable professor to pass along some tips for increasing brain power. Who knows, they just might propel you to the Nobel podium at Oslo.

1. While good ideas can come "out of the blue," they more often come from continually worrying about and working on a difficult problem.

2. Really revolutionary things completely change the way that you think or the way that you do things. It's important to be able to recognize the revolutionary opportunity and be prepared to drop everything you are doing to move in the new direction.

husband-and-wife triathletes Lori Bowden and Peter Reid buckle down to defend their World Iron Man Championships titles.

BC Almanac puts on its fall coat – columnists like Kootenay ecologist Don Gayton return from a summer of discoveries like the Cortesian Spud Gun Militia, and new features come to air. Maybe we'll hit the road to sample preserves and apple pie at a Vancouver Island fall fair, or sip estate wines at an Okanagan festival. But right now I'm craving the simple pleasure of a Keremeos Mac. Drive on, Bruce, drive on.

How I Ended Up in BC

photo: McLean Mill
Photographic Archive (5073)

As a child growing up in Indiana in the 1950s, I would look forward to the summer arrival of my cousin Dan, who picked tomatoes in my grandfather's greenhouse. Dan lived in Ohio, but his father's side of the family lived in Victoria. He would tell stories of Vancouver Island; the ferries, the big trees, and the strange Canadian money that was worth more than our "American" dollars. Dan proclaimed that when he grew up he was going to move to BC.

In the 1960s, the dark clouds of Vietnam threatened as I entered university, and I began to revisit Dan's stories of BC. The reality of war now made me look at Canada as a humane refuge, unlike hawkish and conservative Indiana. My growing interest in nature and wilderness often led to references of British Columbia, and a whole new aspect of Canada began to develop.

Morally opposed to the war, I began to entertain thoughts of escaping to Canada. After graduating from university, and several appearances before my local draft board, I was able to satisfy my "obligation" to my country, as a conscientious objector, pricing furniture in a Goodwill store for two years. In 1972, the overwhelming presidential victory of Richard Nixon over peace candidate George McGovern made me realize that I did not trust "my fellow Americans" to let them determine my future.

I began researching immigration to Canada. I could only immigrate if I could do a job that could not be filled by a Canadian. In 1973, with my degree in education in hand, my wife Joan and I travelled to Canada to visit my cousin's relatives in Victoria, in hopes of finding such a job.

That job turned out to be teaching in a one-room school just being started in a fly-in lumber mill on Takla Lake. In September 1973, the eleven children of the mill helped me unpack the few school supplies that had arrived, and we began Silvacan Elementary School in the mill's recreation hall.

We did a lot of art projects until the chalkboard, textbooks, and other supplies began to trickle in. I was the teacher, principal, and bus (pickup truck) driver. The mill site was 120 miles north of Fort St James. It was inaccessible by road and because of the isolation we were only able to leave the mill site at Christmas, spring break, and summer vacation. We had no radio or television reception or phone, and only periodic mail delivery.

By the second year, the students left the pool table, Coke machine, and ashtrays of the recreation hall behind and moved into a new portable classroom with real desks and chairs. Joan and I moved out of the sixteen-foot camping trailer where we had spent our first Canadian winter, and into a regular-sized mobile home teacherage.

Although deprived of many things, we were happy to have chosen the crisp mountain air of British Columbia to be our home. Now, more than twenty years later, we continue to be happy with our choice.

Dan, my cousin, still lives in Ohio.

David Marchant
McBride

3. While bright people from whom ideas gush are often stimulating, really amazing things can come from an experiment which went wrong.

4. One of the most satisfying things for a professor is to watch a student develop into a researcher who is smarter than them.

5. A great thing about experimental science is that success comes from learning from your mistakes. This can mean that the older you are the better you are. Of course, it is time to quit when you start to think that you never make mistakes.

BC's Nobel laureate Michael Smith died in fall 2000 at age 68. After receiving the half million dollar prize, he donated the money to schitzophrenia research, endowment funds to encourage Canadian women in science, and elementary school science programs.

**GREATEST
RAINFALL
IN ONE DAY**
OCTOBER 6, 1967

A one-day rainfall of 489.2 mm
occurred at Ucluelet Brynnor Mines
a Canadian weather record that
still stands.

Information courtesy Environment Canada.

BC's World Championship Iron Man Team

They must be the fittest couple in the country – if not on the planet. BC's Lori Bowden won the grueling World Iron Man Championship in October 1999; her husband Peter Reid won the men's event the previous year. We reached the dynamic duo at their Hawaii hotel after eight hours of non-stop swimming, biking, and running.

Mark: How's it feel after all that preparation, hard work, and now a chance to rest?

Lori: It's a pretty incredible feeling. This is the highest moment you can ever achieve in our sport. Peter got to experience that last year; just for me to cross that line and see how he felt on that day is pretty incredible.

Peter: It's a great feeling to see Lori cross the finish line, and know exactly how she feels. Now we have this bond of running down the final finishing chute in first place.

Mark: You sound a little bagged. I guess that's perfectly normal, Lori?

Lori: Well, you're pretty tired. We stay up pretty late the night of the race and watch the last finishers, and it takes the last ones seventeen hours. It's also the end of the season so we just go out and celebrate. We might be a little tired.

Mark: Peter, give us a sense of how grueling these Iron Man competitions are.

Peter: It's a really long day. It takes a few years to just do the training to be able to finish one. Now we're actually racing the entire distance. It's an eight-hour-plus event, and we're racing as hard as we can go until we get to the finish line. On the Big Island of Hawaii it is extremely humid, very windy, and just makes for a really tough day.

Mark: What was the toughest part of the event for you, Lori?

Lori: I think the swim was pretty hard for me. I went in with high expectations and I had a pretty disappointing performance. I was fortunate enough to just keep on going, and see what the rest of the day would bring, and hope I'd be strong on the bike and the run. Besides that, there weren't really a lot of low points.

Mark: In the finish photos you look like you're still fresh. How is that possible after eight hours of giving everything you've got?

Lori: You're pretty tired but suddenly you see that finish line and it just gives you a huge boost of energy seeing the crowd. And to see Peter waiting for me was amazing.

Mark: What do you two eat, anyway?

Peter: We basically follow a balanced diet; people are somewhat amazed that we eat just like normal people. We watch what we eat, don't eat too much junk food, but then we don't shy away from it, either. Just a balanced diet.

Mark: How do you top this one?

Lori: I don't know if we can. Now that we've both won it, I think it'll be hard for anyone else in the world to top that accomplishment. It's such a great feeling, and we're really happy about it.

In August 2000, Peter and Lori won the Canada Men's and Women's Triathlon Championships, held in Penticton. It was Lori's fourth consecutive win, and Peter's first.

BOOK SEASON(S)

British Columbians are the most voracious readers in the country, and each year they also write a stack of books as high as Mount Robson. BC publishers send out so many titles during the fall and spring book seasons that mail carriers and couriers must crave back massages when the flurry has passed. Titles found teetering on *BC Almanac's* book desk run the gamut: fiction, history, travel, young adult, mystery, outdoor recreation, politics, gardening. We interview dozens of writers each year, rarely encountering the "moody author" who'd much rather be having his/her wisdom teeth extracted. It's probably because the book publicists have done their job: picked up the author from the airport, chased down a good cup of coffee, made an astute observation about their latest offering, and delivered the guest writer to the studio on time.

BC BIG TREES

Black Poplar
(*Populus balsamifera spp. trichocarpa*)
west of Chilliwack
very old, damaged, many large new
leader shoots
Circumference: 11.9 metres
Height: 43.3 metres
Average crown spread: 29.6 metres

*Information and image courtesy BC Conservation Data
Centre's Big Tree Register: www.elp.gov.bc.ca/rib/wis/cdc.*

Country Fair Goodies

Each fall I anxiously await a call from Robin Nichol, volunteer organizer with the Queensborough Fall Fair, hoping to again be asked to help judge baked goods and preserves at this country fair in the city tucked between New Westminister's condos and the Alex Fraser Bridge. Here are two recipes that come with rave reviews; one is Queensborough's answer to the famous Nanaimo Bar, the other a tasty experiment with Kool Aid. Thanks to Marge Nault, many-time winner at the fair.

Queensborough Treat

base:
2½ cups flour
1½ cups butter or margarine
½ cup brown sugar
2 egg yolks
1 pkg Skor chips

topping:
2 egg whites
1 cup brown sugar
1 tsp vanilla

Mix base ingredients except Skor chips into a soft dough. Spread on a cookie sheet. Sprinkle Skor chips over dough and roll into dough. For topping, beat egg whites with brown sugar and vanilla until peaks form. Spread topping over base. Bake at 300 to 325°F for 25 minutes or until golden brown.

Mock Grape Jelly

4 lbs fresh beets, peeled and cut
4½ cups water
1 pkg grape Kool-Aid
2 oz fruit pectin crystals
pinch of salt
4 cups white sugar

Cook beets in water until tender. Drain and save water. In a large pot, measure beet cooking water plus more if needed to make 4½ cups, add Kool-Aid, pectin, and salt. Bring to a boil on medium heat, stirring until granules are dissolved. Boil for 7 minutes, stirring occasionally. Add sugar and stir to dissolve. Bring to a rolling boil and boil hard for 1 minute. Skim off foam. Pour into hot sterilized half pint jars. Place sterilized metal lids and screw bands on securely. Use the cooked beets for dinner.

Hazelnut grove

TYPHOON FREDA HITS BC'S LOWER MAINLAND
OCTOBER 12, 1962

Remnants of Typhoon Freda struck BC's Lower Mainland, causing seven deaths and damages in excess of $10 million. Twenty percent of Stanley Park was flattened. In Victoria, winds reached sustained speeds of 90 km/h, with gusts to 145 km/h.

Information courtesy Environment Canada.

Fall Harvest
Nancy J. Turner

*Nancy Turner is an ethnobotanist at the University of Victoria,
and contributes to BC Almanac's "In Search of BC" series.*

My earliest recollections are of the hills and woods around Missoula, Montana, where I lived until we moved to Victoria when I was five years old. In Montana, my sister and I spent countless happy hours wandering the thickets and swales near our house. I still remember the enchantment of that place, with its multi-coloured wildflowers, and the sweet scent of the balsamroot and ponderosa pines. Of course, the autumn, when the trembling aspens turned to gold and the long V's of honking Canada geese flew overhead on their southward journey, was a favourite time of year for me.

Moving to Victoria did not diminish my love of the wild places, or of this special season, when the plants and animals are slowing down and readying themselves for winter. My family was always out rambling on fall weekends, when the air was crisp and the sky blue, or even when the soggy drizzle of the west coast had set in. We took our dogs and friends and searched the woods for mushrooms, berries, coloured leaves, and other treasures. I was amazed and delighted then, as now, with the array of different fragrances and soft colours that presented themselves to anyone who sought them out.

Perhaps my favourite of the fall colours is the soft, peachy-coloured blend of orange, pink, and yellow of the leaves of flowering dogwood, our provincial flower. The contrast of the pastel leaves and brilliant red-orange, tight-clustered fruits of the dogwood make both even more spectacular. Sometimes, if you are really lucky, you can find dogwood trees in the fall with a set of creamy-white, late-blooming "flowers" and scarlet fruits together on the same tree. The "flowers" are actually compact button-heads of small greenish flowers encompassed by large white leafy bracts. Dogwood trees are not as plentiful today, but they still grow in the woods around Victoria, and their peachy foliage still highlights any forest stand in autumn.

For British Columbia's First Peoples, the fall has always been a season of intense activity, when the harvesting cycle comes to an end. Many, perhaps most, of the resources that people traditionally required to sustain themselves through the winter and early spring would already have been harvested, processed, and stored away by the end of the summer. Dried cakes of summersweet berries – salalberries, currants, saskatoon berries, raspberries, blackcaps, and soapberries, depending on the location – would be cached in beautifully woven bags and baskets stowed up in the scaffolding of the winterhouses. Root vegetables like camas bulbs, wild onions, yellow glacier lily bulbs, and bitterroots, again depending on the region, would already have been pit-cooked and dried and stored away. Various basket materials – birch bark, cedar bark, basket sedge leaves, and cedar and spruce roots – would also have been dried and stored, to be worked on in the winter.

Still, not all the harvesting tasks of the year would have been completed: many

foods and materials are not ready to be gathered until around the time when the first snows settle on the mountain peaks. Along the coast, people usually waited until the Pacific silverweed leaves started to turn orange and die back before they went to dig these important root vegetables, along with wild springbank clover rhizomes, northern riceroot bulbs, and other types of roots. These were often dug together in late September and October from the tidal flats

mountain (see lingonberry)

currants (*Ribes spp.*)

elderberry, blue (*Sambucus cerulea*)

glacier lily, yellow
(*Erythronium grandiflorum*)

hazelnut (*Corylus cornuta*)

lingonberry (*Vaccinium vitis-idaea*)

onion, wild nodding (*Allium cernuum*)

pine
pinyon (*Pinus edulis*)
ponderosa (*Pinus ponderosa*)
whitebark (*Pinus albicaulis*)

raspberry (*Rubus idaeus*)

riceroot, northern
(*Fritillaria camschatensis*)

salalberry (*Gaultheria shallon*)

saskatoon berry
(*Amelanchier alnifolia*)

sedge, basket (*Carex obnupta*)

silverweed, Pacific
(*Potentilla anserina spp. pacifica*)

soapberry (*Shepherdia canadensis*)

spruce (*Picea spp.*)

BRIAN MINTER'S FALL GARDENING TIPS: SEPTEMBER

Rose care
Keep deadheading your roses. They will look so much better and be stronger, too! Spray regularly to keep them disease-free during the wet fall months, and fertilize them to harden them off and prevent excessive new growth which could be damaged by a heavy frost. If we have an Indian summer, your roses should keep blooming well into November.

Compost bin
With all the fall leaves and garden refuse now available, why not create your own rich soil by constructing a compost bin? Four posts and wire mesh are all you need.

and river estuaries, where they were tended in carefully managed patches. As well as harvesting these roots themselves, people also hunted the geese, swans, and ducks seeking the roots during their fall migrations. Coastal people picked highbrush cranberries and Pacific crabapples in the fall from special moist areas along creeks and lake edges. People also ventured into acid peat bog areas around Thanksgiving time to pick bog cranberries, the small wild forerunners of the domesticated cranberry, as well as lingonberries, or mountain cranberries.

Crabapples and the various types of cranberries were usually stored for winter in cedarwood boxes under water and covered with a layer of oil to seal them. During the winter, they softened and sweetened, but did not rot or ferment. Along many parts of the coast, winter or evergreen huckleberries were the last fruits of all to be harvested in the seasonal cycle. These berries, either dusty blue or shiny black, are small but very sweet and juicy and are eaten fresh in the late fall and winter.

In the Interior, people picked blue elderberries, highbush cranberries, and choke cherries at the end of the growing cycle. Some people would cache the blue elderberries, still in their clusters, under a thick cover of ponderosa pine needles. Here the snows of winter would cover them with a protective layer, and they could be dug out and eaten as needed. Some Interior peoples also sought the large, nut-like seeds of whitebark pine in the fall. This is a timberline species with seeds almost as big as those of the pinyon pine of the Southwest US. People also gathered hazelnuts in the fall wherever they occurred. These tasty nuts were sometimes taken, already cleaned of their prickly husks, from the caches of squirrels and other rodents. People were always careful not to take too many, however, and would leave a gift of some other food behind.

Aboriginal elders and other observers of the natural landscape say that these plants and their habitats are not as plentiful or as productive as they once were, due to urbanization, industrialized logging, ranching, and agriculture, among other factors. This does not negate the value or importance of these plants; they still have the potential to nourish us and are still capable of enriching our lives in many different ways, as long as we recognize and cherish the gifts they provide.

Grape Memories: My First Ten Years in the BC Wine Business

Eric von Krosigk

Eric von Krosigk is a wine consultant in Summerland.

When I started in the BC wine business there were just five large wineries, a dozen estate wineries, and three farm wineries. The flavour of the day was white. Free trade had just had its way with the grape marketing board's lock on the industry, and tariffs and barriers fell for Ronald Reagan's friends in California. In the Okanagan Valley, the grape pull-out was just winding down, leaving deserted landscapes of empty posts and wires. Doom and gloom was felt by all in the business.

I started out building a winery with two partners from New York. In 1991, Summerhill Estate Winery was born, focusing on sparkling wine production. The industry critics said it would never survive. Who would buy a BC-method champenoise, anyway? The skeptics kept saying BC could only grow white wines, and European red grape varieties like Merlot and Cabernet Franc would never survive the winter here.

Ten years ago, the winery business also had image and quality problems. It set out to change this by adopting the Ontario quality program called VQA, or Vintner's Quality Alliance (it assures the wine meets strict standards). The British Columbia Wine Institute was set up to market the VQA program and improve the image of BC wines to the consumer.

Vegetable garden rejuvenation
As each vegetable finishes, take advantage of all the old leaves and stems for your compost. I am a strong believer in using fall rye as a fall and winter crop for valuable green manure in spring. The other great advantage of a winter cover is its ability to prevent severe soil compaction from all the heavy rains we get.

Rhododendrons and azaleas
If we have a warm September, prevent your rhododendrons and azaleas from putting on new growth which will be easily damaged by winter winds.

SEPTEMBER EVENTS

Agassiz Fall Fair & Corn Festival

Bella Coola Fall Fair and
Loggers' Sports

Burnaby Old Time Fall Fair at
Burnaby Village Museum

Chilliwack Annual Bluegrass Festival

Colour it Surrey (multicultural fair)

Colwood Fall Fair

Comox Valley Fall Fair

Harrison Hot Springs World Champion
Sand Sculpture Competitions

Kamloops Annual Provincial
Winter Fair

Kimberley Alpine Folk Dance Festival

Ladysmith Fall Fair

Langford Fall Fair

I remember the first time I sold BC wine to people and what their reactions were like. One comment was that the wine bottle had a cork in it; I was asked if I thought that type of thing was going to be popular – after all, you'd need a special tool to open it! Others where skeptical, having celebrated one too many Schloss Laderheim parties and suffered the effects of consumption by over-indulgence. It really was pretty tough sledding in those days, getting out the message that BC wines had changed.

A great stride forward was the advent of farm wineries. The naysayers from many of the estate wineries said they would never survive and couldn't produce the quality required. I remember this in particular because that's what the large wineries had said about the estate wineries.

From seventeen wineries ten years ago, the industry has grown to sixty-four. Many of my colleagues say this can't be supported, so how is everyone going to survive? This still makes me smile. BC currently has about 4,500 acres of grapes in the ground, and in the world-wide wine scheme of things, this is barely a drop in the bucket.

No other wine region sports as much diversity as ours. With grape varieties from all over the world being made by such a diverse group of winemakers, there's a cornucopia of flavours and styles. Internationally, we've garnered hundreds of medals recognizing the quality of wine from BC grapes. In fact, we may have done our job too well. The European Economic Community is trying to ban our ice wine for export to Europe – for no other reason than being too good.

Cheers.

The Coming of the Grapes

In my neighbourhood in East Vancouver, the coming of the grapes is as much a sign of seasonal change as the turning of the leaves. In our twenty years here, we have learned much from our neighbours, and one joy we have discovered from nearby friends like Luigi and Onorina and Mike and Susan is the annual ritual of winemaking.

During September, there is an anticipation that echoes the excitement of the pre-Christmas season. Are the grapes here yet? Have the varieties we're hoping to use arrived at Bosa's or Colletta's or Spagnol's? Like the first crocuses of spring, the first oak barrels rolled out into the lane and washed out with a garden hose herald a new season.

We make wine with a group of six or seven other families in the neighbourhood. Mike, our fearless leader, knows everything there is to know about the winemaker's craft, from the effect of ambient temperature on fermentation to the dreaded blight of bottle sickness. He is a hard taskmaster, a good friend, and a true connoisseur. An electrician by day, by night and on weekends Mike is a vintner extraordinaire, and the rest of us follow his lead with very few questions.

Once all the grapes reach Vancouver warehouses and we decide what kind of wine and what quantity we'll make, a date is set. It's always a Saturday, rain or shine. We set up the crusher, an electric version of the old mangle washing machine, and wait for the arrival of the pickup truck filled with wooden crates of grapes. Neighbours who have absolutely no interest in wine stop by to observe and chat. We in the winemaking crew pry open the crates and drop bunches one by one into the crusher. Lucky, our Border Collie mascot, snaps at the omnipresent wasps who are wild with desire for the grapes. The crowd of neighbourhood kids is given hammers and the Tom Sawyerish task of flattening the crates. Their reward is an unlimited supply of juicy grapes and samples of Onorina's legendary biscotti.

We watch as the gorgeous purple globes become pulp and juice, filling big plastic vats that sit in Mike's garage fermenting for a week or two before pressing. Then the

Mayne Island Lions' Salmon Bake

Nanaimo Dixieland Jazz Festival And Vintage Car Rally

Nelson's Kootenay Gay Pride

Okanagan Valley Annual Fall Wine Festival

Peachland Fall Fair

Penticton Pentastic Jazz Festival

Port Alberni Fall Fair

Port Alberni Salmon Festival

Port Hardy Regional Fall Fair

Saltspring Island Fall Fair

Sidney and Saanich Peninsula Saltwater (festival of Maritime arts and music)

Telkwa Barbecue & Demolition Derby

Vancouver Fringe Festival

Victoria's Vancouver Island Blues Bash

FALL TRAILS

In 1860, Captain George Henry Richards, who was surveying Howe Sound, saw Mount Garibaldi, which he named after Giuseppe Garibaldi, a 19th-century Italian patriot and soldier who was famous for his valour. Sixty years later, in 1920, Garibaldi Provincial Park was established.

Located less than an hour north of Vancouver, the park region boasts glaciers, lakes, rivers, and masses of fauna.

wine is transferred into oak barrels, racked several times, and bottled after about a year. The cycle begins again when the barrels are washed out before being filled with the next year's vintage.

When all of the grapes have been crushed, the crates broken up, and the seeds, stems, and sludge taken away by delighted composters, the potluck lunch begins. On a table in the garage, cheeses, meats, bread, rolls, fruit, cookies, and other delights appear. Accompanied by samples of past vintages and thoroughly enjoyed by the sticky, tired, but always hopeful winemakers, this working lunch is the highlight of the fall season in our little corner of East Vancouver. No matter how many rave reviews our wines receive at dinner parties around town, no matter how many prizes they win at amateur winemakers' competitions, our Pinot Noir, Sangiovese, and Sauvignon Blanc never taste as marvelous as they do on that magical September Saturday in Mike's garage.

Eileen Mosca
Vancouver

VQA Music
David Grierson

David Grierson is the producer and host of North by Northwest, *which airs on CBC Radio 1 every Saturday and Sunday morning, from 6 to 9.*

> … if it hadn't been studio "A" for a day,
> We might never ever been heard.
> – Bim (a.k.a. Roy Forbes) from *Dance In the Sunlight*

One of my earliest memories of a BC musician goes back to when I was a student. Breaking away from studies late at night in a Calgary dorm, I sought relief in CBC Radio's *Dr Bundolo's Pandemonium Medicine Show*. Amongst the antics of Bill Reiter, Norm Grohmann, Marla Groper, and Bill Buck was a kid full of dreams from

Roy Forbes

Dawson Creek. A kid named Bim who sang the words I just quoted. Then and there I set myself the goal to see studio "A," meet Bim, and make some contribution so others could sing the same refrain.

I'm an unabashed supporter of BC musicians and it's an easy thing to do given the quality of music here. I'm sure you could find folks who drink only BC's VQA wines, or only vacation here, and they would offer the same reasons. I would pick this even if there weren't a worthy reason. It's simply the best.

British Columbians have a history of making music the world wants to hear, be it by Juliette, David Foster, Bryan Adams, Mart Kenny, Bill Henderson, or The Moffatts. There are countless current successes to point to: Sarah McLachlan, the Matthew Good Band, k.d. lang, Farmer's Daughter, Colin James, Spirit of the West, Diana Krall, and others. But there are some pretty substantial success stories of the past in acts like the Poppy Family, Trooper, Chilliwack, Powder Blues, Payola$, Skywalk, and Loverboy.

BC can hold its head high in all forms of music. Pianist Jon Kimura Parker took Britain's Leeds Piano competition in the late 1970s and has spread the good word about BC ever since. Tenors Ben Heppner and Richard Margison, plus soprano Nancy Argenta, are just three of the world-renowned operatic voices to come from our province. Year after year BC choirs win international recognition and the last remaining radio orchestra in North America is resident at CBC Vancouver. Making great music isn't child's play, but BC also has more than its fair share of musicians for young audiences, witness the worldwide success of Raffi, Rick Scott, Norman Foote, and Charlotte Diamond.

While much of the attention is usually paid the performer, one shouldn't overlook the industry that has grown over the years, an infrastructure that supports artists from here and everywhere else. In managers Bruce Allen and Sam Feldman we have two of the most influential people in the Canadian recording industry. Our folk and jazz festivals are second to none in this country. We have some of the finest recording studios in Canada in The Armoury, The Warehouse, Mushroom

Recent volcanic activity is responsible for the formation of many of Garibaldi's peaks, including the famous Black Tusk. Lava spewing from Clinker Peak created The Barrier, a natural dam that led to the formation of the 300-metre-deep Garibaldi Lake.

The dense forest is home to a range of wildlife including fish, deer, mountain goat, marmots, eagles, and ptarmigan. Grizzly and black bears live in the park, but are seldom seen.

While a large portion of the park is only penetrated by the occasional mountaineering or cross-country skiing party, a few areas within Garibaldi Provincial Park have visitor-oriented developments such as hiking, camping, and mountain biking. You should note, however, that in the interest of safety, open fires and dogs are not permitted in Garibaldi Provincial Park.

One world-class backpacking trip through the area is the two-to-three-day traverse from Cheakamus Lake to Garibaldi Lake. The beauty of this hike is that you can start in one spot and finish in another, without retracing your steps. The trick, then, is to coordinate two vehicles.

The hike starts at the Cheakamus Lake trail head (which is located at the Garibaldi Park access south of Whistler) and finishes at the Garibaldi Lake/Black Tusk trail head.

From Cheakamus Lake, the hike starts with a gentle walk through beautiful old-growth forest, then crosses a bridge over Cheakamus River and starts to climb up to Helm Creek, where the trail levels out. There is a basic campsite at Helm Creek, where the first night can be spent, that allows for magnificent views of Black Tusk.

The next day leads through Helm Flats, past such volcanic features as the Cinder Cone and Cinder Flats (and Black Tusk, of course) climbing one more time before eventually descending to Garibaldi Lake. The second night could be spent at either the Garibaldi Lake or Taylor Meadows campgrounds.

Great side trips would include hiking up to Black Tusk lookout or up to Panorama Ridge.

Information courtesy Vicki Haberl, BC Parks.

Studios, and others. And I ask you: what Canadian city wouldn't want a venue like the venerable Commodore to have for their own?

In short, I can't think of a time when buying and listening to BC music wasn't a good thing to do. While I never did see studio "A," Roy Forbes (Bim) has come to be a friend and has introduced me to a lot of fine music over the years. As for making the contribution so others could sing of their "break," Roy is just one of the artists featured on *Eight Thirty-Eight Saturday Morning*, a compilation CD of songs from my weekend radio show currently raising funds to put songwriters into BC high schools.

From Korea to Toronto and Vancouver

I am an immigrant to Vancouver twice over.
My family arrived here with visions of the snow-capped Rocky Mountains scraping the horizon and the thundering waterfalls of Niagara dominating the landscape. Who knew the postcard images of our new home were actually thousands of kilometres apart with a wide prairie between?

What I remember of my journey to becoming a Canadian is captured by a camera lens in frozen moments of time. Framed in a quarter-inch white border, the fading photograph of a two-year-old sitting sideways on a pale green park bench outside the airport terminal is one of the few items documenting my immigration that I still own. The photographer who took the pictures of my departure at Kimpo International Airport in Seoul remains a mystery – an uncle or aunt, perhaps. Looking at the photo, I know I felt a heaviness in my heart at having to leave behind my beloved grandmother, my hal mon ni *who told me old Korean folktales about tigers and poor peasants before I fell asleep for the night.*

Searching further through a pile of dog-eared photos in a shoe box, I discover a second image. This time, I am standing in a well-kept public garden. This photographer also remains unknown, as does the garden's exact location. Only the carelessly scribbled "Vancouver" on the back of the photo helps me place the general location of the scene. My parents are both sporting shirt collars wide and pointy enough to conform to the fashion standards of the day, now considered "retro." We stayed in the city for only a few months before moving on to the "metropolis" of Toronto, as did many Asian immigrants in the early 1970s.

But Vancouver was the first glimpse my parents and I had of our new country after a ten-hour Air Canada flight. I can't say I remember what I may have seen as a child. But on my trips returning from Seoul since then, I've often peered out of my plane window to look down at the sparkling, diamond lights of Vancouver at night and wondered how different it may have looked to them.

My family did finally get a chance to see the mammoth Rocky Mountains up close on our road trip from Toronto to Vancouver. This time, our "immigration" was only from one province to another, but it was a move much more traumatic to me than my first immigration to the West Coast. I was leaving behind close friends as well as the neurotically planned "rest of my life" as a hip and savvy Torontonian.

As the beleaguered family station wagon made its way into Vancouver, I couldn't help but comment under my breath at the relaxed attitude of pedestrians crossing the street, not to mention the other drivers. They would never survive in Toronto, I mumbled, and what was with all the trees and hills? Getting accustomed to the west coast lifestyle did take a few years. But I knew I had mastered it when I phoned a friend in Toronto and she asked me why I was talking at such a slow pace and sounded so relaxed.

The North Shore mountains, Stanley Park, and all the quirky places in between have now imprinted themselves into me. I know they're part of images piling themselves on top of my heap of photo memories of a place I now call home.

Angela Y. MacKenzie

PRINCESS SOPHIA SINKS OFF BC COAST
OCTOBER 23, 1918

A Canadian steamship carrying miners from Yukon and Alaska became stranded on Vanderbilt Reef. Rescuers were unable to remove the 268 passengers and seventy-five crewmen due to a strong northerly gale. The next day, weather conditions worsened and the ship sank, killing all on board.

Information courtesy Environment Canada.

APPLE VARIETIES GROWN IN BC

McIntosh
excellent for every use
tangy flavour; firm and crisp flesh;
cooks soft and smooth
September through May

Golden Delicious
all-purpose
rich flavour; juicy and medium-firm
flesh; best salad and dessert apple
late September to July

Red Delicious
good keepers
highly flavoured for fresh eating
pulp is crisp and juicy
October through July

Spartan
cross between McIntosh
and Newtown
crisp, snowy-white flesh
and small core
distinctive, sweet flavour;
cooks soft and smooth
October through July

Classic Apple Pie

Sufficient pastry for a two-crust 9" pie
6 cups apples, sliced
½ cup + 1 tsp white sugar
½ tsp cinnamon
1½ tbsp butter
1 egg white, slightly beaten (or 1 tbsp milk)
Cheddar cheese

Line pie plate with pastry. Do not trim. Roll out pastry for top crust. Combine apples, ½ cup sugar, and cinnamon. Wet pastry on rim of pie plate with water. Add apples, heaping them up in middle. Dot with Butter. Place top crust on and press crust around edge. Trim and flute. Slash decorative steam holes into top crust. Brush with lightly-beaten egg white or milk and sprinkle with 1 tsp sugar. Bake at 450°F for 10 minutes. Reduce heat to 350°F for 40-50 minutes or until pie is golden brown and apples tender. Serve with wedges of cheddar cheese.

From Okanagan Apple Creations, compiled by Denise Nahirney and Serena Wou. Reprinted courtesy of the BC Orchard Industry Museum, Kelowna.

A Great Northern Adventure

*This story happened almost thirty years ago,
when I had been in Canada less than a month.
Our neighbours suggested that my husband and I
accompany them on a hunting trip. This meant we
had to trailer horses about twenty miles into the foothills of the Rocky
Mountains and then ride another twenty miles. We packed the necessary bedrolls, moose-
hunting rifles, and some food, intending to stay about ten days.*

*We hunted on horseback, riding along the riverbank. I was riding an old, gentle workhorse.
No saddle would fit her broad back, so I was riding bareback, using only a rope around her
neck. The rope was coiled over my shoulder as I carried my rifle in the other hand. I thought
I was alone as I rode the trail adjacent to the fast flowing river, not knowing that others were
riding a short way behind. Suddenly, a dog, which was travelling with the others, ran up
behind me and spooked my horse, causing me to fall backward. As she ran, the rope tightened
around my arm above the elbow. The men behind were helpless as my horse charged along
the trail, dragging me behind. I hollered, "Whoa, mare! Whoa, mare!" but to no avail. She
finally stopped after dragging me through a creek, where I came to an abrupt stop against the
bank. I clung to the edge, fearing that I would drown. But someone came near, caught the
mare, and told me to put my feet down. I stood up in waist-deep water, feeling rather foolish.
I was bruised, but otherwise unhurt.*

*But the adventure wasn't over yet. Even though we all continued to hunt, and very shortly
we would have fresh moose meat, our meagre food supply was running low. We could not go
home as we were not to be picked up until the end of the ten days. It seemed that we would
continue to be uncomfortably hungry when one of the party came into camp with some game.
He had captured a porcupine! Apparently, the only way to cook the thing was to toss it whole
into the fire and let the quills singe off as the meat cooked slowly in the coals. Eating
blackened porcupine with one's fingers may not seem like a feast to most, but to that group
of hungry campers it tasted great! It was my initiation into life in the North.*

Margaret Meutzner
Burns Lake

Royal Gala
sweet apple with excellent
texture and flavour
crisp, firm flesh
September through March

Jonagold
often large in size
firm, crisp, and sweet
great in salads
late October to mid-March

Red Rome
the finest baking apple
available; keeps well
cooks firm; slightly sweet
with firm pulp
late October to February

Newtown
unsurpassed for every use;
very good keepers
rich, tangy, tart flavour with
hard and crisp pulp
November through April

Braeburn
excellent keeping apple
red-on-green colouring;
sweet/tart, firm, crisp,
juicy flesh; superb for eating
late October to early March

Fuji
base colouring of yellow and green with an overlay of red stripes; firm, juicy, and sweet flesh; good for eating and for desserts
late October to late February

Sunrise
very bright, attractive red colour; excellent for desserts
early August through the fall season

Empire
cross between McIntosh and Delicious dark red; creamy, slightly tart flesh; dessert apple
late September to late February

Elstar
firm, tart, and juicy flesh

Granny Smith
green; tart, firm flesh; best in applesauce and pies

Mutsu
good for salads and desserts

Shamrock
tart and firm, great for eating or in pastries

Information courtesy BC Tree Fruits.

Hungry Grizzly Bears Invade Village

The central coast region of BC is remote, vast, and mostly forgotten by British Columbians. In November 1999, the tiny native village of Oweekeno (near River's Inlet) gained international media attention. The sockeye salmon had not returned, and with no fish, grizzly bears had no source of food. They came into the village in numbers never seen before. Frank Hanuse had the sad task of shooting the hungry bears.

Frank: At about 11:30, I just shot a sow and her two cubs who were trying to break into a couple of houses last night. I went to inspect the house and sure enough there was mud and scratch marks all over the window, terrifying all the people in there. Then they went up to a neighbour's, trying to crawl into her window. So she was screeching last night. We phoned the conservation officers and told them of our problems, and they more or less gave me the blessing to go ahead. The bears probably wouldn't have made it through the winter anyway. They didn't have an ounce of fat on them, and usually they're pretty fat by now.

Mark: Have you ever seen it like this before?

Frank: Never, ever. We usually see in the summer maybe one passing through, but never rooting around in the garbage. I've never ever seen it like this. Not with nine grizzlies in the village at once, in one day.

Mark: People must be frightened.

Frank: Oh, the kids are pretty frightened. During the summer there was hardly anybody out for fear of getting run over by a grizzly. They were extremely hungry.

Mark: How do you feel about having to shoot them?

Frank: I really don't like to do it, but when they're that unhealthy and they're terrifying people…. I've been designated the shooter and I've only had to do one bear every other year, but this year I've put down four and the officers themselves have put down nine.

Mark: What do you think this says about what's going on in your area; about food supply?

Frank: Well, the sockeye are way down right in the river where we used to have at least 30,000. The beach is devoid of any life right now. There's no birds, absolutely nothing in the river.

Mark: And for your people, who traditionally caught salmon there, what's that mean?

Frank: Most of us this year haven't had our food supplies. Had this happened fifty years ago we would have had a long, hungry, cold winter. Still, some of us like to have some fish every year but I can count at least ninety-five percent of the village does not have any preserves at all.

Mark: So what will you do this winter?

Frank: Well, I guess we'll just have to dig clams or something. Smoked baloney (chuckles).

THE BEAR FACTS

Any time of year is a good time to spend time in the BC wilderness. In the fall, however, bears tend to be more active as they prepare for the winter. Here are some things to keep in mind as you hit the trails and campgrounds.

Grizzly

Left front

Right hind

26 cm

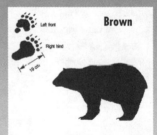

Brown

Left front

Right hind

19 cm

BC is home to two types of bears: brown and grizzly. Bears tend to be more active during the fall, so wilderness recreationists will want to keep the following things in mind:

- bears are not tame, gentle, or predictable
- bears are strong, fast, and dangerous
- bears have good eyesight, hearing, and an excellent sense of smell
- generally, bears go out of their way to avoid people

You can take the following precautions at your campsite:

- camp in designated areas
- always sleep in a tent
- reduce or eliminate odours that attract bears: store food and garbage in air-tight containers and away from your campsite, cook and eat well away from your tent, never bury garbage
- keep pets leashed
- avoid walking at night
- keep children nearby and in sight

Fall Preserves
Pear-Grape Jam

1 lb Concord grapes
½ cup water
5 pears, sliced
1 pkg (57 g) fruit pectin crystals
6 cups sugar

Separate grape skin from pulp, saving both. In a large, stainless steel saucepan, combine grape pulp and water. Cover and simmer until fruit is tender, about 5 minutes. Push mixture through a sieve to remove seeds. Peel, core, and finely chop pears. Add pears, grape skins, and fruit pectin crystals to cooked grape pulp and heat over high heat until mixture comes to a full rolling boil. Stir in sugar. Return fruit mixture to a boil and boil hard 1 minute, stirring constantly. Remove from heat and skim foam. Ladle jam into hot, sterilized 250 ml mason jars, leaving ¼ inch (0.5 cm) head space. Wipe jar rims clean. Center prepared canning lids and apply screw bands fingertip tight. Process filled jars in a boiling water bath canner for 5 minutes. Cool. Sealed lids curve downwards. Store in a cool, dry, dark place. Makes about 9 250 ml jars.

Recipe courtesy Kelowna Orchard Museum.

Rock Hound
Rick Hudson

Rick Hudson operates Mineral World in Sidney. He's the author of
Gold, Gemstone & Mineral Sites of British Columbia: Volume I,
Vancouver Island, *and* Volume II, Within a Day's Drive of Vancouver.

The most successful gold mine in BC was the Bralorne Mine near Gold Bridge, where over eighty-seven tons of gold were recovered, while another forty-one tons came out of the sister Pioneer Mine. Despite the remoteness of the site, there was only one recorded bullion robbery. The culprit was caught, tried, served time, and then re-applied for a job at the mine! (He didn't get hired.)

In 1968, Premier W.A.C. Bennett declared jade the official gem of the province, and the area along the Fraser River between the bridges at Lillooet to Hope as a Jade Reserve, where any citizen can hunt for the rare gemstone between high and low water marks.

Jade isn't always green. Nor is it as hard as a diamond. But it is tough, making it ideal as a tool. Early Salish peoples prized jade highly, and made axes and knives from it. The Chinese and Maori peoples have similar cultures valuing the mineral.

The early Chinese miners to the Gold Rush recognized jade, and sent it home in the coffins of their dead, proving you can take it with you!

BC produces over ninety-five percent of all the commercial jade in the world today. The largest jade carving in the world, a thirteen-ton Buddha, came from a BC boulder, and now resides in a Bangkok temple in Thailand.

The source of jade, the motherlode, eluded prospectors for over a century. Although jade boulders were found in the Fraser River in the 1860s, it was only in the 1960s that it was found in bedrock (near Gold Bridge and in the Yalakom River), and later north of Fort St James, at Dease Lake, and at Cassiar.

Another beautiful BC gem is pink rhodonite (from the Greek word "rhodon," meaning rose), found on Vancouver Island and near Keremeos in the Interior. During World War II, manganese was in great demand to harden steel, and even

You can take the following precautions while hiking:
- heed warning signs
- hike as a group
- let the bears know you are in the area by making warning noises and loud sounds frequently
- stay clear of dead animals
- pack out what you pack in

When you see a bear:
- if it does not approach, and it is in the distance, make a wide detour or leave the area
- if it does not approach and it is at close range, do not approach the bear, remain calm, avoid eye contact, and slowly move away
- if the bear approaches and it is standing up, it is trying to identify you so you should talk softly so it knows what you are
- if the bear approaches and it is growling, snapping its jaws, or lowering its head, it is displaying aggression
- if the bear attacks, generally the response is to do nothing to threaten or further arouse the bear. Do not run unless you are very close to a secure place

Information courtesy BC Parks.

BRIAN MINTER'S FALL GARDENING TIPS: OCTOBER

Fall is for planting!
October is the best time to plant most evergreens, fruit trees, and shade trees. They are now becoming dormant and once planted, they will immediately form new roots. By spring, the roots will be well established and will have put on a full year's growth. Two points to remember: 1) The richness of the soil in which you plant your new trees will determine how well your trees grow. 2) If your trees are in burlap sacks, you *must* leave the sack on the rootball.

Lawn seeding
It is getting late for seeding new lawns and overseeding established ones, but overseeding with a perennial rye grass can still be done if you act quickly.

small deposits were mined. Rhodonite is associated with manganese deposits, and after the war interest in the deep pink gem grew. Today, you often see pink rhodonite bears with salmon in their mouths.

There are now three known deposits of precious opal in BC. One near Vernon is commercially operated. Blue sapphire, blue iolite, and red garnet are found in the Slocan Valley. The resulting cut stones are of excellent quality.

East to West Transplant

I have experienced my life's journey as a mature perennial in a garden. In November of 1994, I took a spade to my roots in Montreal, leaving behind a lifetime of sixty-five years. I walked away from a career doing research for Sesame Street, my home in Senneville, friends, and the rich fabric of a long life in Quebec, and moved west to BC. My husband had recently died of cancer and my four grown children were now living in Calgary and Vancouver.

I waved a last prayer of thanks for my life in Quebec as my son Tim and I drove away. The car was loaded with my Labrador, Torbay, a smiling stone Buddha, and plants. We drove day and night, weaving the long path from east to west, listening to Enya playing softly on a cassette. I replanted myself in Invermere and now new roots are growing each day.

Here, I love to watch the sun rising each morning over the Rocky Mountains and the moon slowly making its passage in a cleft of high, jagged peaks. I have travelled in the last few years — to Indonesia, Nepal, and India — and each time I return through Kootenay National Park and arrive in Radium Hot Springs, I marvel at the gradual emerging of the Columbia Valley and its river spreading fingers north to Golden and eventually on to the Pacific Ocean. There is a tunnel before you arrive at Radium; I call it the birth passage to new beginnings.

One of my special travels in BC was last September. I was in Port Alberni and decided to board the venerable Lady Rose for an unforgettable voyage to Bamfield. With Torbay on a leash, we walked up a rather narrow gangplank and settled ourselves in the bow for a four-and-a-half-hour adventure. The Lady Rose has a long history of connections on this route to deliver mail and freight to settlements along the way, sprinkled with a few passengers. With a toot of her whistle, we moved out of the harbour and down Alberni Sound through changing weather patterns of mist, rain, and sun. The river soon widened into a landscape of mountains, islands, and far away vistas, reminding me of a trip I took on the Yangtze River in China. There were brief stops at a fish farm, logging camp, and eventually at Sechart Whaling Station Lodge. I heard that there was no set schedule and the stops changed according to the weather or freight loads. Wherever we stopped, locals came excitedly down to the dock and we would all hang over the rails and be part of the community for a moment. Then Lady Rose would once again give her departure toot and we would be off. Sea life was abundant, with sightings of eagles, cormorants, and seals bobbing along the inlet in the ship's wake.

We reached the town of Bamfield — two sections divided by an inlet — in the late afternoon. The outer section, where I stayed for two nights, is accessible only by boat. Strangers invited me in for meals; the whole town was a gathering place to meet and share.

My memories stretch back to long ago; to travels with my husband John to the Gaspé area, Perce Rock, and Bonaventure Island in Quebec, near another ocean. I feel profound gratitude for my life, forming links from the east to the western part of Canada. There are more treasures to discover on my path.

Joan Birkett
Invermere

OCTOBER EVENTS

Adams River Salmon Run

Barkerville Haunted Tour

Boswell Fishing Derby

Fort Langley Cranberry Festival

Galiano Island Blackberry Festival

Kelowna Apple Fair

Nanaimo Wine Tasting Festival

Oliver Festival of the Grape

Vancouver International Film Festival

Vancouver International
Writers' & Reader's Festival

Keeping the Stream
Doug McFee

Doug McFee volunteers with the Salmon River Enhancement Society in Langley.

The girls were excited when they heard the splashing in the creek. Their air of resignation ("Why are we going down here again, Dad?") disappeared as we hurried down the last few feet of the steep embankment and scampered along the stream. We were rewarded with the sight of a coho and its distinctive red spawning colour. It thrashed its way up the narrow, shallow creek in water just barely covering its body.

That November morning had turned out well. Although we were enjoying the sunshine, it was the heavy rains of the last couple of days that brought us luck. For it is the rains that bring the coho up the Salmon River in Langley at this time of year. The Salmon River is small, but is the most prolific stream in the Lower Fraser for coho and cutthroat. Despite this, our previous attempts to see the run had been unsuccessful. This is not unusual, as coho and cutthroat are wily species that make their dash to spawn during the higher and murkier waters. They are visible only when they have to jump or when the water is shallow in the small tributaries like the one we visited, Union Creek. These tributaries may be only one metre in width while depths may be less than thirty centimetres (although the higher flows after the rains do expand their size), but they nevertheless provide good habitat for juvenile coho to mature in the river for over a year before migrating out to the ocean. Small tributaries such as Union Creek are actually quite typical of coho and cutthroat streams and are the key to the success of the Salmon River.

The sound and sight of the coho was lost as it pushed only a short way upstream and then, perhaps hearing our approach, it paused. We found it a few metres further along hiding with two other spawners under the large rootwad of an upturned cedar. The cedar had been one of the few big trees left beside the stream but had blown over with its mass of roots standing vertically against the opposite bank of the creek overhanging the water just enough to provide shelter. One of

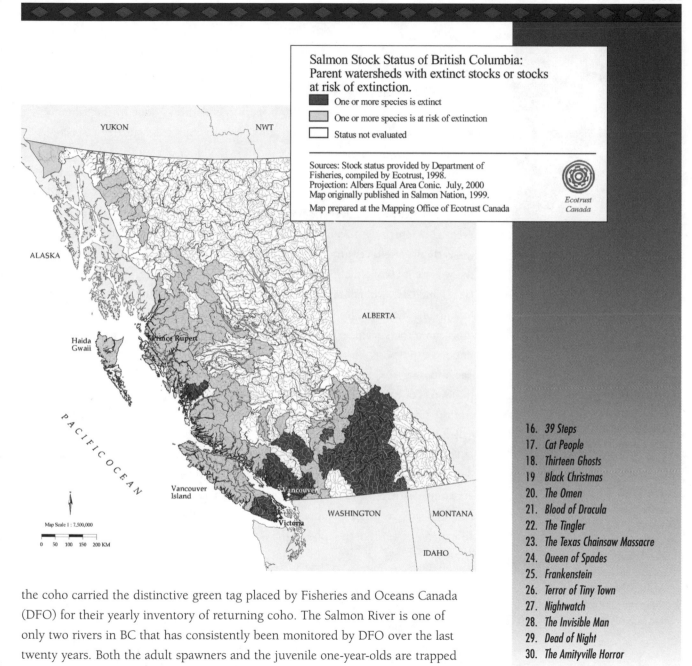

Salmon Stock Status of British Columbia:
Parent watersheds with extinct stocks or stocks
at risk of extinction.

One or more species is extinct

One or more species is at risk of extinction

Status not evaluated

Sources: Stock status provided by Department of
Fisheries, compiled by Ecotrust, 1998.
Projection: Albers Equal Area Conic. July, 2000
Map originally published in Salmon Nation, 1999.

Map prepared at the Mapping Office of Ecotrust Canada

Ecotrust
Canada

16. *39 Steps*
17. *Cat People*
18. *Thirteen Ghosts*
19. *Black Christmas*
20. *The Omen*
21. *Blood of Dracula*
22. *The Tingler*
23. *The Texas Chainsaw Massacre*
24. *Queen of Spades*
25. *Frankenstein*
26. *Terror of Tiny Town*
27. *Nightwatch*
28. *The Invisible Man*
29. *Dead of Night*
30. *The Amityville Horror*

the coho carried the distinctive green tag placed by Fisheries and Oceans Canada
(DFO) for their yearly inventory of returning coho. The Salmon River is one of
only two rivers in BC that has consistently been monitored by DFO over the last
twenty years. Both the adult spawners and the juvenile one-year-olds are trapped
and tagged to keep track of the yearly variations in coho stocks. For this reason

BC MYTHICAL CREATURES: SASQUATCH

The famous 1967 sighting by Roger Patterson and Bob Gimlin, which took place in the backwoods of Northern California, has often had its validity questioned, but no conclusive evidence against the grainy, 16mm film has been found. And there have been hundreds of other sightings across the Pacific Northwest, particularly in British Columbia as well as the Cascade Mountains of the United States. Exact details of the creature's physiognomy differ slightly, but most people report that the creature is very tall — anywhere from six to fifteen feet — with a heavy, muscular build covered in hair, like a huge upright ape. It is often spotted while going about its business seeking food or fishing with its hands,

the fish in the Salmon are all wild with no hatchery fish or fish introduced from other systems.

We watched the three salmon for a while, took some footage on the video camera, and then went on a walk to inspect tree plantings done by the Salmon River Enhancement Society. The girls don't always appreciate our tree inspections but are well aware of the importance of trees; the older one, at the age of four, commented that "Vancouver is nice but it has too many houses and not enough trees. They should cut down some houses and build some more trees." The cedars that had been planted over the previous four years were growing well and would eventually return the streamside closer to its original state prior to the logging of the early twentieth century. The cedar limbs will eventually provide shade to keep the water cool while the roots will help stabilize the banks of the stream. The cedar leaves and bark will fall into the stream to provide food for the multitude of insects that are the main diet for the growing juvenile coho. Even those few cedars that topple into the stream as its course meanders to and fro over the years will serve an important purpose. The cedar's trunk and branches, which can last decades before decomposing, will not create a barrier as so many observers assume, but will force the waters of the stream to find new paths, creating hiding places and pools that suit the small coho well. It is for these and other reasons that the cedar has been called by First Nations "The Tree of Life."

The fate of the Salmon River and the fate of coho stocks around BC rests squarely on whether we are able to protect tiny streams such as Union Creek. These streams are easily destroyed and altered by agricultural and residential development or by activities such as logging and road construction. Will the girls and their children still enjoy the thrill of the coho in the future?

Lone Angler

Typically, we fly fishers are perceived as being an elite bunch; if not by the nature of our sport and its spin-offs, then certainly by the quirks in our behaviour. If I had to pick one characteristic familiar to all practitioners of the sport it would have to be the need to be alone! It is very odd. I meet colleagues in parking lots, retail shops, campgrounds, over back fences, and while sipping a beer in the local pub. We spend hours discussing, debating – even arguing. We meet at our club, trade information and secrets. We even have political clout. We typify human interaction. However, when we go to exercise our fly fishing skills, we get as far away from each other as we can! This quest for solitude is the major challenge in my fly fishing excursions in the Lower Mainland today.

My trips always begin in the dark. So early even the dogs just grumble and roll over in their baskets. It's the sound of the coffee machine, muted pre-dawn CBC, whir of the microwave, and that one dim light on the stove, as much as it is the river. Equipment is always neatly arranged by the back door, ready for a quick load and efficient departure. (Don't even dream of arriving late if you're coming along, and God forbid there are any other anglers on the highway ahead of me!)

Fly tied by Vic Marchiel

Even arriving at the river, in the dark, sometimes in a downpour, is part of it – the anticipation. To a fly fisher, there is nothing like a river waking up. Now you must understand, it's not just any river. You have to have just the right conditions, ambiance, width, flow, water clarity, general surroundings, and of course the fish. Preferably the eager type. Accessibility also helps; just rugged enough to give you the impression you're some place isolated. You can't plan this, either; it all just happens. When you find a place

swimming, or just watching humans. But it has never been reported to attack someone. In fact, many believe the creatures are quite peaceful and docile and therefore should be left alone as they pose no threat to us. In Skamania County, Washington, there is a local ordinance that makes it illegal to harm any member of the Sasquatch population. Opinions also differ as to its origin, but generally, theories fall into two categories. Some believe the Sasquatch is a humanoid creature that has not evolved at the same rate as humans. But others believe that it is exactly what it looks like: an upright ape in the family of *Gigantopithecus,* a species that was thought to be extinct.

141

EXTINCT

The passenger pigeon once existed in huge numbers across North America. The last passenger pigeon died in captivity in the United States in 1914.

ENDANGERED

British Columbia has only one nesting colony of the American white pelican, located at Stum Lake in White Pelican Provincial Park in the Chilcotin region.

- the wingspan of the American white pelican can reach up to three metres
- American white pelicans nest in colonies, and pair bonds are formed when a male can successfully defend his chosen mate from other males
- small islands in Stum Lake are used for nesting, and nests are often built on the bare ground

Fly tied by Vic Marchiel

like this, you commit it to memory and hope the dynamic processes of water, time, and man don't change it too drastically. It becomes your place, and if you're lucky, one of a number of places … it becomes a "BC Moment"!

So do places like this still exist in and around Vancouver? I have one such place: the Indian River at the top of Indian Arm. It's no real secret, but the combination of distance, no retention, and bi-annual runs keep the crowds you'd find at other streams to a minimum. You can get there by road or water. The pinks run every second year and there are resident rainbows … some real suprises! Yes, it's still possible. Have I spoiled a secret? Hardly.

Vic Marchiel
North Vancouver

Lotus Land

Angel Lake
Providence Creek
Paradise Peak
Shaman Creek
Seraphim Mountain
Celestial Reef
Pure Lake
Providence Park
Mount Light
Pure Lake
Eden Lake
Celestial Bluff
Shaman Cove
Paradise Island
Tranquility Bay
Peaceful Bay
Eden Creek
Peace Creek
Expansion lake
Peace Lake
Paradise Lake
Dream Creek
Crystal Lake
Aura Fina Creek
Paradise lake
Eden Creek
Peace River District
Peace Reach
Peace River
Peace Canyon Dam
Providence Lake
Crystal Falls
Paradise Lake
Serenity Mountain
Serenity Glacier
Serenity Creek
Eden Peak
Serendipity Spire
Mystic Mountain
Crystal Glacier
Spirit Island
Providence Point
God's Pocket Marine Park
Providence Passage
Eden Mountain
Loveland Bay
Faith Lake
Love Creek
Love Lake
Paradise Lake
Love Creek
Tranquil Creek
Tranquil Inlet
Providence Cove
Soule Creek
Nirvana Pass
Eden Island
Eden Lake
Inspiration Peak
Eden Point
Paradise River
Cosmos Heights
Spirit Lake
Bliss Landing
Paradise Ponds
Meditation Mountain
Spirit Isle
Mount Loveway
Crystal Creek
Paradise Valley
Tranquille
Paradise Creek
Peaceful Lake
Paradise Lake
Paradise Valley
Inspiration Cove
Crystal Lake
Crystal Mountain
Angels Staircase Falls
Peaceful Pond
Seraph Mountain
Cherub Mountain
Faith Peek
Revelation Lake
Tranquility Mountain
Paradise Point
Crystal Creek
Paradise Creek
Spirit Creek
Faith Creek
Mount Faith
Providence Creek

With apologies to *Geist* Magazine

The Peregrine Falcon once lived on every continent except the Antarctic, but its population crashed in the 1960s and 1970s due to habitat loss and the use of the pesticide DDT.

- the Peregrine Falcon holds the speed record for the entire animal kingdom. Its top speed is over 300 kph
- the Peregrine Falcon usually nests on rock ledges high on steep cliffs, and occasionally on the ledges of tall buildings in urban areas

The Northern Spotted Owl evolved for thousands of year in the old-growth forests of the Pacific Northwest.

- the Northern Spotted Owl is at risk because much of its habitat has been adversely affected by logging or lost due to land development
- the Northern Spotted Owl has an array of at least thirteen calls, including hoots, barks, whistles, and chitters
- BC is estimated to have fewer than 100 pairs

Information courtesy BC Ministry of Environment, Lands, and Parks.

PLANNING THE MENU

Every morning at eight o'clock, producer Laura Palmer prompts us with: "Shall we meet?" Associate producers Elizabeth Hoath, Joan Webber, Laura, and I start tossing story ideas into the pot to determine what will be served up on-air four hours later. Ideas come from a thousand and one sources: that day's news events, personal observations (scribbled on bits of crumpled paper), suggestions from listeners, tips from provincial correspondents, wire services, classified ads, press releases. Each idea is poked, prodded, and considered with our province-wide audience in mind. With luck, determination, copious cups of java, and frequent helpings of colleague Kathryn Gretsinger's banana bread, we always make our 12:08 pm deadline.

Makweelaylah and the Spud Gun Militia

Don Gayton

Don Gayton is a writer and ecologist living in the Kootenay region. He contributes to BC Almanac's *"In Search of BC" series.*

All week the tiny islet of Mitlenatch called to me, as I taught a writing course on nearby Cortes Island. Seeing an uninhabited island, splendidly alone in the middle of the Georgia Strait, and not being able to reach it, is a prescription for fable. Mitlenatch became more and more fabulous to me as my week wore on. First it was an exotic, treeless desert, tucked in amongst wet, coastal forests. Next it was populated by strange and wonderful beasts, and flowers of every description. Then it became a shape-shifter, now appearing close, now far off on the horizon.

In class, I volunteered the information that Mitlenatch was a fabulous ecological marvel and that I, an ecologist from the Interior, had never seen it. Finally, one of my students, Maurice, a grizzled Cortesian oyster farmer, agreed to take me there, but on one condition. "Great. What's the condition?" I asked. "You must witness the Presenting of Arms of the Cortesian Spud Gun Militia," Maurice said, gravely. "Absolutely," I agreed, having no idea what he was talking about.

Maurice's boat was what you call a working boat, an open eighteen-footer with plenty of gas cans and few frills. The seats were eminently practical: de-legged bar stools bolted onto plastic milk crates. Maurice fired up the big old Mercury outboard and soon we were in open water, sliding laterally up and over the long swells in a manner all wrong for landlubbers. I fixed my attention on Mitlenatch in the distance, trying to ignore the periodic alarms in my esophagus.

"The Native people called the island Mahkweelaylah, which means the closer you get, the farther away it appears," Maurice shouted over the sound of the engine. "Do you want a beer?"

Sure enough, the island that at first looked to be just a few minutes away was now quite distant, with lots of open, swollen water between it and us. Finally, we approached the east shore, and I realized the trick Mitlenatch had played on me; with no trees on its horizon, no houses, and no other islands near it, the island gave me nothing to calibrate my depth perception against. A simple trick of perspective, I told myself.

By now we had rounded the south point, and what I first took to be lumpy black rocks turned out to be a fine herd of massive California sea lions. The air above us was thick with glaucous-winged gulls, harlequin ducks, surf scoters, ravens, and crows. Gawky, double-breasted cormorants festooned the rocks, and pairs of oystercatchers picked delicately along the shore. An eagle passed overhead, and as it did so, hundreds of nesting birds swarmed, herding the predator away from their rocky nesting area. As Maurice steered the boat toward a small bay, we passed a clutch of fat harbour seals.

The biological abundance continued as soon as we stepped ashore. Drifts of pink sea blush, interspersed with yellow monkey flower and blue camas, were strewn artistically across the rocky slopes. Tiger lily, alumroot, saxifrage, saskatoon, and Pacific sanicle were all in flower. The lush interweavings of colour were like French Impressionist paintings, but if Claude Monet had seen Mitlenatch, I believe he would have put his brushes down out of sheer respect.

The magical is also fragile; tiny, thirty-six-hectare Mitlenatch and its host of creatures are prone to many human disruptions. As a result, it has Provincial Park status, and volunteer wardens monitor it closely.

I was reluctant to leave the island, but Maurice reminded me that we had to check his prawn traps and get back in time for the Presentation of Arms.

Back at Maurice's snug home on Cortes, we had a delightfully messy feast of oysters, prawns, and beer. By the time we were finally finished, both our beards

COMMUNICATION BETWEEN COMMUNITIES

Janet May

Janet May is the BC Almanac community correspondent in Powell River.

The radio was aimed out the kitchen window toward the woodpile. I half listened and mused while stacking next winter's heat. Like many parents at home, I found CBC my main adult company during those early childhood days. It was, and is, my connection with the rest of the country and the province.

BC Almanac feeds my curiosity about the varied conditions and activities around BC. The people of Keremeos or Dawson Creek, Nelson or Bella Bella, are not very different from each other, but they have adapted to a diversity of climates, topographies, biospheres, and industries. I like to hear what is happening and what people are saying about it.

I got a chance to add my voice to the mix in 1995. I stopped stacking wood, and called up to ask why I never heard about Powell River. Margaret Woodfall asked me to "paint a picture" of my community for CBC Radio.

My community: historically born of the timber and hydropower, locked in the mountains and fjords. Powell River grew with immigrants from many countries who supplied labour

watercolour by Janet May

for the pulp mill. We have surfed the pulp market, up and down, for decades since.

There is a ceremony to leaving and arriving in this town. It takes effort, and it costs money. Plan to be on time for the ferry or plane. The ocean is our moat.

Lakes, islands, and mountains

were smeared with garlic butter, prawn juice, and cracker crumbs. Neither of us cared. Maurice drained one last oyster shell, and settled back to tell the story of the Cortesian Spud Gun Militia.

"Well, you've seen those big yachts cruising by to the east of us, eh? They're all headed for Desolation Sound, which is the playground not of the rich, but the super-rich. The Bill Gates types. Every now and then one of them gets bored, and starts sniffing around our beloved island of Cortes, thinking they can buy up a big chunk of property, fence it off, and build a monster mansion to live in for three weeks every year. Now, we Cortesians are kind of plain folks, nothing fancy, and we aim to keep the island that way. So the Cortesian Spud Gun Militia is ready at a moment's notice to man the beachheads as soon as those hundred-foot luxury yachts start snooping around. And now that you mention it, the time is exactly 11:23 pm, which means it's time to Present Arms."

We stepped outside into enfolding cedar and starlight, and Maurice returned from the toolshed with an eight-foot spud gun, a real beauty, with a five-inch sewerpipe combustion chamber, hard-wired Bic barbecue lighter ignition system, ergonomic hand grips, the works. Following precise instructions, I cleaved a potato in the sharpened muzzle while Maurice vigorously shook a can of hairspray. "Paradoxically, the cheapest brand of hairspray is the most effective propellant," he said, as he sprayed a blast into the combustion chamber, and screwed the gun's breech back into place.

"Present *arms*!" Maurice yelled, and he hoisted the device. A shockingly elaborate cauliflower of purple flame burst from the muzzle, followed instantly by a wet, potato-sounding explosion, like a popgun on steroids, and the humble Russet No. 2 flew deep into the cedar-filled night, in the general direction of the luxury yachts of Desolation Sound.

I should like to take *fabulous* back from the Hollywood public relations people who stole it, and return original meaning to the word. Then I could debate whether the ecology of Mitlenatch was more fabulous than the human culture of Cortes, or whether that is even a valid question for debate. Perhaps the important thing, for both sanicles and oyster farmers alike, is to live on the edge of fable.

Fall Preserves
Prune Plum Relish

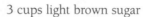

3 cups light brown sugar

2 cups cider vinegar

1 tbsp salt

3 lbs prune plums, pitted and chopped

2 cups onion, coarsely chopped

2 cloves garlic, minced

1 green pepper, diced

¼ tsp ginger

¼ tsp cloves

¼ tsp allspice

¼ tsp cinnamon

½ tsp chili powder

½ cup raisins or currants, rinsed and drained

In a large, stainless steel saucepan, combine sugar, vinegar, and salt and boil for three minutes. Add remaining ingredients and simmer until fairly thick, about 1½ hours. Ladle hot relish into hot 250 ml mason jars, leaving ¼ inch (0.5 cm) headspace. Wipe jar rims clean. Centre prepared canning lids and apply screw bands fingertip tight. Process filled jars in a boiling water bath canner for 10 minutes. Cool. Sealed lids curve downwards. Store in cool, dry, dark place. Makes 6 cups.

Recipe courtesy BC Tree Fruits.

surround Powell River, and this landscape defines our community. A teenager diving from a dry, mossy bluff into Powell Lake, a mushroom picker seeking fungal gold in a damp forest pocket, a diver visiting a wolf eel 100 feet beneath the ocean surface, and a logger stepping out of his truck in morning mist; all use this well-favoured landscape. Our future challenges us to keep the human "footprint" small enough.

Music permeates our community: academy concerts, the annual music festival, the mill choir, and Kathaumixw, which invigorates the town with hundreds of singers from six continents.

As a community correspondent, I relish research. The variety and colour of Powell River and her people give me much more "painting" than I can fit into a radio time slot. I'm thrilled to share their stories and my pride in Powell River with the rest of the province. I enjoy listening to community correspondents relate tales from other places and people. And, I still resort to talking back to the radio, from the woodpile, whenever the mood takes me.

Graeme Bennett is the editor of *PC Buyer's Guide* (www.pcbuyersguide.com) and was formerly the senior editor at *The Computer Paper*. He's also our resident computer whiz and we asked him to track BC-oriented websites our listeners keep going back to.

BC Almanac Listeners' Choice WebSites

Site: **www.altavista.ca**
Altavista Canada is the Canadian arm of the popular Altavista search engine. This tool helps you find Canadian information on the Web and includes useful features such as language translations, the ability to search for graphics or sound files, and much more. Click Altavista's "Help" button for information on how to use it.

Alternatively, www.searchbc.com is a "family friendly" search engine, completely concerned with online British Columbia. With it, you can find BC business and individual websites, BC Internet resources, and media.

Food For Thought
Don Genova

Don Genova is a food journalist who presents "Food for Thought" each week on BC Almanac.

My love affair with British Columbia began in 1983, when as a young broadcaster I moved from southern Ontario to the wilds of northwestern BC: Terrace and Prince Rupert. I've lived in various locations across the country since then, but was always drawn back here. Sure, it was the mountains and the ocean, but it was also the people, and most important to my career, the food.

I'll always remember buying live crabs and just-out-of-the-water shrimp from the back of a truck in a Prince Rupert hotel parking lot. Cracking open the shells and devouring the sweet flesh hooked me on fresh seafood. Later, I savoured smoked salmon from a fish I had caught myself. It doesn't get any better than that.

My career as a food journalist was launched in part on *BC Almanac* about five years ago. As part of my duties as a writer and broadcaster for the show, I prepared a segment called "Don's Deli." Each Friday at noon I would traipse into the studio with the latest, greatest food discoveries I had made in and around Vancouver. One of the best moments was when a listener from Prince George called. She said she was in Vancouver, but she couldn't find Don's Deli anywhere! I explained the deli was a fictitious place which contained all of the great food and food people I met every week in the province.

And we really do have the best. British Columbia is developing foods and wines which are achieving fame around the world. Regional specialties are helping to define Canadian cuisine: Fraser Valley strawberries, Saltspring Island cheeses, Vancouver Island balsamic vinegar. Okanagan wines win gold medals in European competitions.

While the natural resources of our oceans and lands bless us with an amazing bounty, it is what the chefs and processors do to the raw ingredients that makes British Columbia a special place to live. In my travels around the province, I am consistently impressed with the imagination and dedication of the people I meet in the food and beverage industry. It's not an easy industry in which to survive. Ice wine makers sometimes bundle up to snatch the frozen grapes from the vines on Christmas Eve, or whenever the temperature calls. The cheesemakers are out milking their cows, goats, or sheep twice a day, 365 days a year. Chefs routinely work fourteen to sixteen-hour days, most of them six days a week, all so they can share their ideas of good-tasting food for an appreciative audience.

It's been a pleasure for me to bring the stories behind the food and wine to the *BC Almanac* audience on my "Food For Thought" segment every week. And I also thank all of the chefs, farmers, winemakers, and processors who have always been happy to share recipes, secrets, products, and most importantly, their time, to help me tell their stories.

Site: **www.bcyellowpages.com**
Search for business listings. Also links to BC-based travel services, arts and entertainment, community listings, classifieds, and more.

Site: **www.vancouver-bc.com**
Helpful tourist information, maps to an extensive directory of local businesses, classified ads, and an online guide to the entertainment scene.

Site: **www.biv.com**
Business in Vancouver. Here, you'll find market facts, with regional information for decision makers, plus links to the Vancouver Public Library (www.vpl.vancouver.bc.ca) and other local libraries, as well as everything from Vancouver Freenet (www.vcn.bc.ca/welcome.html) to community newspapers.

Site:
www.geocities.com/Athens/ Parthenon/7726
Homework Helper is a great collection of kid-friendly links. If you only let your kids go to one page, this should be it. Its section on Canada (www.geocities.com/Athens/ Parthenon/7726/canada.htm) includes a number of links to useful resources, inluding complete exams with answer keys from 1994 to 1997 in all grade twelve provincial exams.

Site:
www.wlake.com/hicks/
hicks.html
And just in case you'd forgotten what a culturally diverse and wonderfully eclectic province British Columbia is, visit "the Shangri-La of Supernatural British Columbia," to discover a well-maintained list of links to local experts in the esoteric fields of dowsing, healing arts, Kirlian photography, and more.

Site: **www.ufobc.org**
Of course, there's no shortage of "out there" sites on the Net. Here's your complete guide to UFOs and other phenomena in BC.

Site: **www.cbc.ca**
Perhaps it's no surprise that *BC Almanac* listeners would vote for the CBC website as one of their favourites, but worth mentioning are some of the state-of-the-art advancements that make this site unique. Streaming digital video is now available, allowing you to experience CBC Radio or Television programs from anywhere in the world with an Internet connection. Recently added is support for the SMIL (short for Synchronized Multimedia Integration Language) standard, which allows broadcasts to pop up web links of related materials while you're watching.

Kicking Horse River
Greig Bethel

Greig Bethel is the editor of Coast, *the outdoor recreation magazine. He lives in Golden.*

I always listen to music while I'm writing. It helps my thoughts flow. One verse in particular seems to resonate with me. It's from Jim Cuddy's CD *All in Time* (yes, I'm a sucker for sappy love songs) and it goes like this:

> I wish I was a river
> A river running free
> and running wild

* * *

Rivers can make music, too. They thunder through rapids, gurgle in slow back eddies, hiss with glacial flour, and sometimes they are quiet, nothing but perfect silence. The Kicking Horse River, a Canadian Heritage River, is close to where I live in Golden. The Canadian Heritage Rivers System was formed by the federal government in the mid-1980s to ensure the long-term management and conservation of twenty-eight rivers which were deemed to have important natural, historical, and recreational values.

The Kicking Horse, which tumbles west from the Continental Divide, is covered in ice and snow for half the year. But during the summer months its waters are jam-packed with thrill-seekers in whitewater rafts and kayaks. Just past where most of the rafters and kayakers pull out of the river, the Kicking Horse empties into the Columbia River.

At the rivers' confluence, the Columbia is only about 150 kilometres into its 2,000-kilometre journey to the Pacific Ocean, and gently meanders back and forth between the skyscraper peaks of the Rocky and Purcell mountains.

"Rivers tie mountains to the sea," author Mark Hume wrote in his 1991 book, *The Run of the River*. "On Canada's western edge, they send back to the ocean, through

The Fraser River is still flowing.

an infinitely complex system, the rain that was drawn up from the Pacific and showered down onto forested slopes and granite peaks." Appearances, however, can be deceiving. The Columbia is not a river running free and wild.

Thirty kilometres downstream of Golden, the river enters the tail end of Kinbasket Lake, the first in a series of slackwater dam reservoirs that hold back the river's once mighty flow. The Columbia is a river in chains, a river lost. Fourteen dams block the river's progress to the ocean. Roughly 1,300 kilometres, or sixty-five percent, of the river's length is impounded behind these dams.

I have also been listening to another CD quite frequently – Billy Bragg and Wilco's *Mermaid Avenue*, in which they cover fifteen songs written by American folk singer Woody Guthrie during the 1930s and 1940s. Guthrie, incidentally, had a Columbia River connection. He was hired by the US government in 1941 to write songs promoting the wonders of the Grand Coulee Dam, located in northeast Washington state:

> Green Douglas firs where the waters cut through
> Down her wild mountains and canyons she flew
> Canadian Northwest to the ocean so blue
> Roll on, Columbia, roll on
> And on up the river is Grand Coulee Dam
> The mightiest thing ever built by man
> Your power is turning our darkness to dawn
> So roll on, Columbia, roll on

* * *

Site: www.120seconds.com
The home to CBC Radio 3, the new radio network, one of the most advanced websites in existence when the Beta version was launched in the summer of 2000.

Site: www.maikon.net/wcfma/Foundat.htm
The West Coast Foundation for Modern Art provides information on West Coast artists, a guest artist gallery, gift shop, and a section for critical writings.

Site: www.userfriendly.org
User Friendly is a daily comic strip created in BC.

Site: www.cap.ic.gc.ca
The Canadian Government's Community Access Program links communities across Canada. An example is "the Virtual Village" at www.monashee.com, serving the community of Lumby.

Site: www.mac-conflicts.com
If you're a Macintosh user, you'll find useful troubleshooting tips in the Complete Conflict Compendium, based on Vancouver Island.

Site:
www.evandelay.com/vancouver/stanleypark.htm
Everything you ever wanted to know about Vancouver's urban park. Includes a huge list of related links, including another of our favourites: Raymond Kam's Vancouver VR, a tour of Vancouver's most scenic sites using QuickTime VR, which allows you to view 360-degree panoramic photographic scenes. It's at www.hotel.cprost.sfu.ca/vanvr

Other useful sites about British Columbia worth checking out include: Telus' **www.mybc.com** and the "Recommended Sites" page at **www.beautifulbc.ca**

Please note: All good websites change their design from time to time, so there is a possibility that pages listed here may have changed or been removed. If possible, refer to the site's main directory (e.g., remove everything after the "dot-com" part of the name) and try again. If the site provides a search function, use it to look for the information you are seeking, or use an Internet search engine such as www.altavista.ca. Happy surfing!

In 1998, the BC government included the Columbia as part of its heritage rivers program. That same year, the river was also included on two other lists as well: the Vancouver-based Outdoor Recreation Council of BC placed the Columbia on its ten most endangered rivers list due to irregular water flows from the dams, and it was also named the number one most threatened river in the US by American Rivers, a Washington, DC-based conservation group.

Ironically enough, that group wanted to protect an eighty-three kilometre stretch of the river in Washington state known as Hanford Reach, a place where nuclear waste is stored and has, in the past, seeped into the river.

So why is the Columbia a heritage river if it is endangered? And conversely, why is the Columbia endangered if it is a heritage river?

"Rivers spin our turbines, powering industry and lighting the cities. They carry away our industrial and residential waste. But they do not wash away our sins," Hume wrote. "We must pay attention to the whispering voices of our rivers, for they are speaking about our future." Good idea. I think I'll walk a couple of blocks and take a listen.

The choice of my favourite BC river became clear enough when I realized the range of adventures and emotions I have experienced on the Chilko-Chilcotin River.

This is a river where I have had two near-drowning encounters. I have baked in the summer heat, and watched from a tent as days of rain virtually obliterated the landscape. A river where I have met what were to become life-long friends. A place of discovery — my first golden eagle, bald eagle nest, and beaver dam. I have ridden on horseback along its canyon rims amongst the rocks, cactus, and jackpine, and looked down on the glacial blue-green waters from on high. I have watched bighorn sheep grazing on their protected corner of rangeland.

I have hiked down to near inaccessible places where the local Indians set their dip nets to catch migrating salmon – the Chilcotin being one of the more important salmon spawning rivers in the Fraser system. During the winter I have skied along its banks and benches, fascinated by how different the river looks in the snowy season – how terribly cold and crisp, but no less inviting in its own starkly beautiful way. I've spent hours changing irrigation pipe, hauling bales of alfalfa hay, and splitting firewood on a small ranch which hugged the banks of the river.

Khutzeymateen River

But most of all, of course, I remember the days on the river itself. Days of drifting on the silt-laden, silk-like water, past groves of aspen and stands of pine; waking to full attention at the various rapids and negotiating these hazards with skills learned on this and many other rivers. At the end of a long day, having still not had enough of the river, jumping in at the head or a rapid and drifting, swimming, downstream, buoyed by a lifejacket. Finding the delicate mariposa lily carpeting the forest floor between craggy anthills, marvelling at its resilience and ability to survive in this environnment of extremes. Coming almost eyeball to eyeball with a black bear about to navigate its way across the river but thinking better of it as this strange object floated the current, blocking its own objective.

I delighted in new friendships, faced fears, and experienced the exhileration of being "on the edge" and surviving. From just below Chilko Lake down to the confluence with the Fraser River, this river has been the source of many memories and of much learning.

Suzie Sims
Armstrong

153

BRIAN MINTER'S FALL GARDENING TIPS: NOVEMBER

Trees and shrubs
All the deciduous and evergreen trees are now dormant, so it's a great time to begin planting. Fruit, flowering, and shade trees, planted now, will develop terrific roots even through winter months, and will reward you with tremendous growth next spring.

Garden colour
Untidy perennials and late flowering shrubs can be clipped back. Plants under the eaves of your house should be well-watered now. Don't forget to add lots of winter colour to your garden. Violas, winter pansies, Dusty Miller, and flowering kale are terrific, as is a "winter" flowering English Daisy. Don't forget the hardy winter flowering trees and shrubs.

The Comic Book Murder: Dawson Creek, November 1948

Jon Swainger

Jon Swainger is Associate Professor of History at the University of Northern British Columbia, Fort St John Campus.

World War II and the decade that followed ushered in an era of enormous change for the residents of British Columbia's Peace River country. No longer beyond the reach of passable roads and soon to be connected to the rest of the province by rail and highway, the region was linked to the outside world in a fashion unheard of a generation before. For some residents, these new connections were indications of future opportunity and prosperity, whereas others were decidedly of the opinion that the changes were, at best, a mixed blessing.

Driving home to the small community of Kilkerran after watching Errol Flynn and Ann Sheridan in *Silver River* on the evening of November 12, 1948, the James Watson family was confronted by two masked bandits alongside the Alaska Highway. Rather than stop in response to what was later described as a warning shot, driver Fred Watson reversed his course and sped back towards Dawson Creek. Armed with a stolen 30-30 rifle, one of the bandits fired at the fleeing vehicle. The bullet passed through the car's trunk and rear seat, striking sixty-two-year-old James Watson in the back. Watson died from his wound four days later in St Joseph's Hospital in Dawson Creek. When it was revealed during the subsequent coroner's inquest and delinquency hearing that the youthful bandits had been reading between thirty and fifty American crime comics a week, a moral panic erupted across the Peace country.

Reaction to the fatal shooting, the youthfulness of the accused, and the apparent role of American crime comics was immediate. Calls for an import ban of such comic books were initially matched with pleas for parents to be more vigilant in supervising their children's reading materials and activities. However, while parental duty remained a common theme, increasing attention was concentrated on the message these American crime comics carried: "Most comics portray the villain as a man of property or position. Comic strips portray all congressmen or other holders of public office as pot-bellied imbeciles wearing string ties and funny hats. Clergymen are useful as the butt of jokes of the inspired comic book artists. Judges and magistrates are portrayed as individuals out to take the joy out of life. The police are held up to ridicule wherever possible." Not only did these comics encourage disrespect for authority figures and law enforcement officials, the literature undermined the western way of life: "… we are playing our children into the hands of our enemies when we destroy in their minds all respect for law, religion, property, and the virtue of girls. We are playing the communists' game and are parties to a dreadful undermining of the morals of the on-coming generation, so that they will be easy prey for the enemies of Christendom and democracy." Apparently, crime comics represented all that was evil in an increasingly complicated world.

Shock and outrage over the "comic book murder" fed into an existing debate over the role of American crime comics and the perceived rise in juvenile delinquency across North America and Great Britain. Led in Canada by E. Davie Fulton, a Conservative MP from Kamloops, the campaign was reinvigorated by Watson's death. Although much of the local furore over the shooting resonated with language drawn upon the wishful notion that the Peace region had been essentially crime-free, the comments of George Murray, MP for Cariboo and part owner of the *Alaska Highway News*, were especially notable for attributing blame for the shooting to the Americans. Claiming to be a "humble publisher," Murray stated that "this country is deluged with filth from the publishers of the United States and no effort is made to stop this material coming past the border." Although Murray's comments echoed similar sentiments uttered by his parliamentary colleagues, they were also consistent with the ideal of the crime-free Peace and the parallel assertion that criminality was foreign to the well-ordered and law-abiding community. Fulton's bill banning the importation of American crime comics into Canada received third reading and was passed on December 5, 1949, slightly over one year after James Watson died from the wound he received in the comic book-inspired hold-up just off the Alaska Highway. While some in the Peace may have taken a measure of comfort in the Fulton legislation, an equal number undoubtedly wondered what other influences would soon arrive in what had once been an isolated corner of British Columbia.

Spring bulbs
You won't be able to enjoy those gorgeous spring bulbs if they aren't planted soon! November is an ideal planting time. At Minter Gardens, we plant over 100,000 bulbs in November!

Summer bulbs and tubers
All your summer bulbs and tubers should now be lifted, cleaned, dusted with sulphur powder, and stored away for winter. Remember: most bulbs and tubers prefer to be stored cool except for gladiolus and begonias that need warmth.

BC WEATHER EXTREMES

Total Precipitation (Rain and Snow)

Most rain in 1 hour
49 mm
Oct. 29, 1966
Bear Creek

Most precipitation in 24 hours
489.2 mm
Oct. 6, 1967
Ucluelet Brynnor Mines

Most precipitation in 1 month
2235.5 mm
November, 1917
Swanson Bay

Compiled by Jamie McDuff and Anne McCarthy, of Victoria's Environment Canada weather office.

While exploring the Charlottes, a friend and I spotted an eagle swimming across a small river. We decided that it had a salmon in its talons and, unable to fly, was towing the fish to a gravel bar on the far shore. As several eagles were in a tree above the bar watching, we decided to make our way through the slash to photograph the proceedings.

On arrival at the river's edge, we observed the eagle had pulled the fish to shore, had dispatched it by pecking a hole through its side, and had then flown up into the tree to join the others.

A staring match ensued. We waited. Occasionally an eagle would fly from the tree, circle our heads, emit a small cry, and regain its perch.

After twenty minutes, motivated by thoughts of tinned stew, I decided, brazenly, to wade the river and lay claim to the fish. As I crossed the stream, I was observed with heightened interest, a more intense stare. My friend was thrilled with the prospect of photographing an eagle attack on a human, but fortunately this did not happen.

We barbecued the six-pound pink for supper. It was delicious.

Did I feel a twinge of guilt? Yes. But I assure you the river was loaded with fish that day.

Glen McNie
Shawnigan Lake

An Explosive Experience

What to do when a live grenade is discovered in your apple orchard? It happened to Gordie Ivans of Kelowna in the fall of 1999. We called him and the bomb disposal expert who came to the rescue: Lieutenant Clay Cochrane of CFB Esquimalt.

Mark: Gordie, who found this thing?

Gordie: I had a couple of friends picking up windfalls and one was crouched down by this tree and looked at it. I happened to be out in the orchard spraying at the time and they came running over to me and said, "We've found a grenade." So I said, "Right, what have you guys been smoking today?" My first thought was it was a kid's thing, I didn't think it was real. When I did grab hold of it, and felt the weight of it, I thought, "Jeez, this thing might be real."

Mark: Did you hold onto it?

Gordie: At the time I wasn't really sure so I carried it to the roadside, probably a couple of hundred yards, set it down by the tree, went into the house, and called the RCMP. They showed up, looked at it, weren't sure, then called Clay and his partner. When they looked at it they said, "Yup, she's the real McCoy, eh?"

Mark: Lieutenant Cochrane, when you looked at that what did you think?

Clay: We did a long range look and I immediately identified it from my training as a live US hand fragmentation grenade. We immediately secured the area and called in the support we needed.

Mark: What could have happened if it had gone off?

Clay: Obviously, it wouldn't have been a good situation. I guess where Gordie had put the grenade was inside a shed. Unfortunately, the shed had a 500-gallon drum of diesel fuel right on top of it. Inside, the grenade was sitting nicely upright on a work bench, but scattered throughout the shed was a whole pile of fertilizer, which he

BC BIG TREES

Bigleaf Maple (*Acer macrophyllum*)
North Vancouver District, Roche Point
Healthy, excellent crown,
height record
Circumference: 3.9 metres
Height: 42.7 metres
Average crown spread: 24.4 metres

Information and image courtesy BC Conservation Data Centre's Big Tree Register: www.elp.gov.bc.ca/rib/wis/cdc.

obviously uses for his orchard. So we had quite a mixture on our hands there, and a live grenade with basically eight ounces of explosives.

Mark: So did you defuse it? What did you do?

Clay: We have a whole series of procedures we follow and are trained in. I can't get into them in detail because they're actually confidential, but I can tell you we basically carry out a "render-safe" procedure. My partner Gary and I then carried out a remote pole, set up a series of lines and pulleys, and used some stainless steel troughs the neighbour had, to pull the grenade off the work bench; almost like a sled to help pull it safely away from the fertilizer and fuel. We were able to do that, got it out in a safe area, gave it the proper wait time. Everyone was well back 500 metres away, cleared a bunch of local houses, and got it in a safe spot and I was able to complete the render-safe procedure and secure it in a strong reinforced steel box.

Mark: Inside the grenade, was there still TNT in there?

Clay: There would have still been explosive in there. No one will ever know, because we immediately took it to a disposal site in a remote area in the adjoining hills.

Mark: And you blew it up.

Clay: We blew it up. We set a charge beside it and were able to counter-charge the grenade, and had quite a nice detonation that went off right on time.

Mark: Gordie, what was it like when you realized this was live – potentially live – and you're walking around with it?

Gordie: Well, actually today I feel kind of sick about the whole thing. I guess it's the old saying, "What you don't know won't hurt ya." If I do stumble across another one I certainly won't be transporting it anywhere. I'll be getting hold of these guys again.

Mark: No kidding. The question is, how did it get there in the first place? What's the speculation?

Clay: This particular area was used extensively in the Second World War and Korean War by the Canadian Army for training for soldiers going abroad. So an extensive training area was set up here.

Gordie: Clay, maybe you can explain about the wire and stuff, and handle that was busted off.

Clay: Essentially there's a handle or what we call a spoon that holds the safety lever or striker from firing the grenade. That's the thing you see in the movies where they pull the pin and the spoon goes flying off. Well, there was no pin with this, that's what made it precarious because it was sitting upright and the striker was cocked back in a firing position –

Mark: No.

Clay: – impinged basically by a small thin wire we're assuming someone put in there to help hold back the cocked firing hammer.

Mark: And you do this for a living, Clay?!

Clay: Yeah, I do, actually.

Mark: Any jokes around the orchard, Gordie?

Gordie: They're calling me Rambo up here now.

Mark: And you're thanking Clay and company today?

Gordie: Well I've got some Spartan and Golden Delicious apples that I'm going to send back with these boys.

The Selkirk Mountains loom on our right as my mother and I drive over dusty, badly rutted roads. We are on a journey to walk the path of her childhood and revisit the place of my birth in Longworth. "There was a lookout up there during the war," she says as she points to a high peak in the Selkirks. We drive along the Canadian National line, once one of only two ways of getting to Longworth. My mother reminisces about the train, telling me that it was the only way in or out fifty-four years ago, when I was born. The roads and power were only about eight years old. We finally pull up to the gate, which encloses the vast expanse of land that knows my origins, and it rolls gently downward to the murky Fraser River. I know that two of her brothers drowned in that river and today is the day that we will remember these events in the places they happened. We pass rotting wood that was once a log cabin, where a lone willow tree spreads its branches protectively over the remains of my birthplace. Although the property gates are closed and warning signs are plastered everywhere, my mother flags me through. "When you own a place for a century, it always feels like yours," my mother rationalizes to no one in particular.

From the CN tracks we revisit the spot where her schoolhouse once stood, only fifty feet from the Fraser River, in a vacant, desolate spot that gives no indication that happy children ever inhabited it. I stand quietly in reverence to my mother's memories. About a mile down the road we come to the one lone house still inhabited by an original owner. Beside the house, the tiniest post office I have ever seen boasts that it is an "Official Post Office." It is the size of an outhouse. A very old lady peers around the corner of the weathered yellow house. "Is that you, Therese?" my mother hollers. Aside she says, "Geez, I thought she'd be dead." My mother and her forgotten friend sit in a kitchen and look at photographs of their children, some more than half a century old. I feast my eyes on a kitchen that hasn't been updated from the thirties, while Johnny Cash blares from the radio. I look through a Watkins cookbook older than my mother. My mother wants to know about the cemetery and why it is all grown over with tall grass and weeds. Old Lady McCoy, as my mother refers to her friend, tells her that Canadian National owns the property and they are waiting for papers so it can be turned over to the community.

We stop at the cemetery and look at my uncle's headstone. It reads, "March is a windy month." Another one tells us that a Swedish immigrant was eaten by a grizzly bear. On the ride home there is a sense of completion. My mother points to the place where she helped her father with a trapline. I feel a sense of loss, and wonder if my mother and I will ever walk the path of her childhood again. "I'd sure like to see a train on these tracks," my mother mumbles. As we drive alongside the tracks, something magical happens: three train lights appear around the bend, caught in the sunlight as the CN blows out a mournful whistle. We stop and watch as it winds along the tracks through a town with many stories hidden in its history. The train all but disappears, but gives one last fading whistle, a tribute, I feel certain, to the lullaby of my mother's youth.

Megan Hutton

"The Royal Hudson," by Carl Chaplin

Coastal winters have two distinct features: wet and windy. Storms lash our coast with such force that some lightkeepers report walls and beds that shake; one north coast lightkeeper watched the wind blow the chickens right off his island. Meanwhile, in the mountains and interior, ice and snow prevail. Avalanches cut off mountain highways and rail lines, black ice makes trouble for drivers, and in some places it's so cold your tires run square. But the marvelous flip side to this is how adept we've become at making the most of winter: snowboarding, hockey, curling, ice climbing, dog sledding, skiing – if it's frozen, we'll play on it.

My ski gear dates back to the 1970s. Very retro. As my snowboarding sons remind me, also very uncool. Riding up the Manning Park chairlift, a skier glances at my chipped Strato 105s and suggests they belong in a museum. I vow to blow past him on the next run, then realize he probably isn't skiing the slowpoke blue runs. Skiing is an expanding enterprise, and as Whistler potter and community reporter Vincent Massey reminds us, the industry has a tremendous impact on how towns evolve. Some flee the upmarket scene for more laid-back lifestyles in places like Rossland – which is where I interviewed local legend Booty Griffiths. Booty has skied Red for sixty-five years – before lifts, when skiing meant a two-hour hike, but then a heavenly reward.

Winter does find many of us indoors, preferably curled up with a good book. *BC Bookworld's* Alan Twigg provides a reading list that includes M. Wylie Blanchet's *The Curve of*

Salmon River, Fort Langley

Miner's Hall, Rossland

Winter

BC BIG TREES

Ponderosa Pine (*Pinus ponderosa*)
beside Kettle Valley Railway,
north of Princeton
ancient, large bole with no taper,
broken top
Circumference: 5.2 metres
Height: 29.9 metres
Average crown spread: 18 metres

*Information and image courtesy BC Conservation Data
Centre's Big Tree Register: www.elp.gov.bc.ca/rib/wis/cdc.*

Time – a BC classic that still surfaces on the bestseller list four decades after being published. Noted historian and "In Search of BC" contributor Jean Barman reminds us why a sense of BC history is essential to feeling rooted: "The past is part of us and unless we acknowledge its presence, we are not all that we can be." Brian Minter points to other roots: those of plants, and how to keep them alive through the darkest months of the year.

This is also the season when thousands of eagles congregate at Brackendale to dine on salmon – generating more inspired letter-writing about contact with the wild from listeners. Christmas triggers memories of cherished meals, friendships, and treks to locate a Christmas tree. Carol ships take to the water in various communities, while winter carnivals keep the blood flowing in others. The annual food bank broadcast on CBC Radio brings with it mixed emotions as it highlights both a growing need each year, and our listeners' extraordinary generosity.

As winter creeps southward, I'm hoping for a cold snap – long enough to freeze the fields on the flood plain below my home. We'll lace up skates, chase pucks till dusk, and realize dreams of breakaways that always find the top corner.

Oliver Lake, near Prince Rupert

photo: Lynn Thompson
Snowed in on Denman Island

It all started in the spring of 1998. I started looking for a piece of property in the Cariboo. The place had to be just right, large enough to have space for the horses and a few other critters. By June I had found just the right quarter section, just east of Lone Butte near Sheridan Lake.

My husband Peter referred to me as the terrier as I pursued the property over the next four months. I negotiated with the bank, the real estate agents, and the property owner, with our dream property as the ultimate goal. Finally, in November of 1998, we had a completed agreement. My friends thought I was crazy. Here I was moving up to the Cariboo with five horses and two dogs in November. Insanity, they thought. My husband Peter would remain in Squamish and commute up to the ranch on weekends. Every weekend over the Duffy Lake Road. They thought he was crazy, too!

The house is a 1906 square log timber homestead. There used to be a steam-driven sawmill here and we are constantly finding or digging up old pieces of machinery from days gone by. There is a large covered front porch where we sit to start the day or finish it.

The first winter was hard. Lots of wood to chop and snow to shovel. The half-mile-long driveway was interesting. No, I didn't shovel that, a neighbour came and plowed it. Taking hay out to the horses twice a day and hauling water. But it was marvellous. During the day, the white snow in contrast with the blue sky; the frost decorating the aspens and the snow icing on the pines and spruce. At night, the myriad of stars, the Milky Way, and occasionally the Northern Lights. On a night with a full moon it was magical. The horses running across the field to greet me, the dapple-grey Arab glowing in the moonlight.

The wildlife that occasionally drops by to visit us seem to know that we won't hurt them. The red fox that sits out in front of the house watching us or having a nap at the back of the house with one eye open and the other shut. Its beautiful red fur coat with the long black stockings and delicate feet. The two coyotes up in the field prowling, listening, and

DECEMBER EVENTS

Comox Polar Bear Swim

Fort Nelson's Canadian Open Dogsled Races

Grouse Mountain Winterfest

Kamloops' First Night

Mission's Candlelight Parade

Qualicum Beach Festival of Trees

Vancouver Christmas Carol Cruises

Vancouver Festival of Lights

Vancouver's Christmas at Canada Place

Victoria's Christmas Festival

Victoria's First Night

Whistler Start (World Cup Skiing & Snowboarding)

COLD WAVE FREEZES VICTORIA AND BC'S LOWER MAINLAND

JANUARY 19 - 29, 1935

Winter weather gripped Vancouver, with temperatures dipping to -16°C and snowfall greater than forty centimetres. While the extreme cold caused fuel shortages and frozen water supplies, a quick thaw followed by 267 millimetres of rain over the next four days added extensive roof damage across the city, including the collapse of the Forum — the city's main hockey and curling rink.

Information courtesy Environment Canada.

then pouncing on the unsuspecting mice. The wolf who lies up on the hilltop of the upper meadow watching everything and everyone. The moose cow with her newest arrival and the bull moose not far away. In the summer, the variety of birds that make their home here is vast. The red-tailed hawk, the eagle, juncos, grey jays, woodpeckers, owls, and the incredible sandhill cranes with their loud cries.

The neighbours are the best. Though they are not as close as in the city, they are but a phone call away and always eager to help out. The community is incredible, with all sorts of interesting courses at the local school in the evenings for souls of all ages, and organizations from 4-H to quilting socials and everything in between. There is a local volunteer fire department with the motto "Neighbour Serving Neighbour." It seems to be the motto for most people in this community!

This year we will start raising Scottish Highland cattle, a longhorn breed with very lean meat. With fresh eggs from the chickens and a few pigs, sheep, and goats, we are becoming quite self-sufficient. The well water is excellent and we will be putting up a greenhouse this summer to lengthen the growing season.

Okanagan Winter

Next year we will be teaming up with one of our neighbours to provide adventure horse holidays and bed and bale facilities with a riding ring, round pen, and all the trails you could wish for.

The old motto of "Where there's a will, there's a way" is very true. If you have a dream, dare to pursue it. For us, it was a quarter section with a small creek running through it.

Jane Murray
Pine Hills Ranch

When in Whistler

Vincent Massey

Vincent Massey is a potter and
BC Almanac's *community correspondent in Whistler.*

My family and I feel lucky to be living in Whistler. I have always had a great addiction to the outdoors, especially the mountains, whether skiing or snowboarding in fluffy powder snow, or experiencing the ambience and spiritual energy of being in ancient, old-growth forests that still blanket parts of Whistler and Blackcomb Mountains.

Whistler has the reputation of being a playground for the rich and famous. This is true to some degree, but the rich and famous still have to go to work on Monday, leaving Whistler to us locals to enjoy some quality time. To me, the variety of local characters, especially my neighbours, add some spice to our town. We have heli-pilots, guides, commercial fishermen, ski patrols, photographers, professional skiers and snowboarders, all of whom have some spiritual connection to mountain life.

Myself, I am a potter. I first came to Whistler in the seventies to fuel my vertical desire, but now I find the most stimulating pastime is making pottery. Big pots, little pots, wide, long, you name it, all fired in my giant gas kiln, which gives me an ever-changing palette of rich colours. The market to sell pots in Whistler is huge. People from all over the world arrive at our little gallery on the side of Rainbow Mountain. My wife Cheryl is a basket weaver and weaves from local materials that she gathers herself, such as cedar bark, tule grass, and bull kelp, and together we eke out a living by working at home.

EXTINCT

The Dawson Caribou, which once lived in the muskeg habitat on the Queen Charlotte Islands, were last reported seen in 1908.

ENDANGERED

Restricted to the mountains of Vancouver Island, the Vancouver Island Marmot is one of the rarest animals in North America.

- the Vancouver Island Marmot is entirely confined to Canada, and is one of fourteen marmot species found around the world

- because their habitat is so small, most colonies contain fewer than five adults

- their 1998 population was fewer than 100 individuals

- family groups hibernate together in deep burrows for six months or more each year

Information courtesy BC Ministry of Environment, Lands, and Parks.

Our children, Tyler, fourteen, and Michela, eleven, are growing up in what we feel is a clean, safe, sports-oriented environment.

Affordability is still something that may not keep us here forever, but in the meantime Whistler is still a fast-paced, semi-rural town where we can rip mile-high mountains before lunch, and come back to our studios full of creative juices to apply to our craft.

We are content where we are and wouldn't have it any other way!

British Columbia Needs No History. Or Does It?

Jean Barman

Jean Barman is a Professor of History at UBC, the editor of BC Studies, and an "In Search of BC" contributor for BC Almanac.

British Columbia needs no history, goes a common refrain. We are a province of the present looking to the future. To the extent we seek out larger meaning, we have a geography that is bigger than life to sustain us. Be it mountains, rivers, lakes, or ocean, we are surrounded by a natural beauty that is sufficient for our needs. I don't agree. We are who are by virtue of who we have been. We are always in a state of becoming as well as a state of being. Every aspect of who we are, what we are, where we are, has a past. That past is part of us, and unless we acknowledge its presence we are not all that we can be.

photo: Barry Peterson & Blaise Enright-Peterson

It is not just ourselves who are embedded in history. The environment around us is constantly changing, both in and of itself and as moulded by our actions. As British Columbians, we have fished the rivers and the oceans, cut down the trees, mined the mountains and hillsides, and littered the sides of the paths and walkways that we have made. The "pristine wilderness" in which we take so much pride is as much a product of ourselves as it is some "natural" phenomenon.

Each day, as we pick up a newspaper, listen to the radio, watch television, or search the Internet, we are reminded that we live in a place called British Columbia. The social, economic, and political quirks that caused this place to become British Columbia, as opposed to, let's say, Alberta or the United States, are part of a common inheritance that we share by virtue of living here.

As families and individuals, and as members of communities, we have a history in this place called British Columbia. Our physical selves are a reflection of a parentage and a personage going back, and even further back, in time. Some of us are recent arrivals, others have been here much longer. For those of us who are Aboriginal, that time is so far back in the mists of the past that it is lost to us as individuals and as peoples. Many of us have multiple entry points. We are hybrids, part of families with diverse ethnic and racial origins, each with its own trajectory into the province. We embody our pasts, whether or not we acknowledge their presence.

History comes in two sizes, it might be argued. The first percolates down to us from larger entities, from the world, Canada, and British Columbia as a province. We sometimes feel that we are entrapped in larger forces over which we have no control. These entities impose on us interpretations of how things ought to be, in other words a history of how these entities came to have an importance that is in good part assumed or taken for granted.

Against this "big" history there is another size of the past that can give us hope. It begins with ourselves, with our finding out who we are and how we got to where we are today. The immense popularity of family history and genealogy grows out of a need that we all have, as outside forces sometimes seem to overwhelm us, to know ourselves. "In Search of BC" on *BC Almanac* opens up new possibilities for exploring ourselves in this place called British Columbia. Ethnobotanist Nancy

1908
Manufacture and sale of opium is banned in Canada

1910
Annual provincial surplus peaks at $2.4 million

1919
University of British Columbia establishes the first nursing degree program in the British Empire

1922
BC drivers change from driving on the left side of the road to the right

1917
Provincial prohibition takes effect

1920
Provincial prohibition is repealed

1928
First drive-in restaurant, White Spot, opens in Vancouver

1938
Lions Gate Bridge links Vancouver with North and West Vancouver

1964
BC Lions win the Grey Cup

169

BRIAN MINTER'S WINTER GARDENING TIPS: DECEMBER

Winter evergreen protection
If you have fast growing evergreens, you might wish to put a handful or two of a winterizer around the base to harden them off and prevent windburn. It might also be wise to tie up cypress and Globe cedar trees to help prevent heavy snows from destroying their shape. Plant "berried" trees and shrubs this month to brighten up your landscape and provide valuable food for birds.

Turner told me, as I was driving along one day, more about the lore of cattails than I had ever imagined, despite a childhood in which they figured prominently.

My own segments on *Almanac* have introduced some of my favourite persons and places in British Columbia. I've talked about Fort Langley, Wild Horse Creek, and Powell River. All three originate in our long-lived economic dependence on the exploitation of natural resources. Fort Langley, now a national historic site, was from 1827 a crossroads. There, a handful of newcomer men traded furs with local peoples, and with their daughters raised families whose descendants figure prominently across the Fraser Valley. Wild Horse Creek in the East Kootenays, now a heritage site to be explored on foot, was for a brief moment in the 1860s a gold rush boom town. Still a vibrant coastal community, Powell River exemplifies the province's "company towns." Its men and women enjoyed a high standard of living at the cost of being supplicant to the American company that both built the town in 1910 and long operated its large pulp-and-paper mill.

Another economic enterprise with ripples into the present day is whaling. Before ground oil was discovered, to be refined into petroleum, whales were a principal source of the oil that, among other tasks, lit the lamps of early Nanaimo coal miners. As I explained one day on *Almanac*, Whaler Bay on Galiano, Whaletown on Cortes, and Blubber Bay on Texada Island, just across from Powell River, all got their start as places where whaling ships anchored or whales migrating along the coast were cut up and their blubber rendered into oil.

Whaling's impact extended into Stanley Park and to the Silvey family, both of which I've talked about on *Almanac*. "Portuguese Joe" Silvey was one of the many thousands of men attracted by the gold rush who, when riches proved elusive, turned to other means of making a living. Drawing from his childhood in the Azores, he whaled, but, like so many others, did a lot of other things. "Portuguese Joe" competed with "Gassy Jack" in running one of the first saloons in Vancouver's "Gastown," and he lived for a time at the edge of Brockton Oval in the future Stanley Park, where his first wife, a Musqueam woman named Khal-ti-nat, would take their young daughter to potlatch.

The Silveys were among numerous families of diverse origins to make Stanley Park their home, mostly surviving by fishing or whaling, well into the twentieth

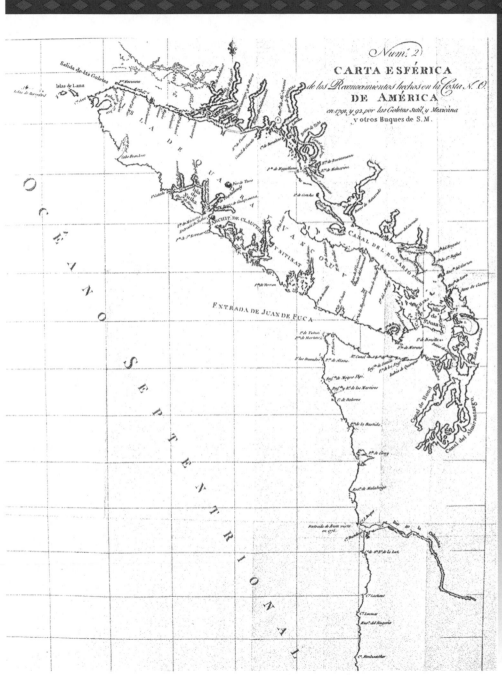

Winter indoor plant care

You must realize that the growing conditions for your houseplants have completely changed. They are going through a difficult stage. You must increase the amount of light they receive, keep them cooler to improve the humidity, and make sure they are pot-bound going into winter. When you water, use warm water and soak the plant thoroughly until water runs out of the bottom of the pot. This will prevent any salt burn.

Christmas plants

Without exception, keep all your Christmas flowering plants in the coolest part of your home. Azaleas need water at least twice daily, and frequent misting on the foliage as well. Cyclamen need to be on the dry side, and in a very cool window. All your flowering plants must be near a window to take advantage of maximum available light. Water all your flowering plants thoroughly with warm water only, then allow them to become dry to the touch before watering again.

map by Dionisio Galiano, 1792, from *Relacion*, 1802, courtesy Derek Hayes (*Historical Atlas of British Columbia and the Pacific Northwest*)

Caring for your poinsettias
To keep your plants looking their best all the way through the holiday season, place them near a window with indirect light. Also make sure to keep them away from heat vents, fireplaces, or any drafty areas in your home. A temperature of 17°C is ideal to maintain the flower buds and colour. Water with warm water only! Give them a good drink, then let them dry out slightly before thoroughly watering again. Lifting the pot to feel the weight is the best indicator. Heavy pots don't need water; light weight pots need water. Fertilizing is not required. If plants are being moved outside, gently cover them with a light plastic bag. Do not touch the bracts or brush against them for fear of bruising or breaking them, thus allowing the white sap to flow out. Remember: poinsettias are *not* poisonous.

century. Their presence irked Vancouver politicians who wanted the "wilderness" to be pristine. So in the 1920s, the so-called "squatters" were legally evicted, apart from Tim and Aggie Cumming, the children of a Scottish fisherman and Bella Coola woman. Loyally raising the flag each morning and lowering it at night, they continued to live in their neat little cottage on the northern shore of Brockton Oval until their deaths in the 1950s. Linking past and present, who should have been the loudest voice demanding the cottage's demolition, but then park commissioner George Puil.

On *BC Almanac* I've sought to give voice to people and places that often get overlooked in the "big" history. Be it British Columbia or more generally across Canada and beyond, women were long expected to stay in the background. Some women pushed the boundaries through political action, as with longtime Vancouver CCF/NDP MLA and MP Grace MacInnis. Others made their mark in economic life, as with Sophie Morigeau (pronounced Mar*joe* by those who knew her), a remarkable free spirit of mixed Quebec, Scottish, and Aboriginal ancestry who, as a young woman, ran her own pack train of trade goods into Wild Horse Creek. As a great-grandniece has put it, "undismayed that no woman, either white or red, had done such a thing before," she traded all her life from Revelstoke and Invermere in the East Kootenays south to Colville and Tobacco Plains in northern Washington and Montana. Women like Grace MacInnis and Sophie Morigeau had an impact far beyond their numbers, for, as a man employed by her as a youngster recalled in old age, "Sophie was a friend to everyone and always helped the sick and needy."

We each have a history in this place called British Columbia, just as the place itself has a past. It is by exploring that relationship that we acquire a new pride in ourselves and in our families and communities, our province and nation. Comfortable with who we are, we can even, should we desire, begin to challenge, to reinterpret, the "big" history that we too often simply take for granted. British Columbia needs a history, yes, and that history is us.

Winter Preserves
Pear Chutney

8 cups pears, peeled, cored, and diced
1 cup onion, finely chopped
2 cups raisins, coarsely chopped
3 cups granulated sugar
3 cups white vinegar

In a large, stainless steel saucepan, combine all ingredients. Stir over medium heat until sugar dissolves. Bring to a boil then simmer about 1 hour or until thick, stirring more often as it thickens. Ladle hot chutney into hot 250 ml mason jars, leaving ¼ inch (0.5 cm) head space. Wipe jar rims clean. Apply prepared canning lids fingertip tight. Process in a boiling water bath canner 10 minutes. Cool. Sealed lids curve downwards. Store in cool, dry, dark place. Serve with poultry or pork, or as an appetizer on crackers covered with cream cheese.

Recipe courtesy Kelowna Orchard Museum.

Unfortunately, I missed most of today's "Open Line" on canning because, believe it or not, I was busy making peach chutney. My friends have dubbed me the Chutney Queen. You name it, I have "chutney-ed" it: strawberries, blackberries, plums, apples, pineapple, mangoes, cranberries. Even our eighteen-month-old daughter loves the stuff so much that she has been able to say "chutney" very clearly for over two months now, and her Grandma calls her the Condiment Kid. I love to hear the sounds of the lids popping as they form their seal. My husband likes to tell everyone that if he leaves anything lying around too long, I will "boil it within an inch of its life and put it in a jar."

Kerry Heckbert
Victoria

Caring for your living Christmas tree
In spite of all the care you may have taken with your living Christmas tree, the time inside has been difficult for it. If the weather is cold, place it in a protected location for at least a week until it has a chance to acclimatize to the outdoors. If it remains mild, however, plant it as soon as possible and get moisture back into those needles. When planting the tree, the burlap sack must stay on, but any type of pot must be removed. Root growth can begin quickly, so add a root stimulator to the root ball, and water the tree well.

Cut Christmas trees
These are still my favourite because of the tradition and fragrance! Cultured trees, grown on Valley tree farms, are usually fresher than northern Interior trees, but treated with care, any cut tree should last two weeks indoors. The latest research has revealed that clear water is all cut trees need for optimum lifespan indoors. It is, however, essential that one inch be cut off the bottom of the trunk so the tree can drink. A little bleach added to the water will kill bacteria that slow down the capillary action. A tree with good moisture levels will drink about one litre per day per one-inch diameter of trunk. In other words, an average tree with a four-inch trunk should drink about two to four litres of water per day! Does your stand hold about one gallon? A tree with good moisture levels in the needles will stay far fresher, longer.

My Bike

I would like to share a memory of the best Christmas present a little four-year-old boy could have: a Gendron tricycle.

There it was, under the tree, just what I asked Santa for. The bike wasn't new, but it had a new yellow paint job. The door to the front room was closed because we had to have breakfast first. It was the longest breakfast I ever had. I could have killed my father when I heard him say, "I think I'll have another piece of toast."

I couldn't try my new bike outside because of the snow, and our house wasn't big enough to ride it inside. Instead, it was stored until spring. What a long winter. Every day I would go down into the basement and sit on the bike, waiting for the snow to melt.

When spring finally arrived, and I was allowed to take the bike out, my dad helped me get it up the stairs and out to the front sidewalk. He had to put wooden blocks on the pedals so I could reach them.

As I rode my bike, year after year, I had one secret wish. When I grew up, got married, and had a child, I wanted to give the bike a new yellow paint job, and have Santa put it under the tree just as he had put it under the tree for me.

When I outgrew the bike, I hung it up on a nail in our basement. Years passed. One day I came home from work and saw a station wagon driving down the street with my bike in the back. My mother, nice lady that she was, loved to give things to people. She had given away my bike.

And I've spent years since looking for a replacement, to no avail.

Mike Brereton
Grafton Lake Valley
Bowen Island

A Christmas Tree to Remember

A few years back, my son, Jake, his dad, Brett, and I went out on our "back forty" to find a Christmas tree. We could not find a tree that had branches evenly distributed around the tree, so I got the idea of taking two or three scrawny tress and tying them together. Jake was not too keen on this idea, so we continued our search for a while longer. After another half-hour, Brett said, "That's it, Jake. We have to go with Mom's idea and tie some trees together."

Jake said, "Oh sure. Then we can tell everyone to come see our slash pile."

But it worked.

Carolann

Winter colour

Winter flowering shrubs add an entirely new dimension to your garden. Colour is very important during the winter months, and there are numerous plants and shrubs which provide unusual winter fragrance and colour: viburnum "pink dawn" (Nov. - Apr.), winter heather (Nov. - Apr.), Chinese witch hazel (Jan. - Mar.), French pussy willows (Jan. - Mar.), Christmas roses (Dec. - Apr.), winter jasmine (Nov. - Feb.), and contorted filberts, or catkins (Nov. - Apr.). Berried plants and colourful barked maples, cherries, and birch also provide excellent winter colour.

CHILDREN'S BOOKS

Kids' books can be colourful and cute, or poetic and profound. And there's a dizzying array to choose from -- as you see when you head into any library or children's book store. On the "Open Line" we asked for your favourite kids books. Here's a great list of bedtime reading suggestions

A Place for Margaret
Bernice Thurman Hunter

A Wrinkle in Time
Madelaine L'engle

A Visit by Rudy Beaver and **Fire in the Bramblewood**
Barbara Duvall

Amelia Bedilia
Peggy Parrish

Among the Hidden
Margaret Haddix

Black Nell and Kit: The Adventures of a Raccoon
Shirley Woods

The Black Stallion
Walter Farley

A Winter Morning

The sun has not yet risen as my old Honda comes to a halt at Sombrio Provincial Park, and I trade the sounds of my engine for the silence of the crisp December air. I close my eyes, rest my head against the steering wheel, and contemplate whether I really want to struggle into my still damp wetsuit. Then I hear it: a far away rumbling I just barely sense in my still sleepy head and feel in my tired bones, rising and fading, rising and fading. My pulse quickens and my stomach rises just slightly higher in my body. The swell is big. Very big. A storm begun off the coast of Japan has thrown up a swell so large it has travelled the length of the Pacific and is at this very moment erupting onto the reefs off Sombrio Bay. I brace myself for the cold, try not to think about the blueness already seeping into my hands. I fumble to pull five millimetres of neoprene over my shivering body, free my surfboard from the roof rack, all the while listening to that distant rumble, rising and fading.

Tofino

As I walk down the path to the shore I am surrounded by the darkness from thousand-year-old firs and cedars, towering overhead like a cathedral — so high I cannot see their tops. This is my cathedral, one no person could ever construct, built over millennia. The rumbling grows louder.

Darkness turns to grey as I walk out onto the beach to see walls of water ten feet high exploding onto the reefs. The noise is so loud I can barely hear myself think, and I sit down to watch in awe. I'm alone as I sit looking across the Strait of Juan de Fuca to see the Olympic Mountains give way to the Pacific.

Then, the entire strait is bathed in gold. The sun has burst from the east with the dawn, sunlight has spread across the ocean like the touch of Midas. Trees and mountains come alive with light, waves are lit up like walls of green stained glass in the freezing air. I stand, my soul overwhelmed, and begin to sing. No one can hear me and I sing at the top of my lungs. I sing in thanks, in awe, so that I might join in with this symphony that mother nature has written for me on this day.

I step into the frigid water, climb onto my surfboard, and paddle out towards the reef, my soul and my heart full to the brim. Ready to dance in paradise.

Jacob Malthouse
Victoria

Blood and Chocolate
Annette Curtis Klaus

**Blueberries for Sal,
One Morning in Maine,
and Time of Wonder**
Robert McCloskey

**Bunnicula and Celery Stalks
at Midnight**
James Howe

Child's Garden of Verses
Robert Louis Stevenson

**Complete Works of
Beatrix Potter**

The Cure
Sonia Levitin

The Dorrie Books
Patricia Coombs

Emily of New Moon
Lucy Maud Montgomery

Galax Arena
Gillian Rubenstein

The Giver
Lois Lowry

Good Night Moon and
The Runaway Bunny
Margaret Wise Brown

Guess How Much I Love You?
Sam McBratney

Jelly Belly
Dennis Lee

Stuck in the Studio

CBC Radio British Columbia used to broadcast its daily radio programs from deep within the "bunker" at 700 Hamilton Street. Studio 5, buried two floors beneath ground, was so quiet you could hear a flea flex its wings from twenty paces. Hosts (including yours truly) were notorious for whining about this dungeon, praying for a periscope, a skylight, anything to lift their spirits above ground. Eventually the Mother Corp relented. A third-floor studio was built right beside our news and current affairs crews.

One morning after taping an interview in our newly christened studio, I tried to leave. The heavy, soundproof door would not budge. The locking mechanism had jammed; I was now a hostage. Two men from building maintenance arrived, peered at the door, and walked away. They returned with a screwdriver and hammer. The hinges merely scoffed.

Now people were gathering around the studio windows ... pointing. Banners and placards taunted me: "Save the Almanac One," "Free Mark," "First In Our Hearts." This was followed by a Yellow Ribbon campaign. *Basic Black* host Arthur arrived with his camera.

A locksmith – who just happened to be in the elevator – took one look at the CBC issue door and solemnly pronounced, "They stopped making parts for those years ago." When airtime arrived I found myself explaining this predicament to listeners – on a full bladder. Producer Laura Palmer, sensing a programming opportunity, played "Stuck in the Middle With You." An hour and a half after walking into Studio 31, a crowbar finally pried the door from its frame. I escaped without injury.

Then there was the time I was stuck in the elevator for forty-five minutes....

photo: Arthur Black

An Immigrant Story

We arrived in Canada from South Africa via Australia on September 17, 1951. I was eight years old. I recall visiting an office in Johannesburg with my mother and seeing on the wall a beautiful picture of geese flying over a sparkling lake that was fringed with rushes. "That's where we're going to live," my mother had said. I'd also heard my new stepfather tell about the island we would live on in Canada. He'd stated that it was quite a small island. I pictured it about the size of a city block, of some amorphous shape, and with little or no vegetation. Imagine my surprise when we arrived on Gabriola Island and it was miles long and wide, and virtually covered with tall trees.

There was so much to learn about on Gabriola Island, and such incomparable beauty to be appreciated. I remember the glorious Indian summer we enjoyed, the brittle browning bracken and the maple leaves turning colour in the warm sunshine. Our closest neighbours were the deer, raccoons, and mink that thrived on the island. I learned to eat fresh oysters right on the beach, and to pick ripe Saskatoon berries. We got our water from one of three wells on our property. A hand pump had been installed in the kitchen of the house. There was no electricity, so we needed to learn about kerosene lanterns and the delicacy of the mantles they needed. The outhouse was fairly close to the house, but it smelled badly, and was infested with spiders and insects. A farm neighbour who lived some miles away from our homestead brought us a grand present: a box of the finest-tasting apples he'd picked and stored from his own trees. As winter approached I learned about cutting firewood, chopping kindling, and keeping the ash box clean in the kitchen stove. When a heavy frost came and the pond in one of our hayfields froze over, I decided to act on the stories I heard about hardy Canadians who braved the winter chill to swim in frozen lakes. I stripped to a pair of underpants, ran to the frozen pond, cracked the surface ice, sat down in the frigid

Fifteen years ago, BC filmmakers produced a handful of movies; today, it's a billion-dollar industry employing thousands. Ian Caddell has watched the boom for *Variety, Hollywood Reporter, Georgia Straight,* and today edits *Reel West Magazine.* He also watches about 100 movies a year (while working for *Variety* and the *Georgia Straight,* he logged 470 in one year — a lot of popcorn), and keeps an eye out for homegrown productions. We asked for Ian's ten favourites — most you'll find on video if you search hard enough. Here are his suggestions for a cold winter weekend:

Caddell's Top Ten

1. *My American Cousin,* 1985. Directed by Sandy Wilson. Arguably the best English-language Canadian film ever made, *Cousin* captures its time (1959) and place (the Okanagan) in such a vibrant way it makes you want to leap into the screen and live life with the Wilcoxes. If there is a moment that will last forever in the memory it is the contradiction of cousin Butch's bright red Caddy shimmering against the rich and luscious

backdrop of beautiful BC Gorgeous.

2. *The Lotus Eaters*, 1993. Directed by Paul Shapiro. Peggy Thompson's Genie Award-winning screenplay sets an awful moment — the betrayal of a young girl by the two people she trusts the most — against characters and plot that are as delightful and quirky as those of *My Life as a Dog*.

3. *The Grey Fox*, 1983. Directed by Phillip Borsos. After thirty-three years in jail, a gentlemanly wild west stage coach robber emerges into the turn-of-the-century world of trains. Borsos is never judgmental here. Instead, he lets his screenplay and Richard Farnsworth's compelling performance tell the true story about one man's solution to career disruption.

4. *Double Happiness*, 1994. Directed by Mina Shum. Shum's screenplay and creative directing, and Sandra Oh's Genie Award-winning performance combine to turn what could have been a difficult story about interracial relationships into a poignant, relatable, and often funny examination of family life.

5. *The Outside Chance of Maximilian Glick*, 1988. Directed by Allan E. Goldstein. The humour comes from odd places in this story about a Jewish boy who falls for a

water, then scooted back to the house where my mother was waiting with a towel to dry me off. I really don't remember feeling cold. Ah, the joy of being a kid!

While my mother and I sorely missed our large family and many friends in Johannesburg, it was wonderful learning to live in new and different ways in our adopted home.

Ray Silver
Coquitlam

Surf's Up: Stand Back, Here Come the Fast Cats

"Fast Ferry Fiasco," "Sinking In A Sea of Red Ink," "Pacific Fat Cats." The headlines were blunt as BC's turn-of-the-century experiment with high-speed ferry technology backfired. It wasn't only cost overruns and design issues that had British Columbians in a lather. As Mary Wohlleban's family on Gabriola Island discovered, the wake from the aluminum-hulled ferries can pack an unexpected and potentially dangerous punch. Here's part of what she told *BC Almanac* following a fall trip to the beach with her two young children. They arrived shortly after one of the fast cats had sailed by on a test run.

Mary: Off we go, had our swim, everything went fine and my son was doing a bit of fishing. He handed me his fishing rod across the rocks, and just as I went to cast out, I heard this scream out of him. I turned around and there were waves coming in — the third wave hit him and knocked him off the rock into the water. It started to suck him out around behind it. I jumped in, grabbed him. There was another lady at the beach at the time, so she jumped in and I was able to pass him to her.

She put him up on the rocks. At the same time I was holding onto my other daughter, we sort of crouched over a rock as these waves were breaking over us. Once everything subsided I was able to lift her off and get her onto the main rock.

Mark: How frightened were they by this?

Mary: Oh, totally blown away. They didn't expect this, they'd grown up their whole life on these rocks. The lady with us had this remarkable ability to calm my son down. He had some pretty good scrapes down one side, and some good gouges around his knees after being bashed against the barnacles. I then realized I'd received a good scraping myself. From the back of my derriere down to my ankles there were forty to fifty cat gouges – with two or three good pieces taken out of the back of my knee. But you didn't feel it at the time, you were just getting in there and grabbing your child.

Mark: Yes, the adrenalin is flowing…. How much higher was the wave than the normal surf where your son was?

Mary: The way these archipelagos go, the rough water is on the outside. You don't go out there because when there's water on the rocks they're slippery, so it's just a no-go zone. But on a beautiful, calm, sunny day, the tide was slightly rising, so the rocks were very dry and safe to be on. These waves were not what you'd expect for around here … and you can't see them coming.

Mark: How steep are they?

Mary: It depends on the reef structure. At Tinson Point where the fellows surf, they get up to eight or nine feet. It's the same reef that runs all along that northern side where we were; so for the surfers who are six feet tall it's a thrill – but not when you're four feet tall, and your back is turned to the water. My son just flew like he was a piece of plastic.

Mark: Fortunately with your reaction, your kids are safe. I hope those scrapes heal quickly….

Mary: Oh, they will – although I'll be in shorts for weeks.

Christian girl in the rural Manitoba of the 1950s. Humour it is, however, as Saul Rubinek plays funny rabbi to Noam Zylberman's quizzical kid.

6. *Kissed*, 1996. Directed by Lynne Stopkewich. Molly Parker "sees" dead people in this dark but mesmerizing fantasy about a young woman who has sex with the cadavers that end up in the morgue in which she works. More irony than in any given year of American films.

7. *Skip Tracer*, 1977. Directed by Zale Dalen. The title character has a "wild west" quality to him. Charged with finding those who have "skipped" their loan payments, he appears to see himself as a modern bounty hunter. Both the comedy and the drama of this film, arguably the first great BC-produced movie, come from his sense of duty.

8. *The War Between Us*, 1995. Directed by Anne Wheeler. While there have been several movies about racism in the interior American and Canadian towns that were turned into Japanese internment camps in World War II, this film is better because it sets the racism against the backdrop of a class war between the educated, middle-class Japanese and the rural whites, and treats all of is characters with dignity.

BC's Giant Waves

Imagine a cresting wall of green water and foam nearly thirty metres tall (101 feet) – that's higher than a ten-storey building. The giant crashes and roars with a life all its own. A freak wave this size was recorded at the East Dellwood marine weather buoy west of Cape Scott back in 1993. Two years earlier, a South Hecate buoy registered a wave of thirty metres; both are amoung the largest recorded on the planet. They often arrive without warning.

Intense Pacific storms can erupt with little notice, packing hurricane force winds (sixty-four knots on the wind scale) transforming the Pacific into a chilling graveyard. In recent years, the fishing fleet has taken the brunt of these storms – thirteen fishermen were lost during a sudden storm in 1975; the 400-boat halibut fleet was caught off-guard in 1985, the ocean claimed seven vessels and three lives. In 1987, the trawler *Scotia Cape* just disappeared. Seven crew were aboard. Freak waves had been spotted near Northern Vancouver Island where the vessel was last seen.

Researchers like DFO oceanographer Dr Jim Gower and Environment Canada metereologist David Jones describe how these freak waves get wound up: "Waves form and grow as the wind transfers energy from the atmosphere to the sea … when several wave trains converge to a point, the resultant wave may be much larger than the surrounding waves. Occasionally the resultant wave may seem outrageously disproportionate – hence the expression freak wave…. The interaction of the seas with prevailing tidal and ocean currents and the sea bottom can create especially conducive conditions for freak wave development."

These giant waves have a short, intense life – only a minute or two. Today a network of moored marine weather buoys helps provide advance weather warnings for mariners, but the unpredictable nature of these monsters suggests other souls will be caught in their ferocious grip.

Information courtesy Marine Weather Log, Spring 1994.

Somewhere Near Sicamous

photo: Kathy Chapman
Kootenay River

My computer screen partly blocks the view through the window and glass door leading to the sundeck of our apartment. I often turn my eyes from the screen, and no one blames me. In the whole area, there isn't a view to compare.

Below me, a finger of land pokes out into a wide bay to change the bay's shape into a sort of lazy "W." The land marks the Eagle River, which clings to its shores until it finally releases itself into Shuswap Lake. This is a favourite spot for fishermen to spend hours casting for trout. Canada geese and trumpeter swans feed along there and the shore of the bay in the winter.

The lakeshore is lined with sandy beaches that will delight tourists, come summer. For now, the lake winds around the base of forested mountains still topped with snow, where "sledders" delight to spend winter's daylight hours.

The sun's rise lights my kitchen; when it sets, the glory of it is framed in my living room window. I mark sunset's passage along the mountain tops as the year progresses: on the right towards Salmon Arm in the winter, moving a little further east and north each evening until in June it sets far up the lake.

In the other direction, across the parking lot, I see Sicamous, Mara Lake, and the narrow channel between that lake and the Shuswap. Along the channel sit rows of houseboats waiting for summer, when they will slip into the water, ready for the tourists.

My bird's eye view is sometimes shared by eagles, rising in the sky against the hillside's air currents. At night, deer leave their tracks on the driveway, and in the spring, bears come to feed on young dandelion leaves. We try not to disturb them, though the marmots who sun themselves on the rocks still dive into their holes when we drive by on our way to town.

Cupid, draw back your bow. This call about meeting the one you love came through our Valentine's Day "Open Line."

We got together in the summer of '98 … we were both protestors at APEC. We were going to be Street Theatre for that day and Garth dressed up in his suit to represent capitalism. I dressed up as a police officer. We went and had a rally at the City Hall — ended up getting arrested, dragged off by the police. We had to go to jail and got processed at the romantic Downtown Detention Centre at Main and Hastings. We spent the day locked up in separate cages, but really made a connection in the paddy wagon on the way over. We were banging on the doors and singing Black Flag punk songs to each other. When we got out from jail he was waiting for me. We've been together pretty much ever since.

Alyssa Westergard-Thorpe
& Garth Mullins
Vancouver

COUGAR MAN CHASE

Here's how associate producer Elizabeth Hoath describes tracking down a man who survived a cougar attack:

All we knew in the morning at our story meeting was that a man was in hospital in Bella Coola after a cougar attack. No name. No real word on his condition. Naturally we decide to chase the story. First stop: RCMP. The officer could tell the story just fine, and he freely offers up the name Clarence Hall. He's the man who was attacked and is now in the hospital. The chase is on.

It doesn't take long to reach the nursing station closest to Mr Hall's room. This is the tricky part. I have no real idea how injured this man is or how traumatized he might be by the experience. And I'm asking a nurse to put me in touch with him.

It is quiet here; some folks describe it as "therapeutic." Visitors from the city often come with a "rush hour" attitude, and spend a day or so thinking they've fallen off the edge of the world. Given time, they relax and eventually leave considerably calmer, having discovered the secret of this place. Part of the secret is taking the time to appreciate the wonderful view, which I gratefully do every day.

Olga McCormick

Some years ago now, I went hang-gliding with my "flying" buddies at our prime site on Mount Woodside, a great place overlooking the Fraser Valley where the Harrison and the Fraser Rivers meet. Besides Brackendale near Squamish, the Harrison at that particular place is visited by many eagles as well. In spring the juveniles like to try out their soaring skills just like we do.

On this day the conditions were great, as it is so often that time of year; strong thermals, and fairly easy to stay airborne.

After playing around for a while in the air currents and marveling at the beauty and awesomeness of nature all around me, I noticed some eagles below me perched in some of the snags that are prevalent on the mountain.

Getting air off Grouse Mountain

While I was circling in a thermal, I could see one of the birds flying out of a tree and turning into the same updraught that I was in. I knew that something very exciting was about to take place. The eagle did not waste any time and soon was right under me, showing me how flying is really done. Then, just as I was wondering what would happen next, it moved to my right wingtip and stayed there, circling with me and looking at me with its big yellow eyes. It truly was an incredible moment almost too fantastic to be true.

When the king of the air had enough of me it went up higher and disappeared, leaving me with a thrilling feeling of having been part of something truly great.

Herman Bosman
Burnaby

Man Fights Off Cougar

How do you fight off a cougar latched onto your neck? Stick your hand in its mouth. That's what tracker Clarence Hall resorted to as a survival tactic. From his hospital bed where he was nursing 100 stitches, the feisty seventy-four-year-old from Bella Coola told *BC Almanac* listeners how he fought off a hungry cat that attacked him from behind:

> … *this cougar hit me so hard it was like getting clubbed on the side of my neck. Down I went on my back, she began munching on my neck and I realized it was a matter of seconds before I wouldn't be here. I put my right hand in the cougar's mouth – behind the lower canines – and pulled that cougar over on my chest away from my neck. At the same time I had her paws pinned down so she wouldn't cut me. I was calling for help and she's chewing my right hand to pieces – I've got broken bones in my hand right now. I planned to choke her to death. Bare handed. When I went to do this, I took my hand out of her mouth, and in a split second she grabbed the top of my head. The right top front canine tooth went right out of sight into my skull. About that time the neighbour came over with a .22 rifle, and at point-blank range he shot it four times. The last shot broke the cougar's spine. It was a matter of life and death.*

The young neighbour who came to Clarence's rescue was Barry Mack. 1999/2000 was an especially bad winter for cougars unable to find food sources in the Bella Coola Valley. Some biologists worry that adult cougars – often the mothers – are being shot so the young aren't properly trained to hunt, and they attack easy pickings: livestock and humans.

But she's open. No, there's no phone in the room, she explains. I ask if there's any way to get him to a phone. The handset is muffled for a minute. She's back and instead offers to move a phone into his room so he can talk to me. My heartbeat speeds up a pace, I'm almost there, he must be willing to talk or she'd never put him in that position. Minutes pass, there's clicking and buzzing on the line. Finally an extension picks up and a strong, lively voice chirps, "Clarence Hall here." At that point, I knew I had the makings of an unforgettable interview; great story, great storyteller.

BEST BC BOOKS

Ask the publisher of *BC Bookworld* for a list of ten favourite BC titles, and Alan Twigg will give you twenty. An author, journalist, and critic, Alan launched *BC Bookworld* in 1987 to promote BC writers and publishers because while growing up here he could count most of them on his left hand. British Columbia now has a thriving $58 million-a-year book industry, and *BC Bookworld* is among the country's premier publications about books.

Alan Twigg's Best BC Books (Listed chronologically)

1. *Legends of Vancouver,* E. Pauline Johnson, 1911

2. *Under the Volcano,* Malcolm Lowry, 1947

3. *Measure of the Year,* Roderick Haig-Brown, 1950

4. *Mist on the River,* Hubert Evans, 1954

5. *Desert of the Heart,* Jane Rule, 1964

The Bird Woman
Brenda Mallory

Brenda Mallory is the BC Almanac community correspondent in Telkwa.

It was late in the summer of 1986 and time once more to leave the placer mining season behind. Already ice was skimming the sluice boxes and the first snows of the season were not far behind.

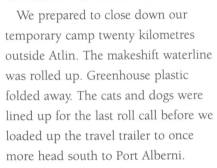

We prepared to close down our temporary camp twenty kilometres outside Atlin. The makeshift waterline was rolled up. Greenhouse plastic folded away. The cats and dogs were lined up for the last roll call before we loaded up the travel trailer to once more head south to Port Alberni.

This year had a feeling of anticipation as I remembered all the paintings I had completed in the old miners shack. Paintings all ready for a show for my home-town crowd.

The trip was basically uneventful. No problems with vehicles or the animals. No crowds in the gravel pits we would use for camping.

Finally we hit pavement and headed down the smooth highway to the Hazeltons. As before we were impressed by the beautiful, rugged mountains and the rivers. As we came closer to Smithers we enjoyed the rural atmosphere and mountains. Then came picturesque Telkwa, the little town where the rivers meet. The log-built library and the gazebo facing Hudson Bay Mountain, the quaint houses with heritage home designations, seemed to be just what we needed.

We had friends in the area who had just bought a home and as luck would have it, five acres were for sale right next door. In a flash we decided to buy the property. No cash but a coffee jar of gold was all we needed to secure the place as we carried on with our journey to Port Alberni.

As the years went by I had the opportunity to share my views about this little place on *BC Almanac*, first with Cecelia Walters and then with Mark Forsythe.

I could tell the people around the province about the moose who chased me or the new birds at the sanctuary.

No matter how many times I have been heard over the radio, there has been some response. I am stopped on the street or called from another place. It might be a comment about the piece or a friend from long ago.

Talking about this beautiful place is always fun and rewarding. Hearing from the listeners is just a pleasant bonus.

I can remember sitting in a coffee shop in Atlin after I was told some of my letters were read on air at CBC Whitehorse. An old sourdough summed things up nicely: "At least I can shut the radio off."

BRIAN MINTER'S WINTER GARDENING TIPS: JANUARY

Trees and shrubs
Your second and third sprayings of lime sulphur and dormant oil should be done in the month of January. Remember: these sprays stain buildings, so put plastic behind shrubs and trees which are against walls. For the best results, use only a pressure sprayer to get the spray into all the cracks and crevices of the trees, and spray all branches thoroughly until the spray begins to run off. Certain trees are adversely affected by some dormant sprays, so please read the labels before you spray. Lime sulphur and dormant oil should not be used on maples, nut trees, or viburnums. Copper spray is better for peaches, nectarines, apricots, and apples with European canker.

River of the Angry Moon

Descending Highway 20 into the Bella Coola Valley is like experiencing free-fall without leaving ground. Locals may scoff, but the nearly vertical "Big Hill" warrants a five star white-knuckle rating.

The road links dry, grassy Chilcotin plateau with a rainforest so rich and verdant it reaches out to embrace you. Separating them is the mile-high Coast Mountain Range, a barrier so steep and rugged that the provincial government refused to spend money on a road. Residents of Bella Coola and Anahim Lake built a road themselves in the early 1950s.

The Bella Coola River and its tributaries, tumbling from the same mountains, are revered for unsurpassed fishing: steelhead, cutthroat, coho, and chinook. But the pulse of the river grows ever fainter. A ban on steelhead fishing – the most treasured of sportfish – was recently imposed.

* * *

"Nature is resilient and salmon are incredibly fecund," says Mark Hume in *River of the Angry Moon* (Greystone). "The waters should abound with fish. When they do not, it's a sign of terrible mismanagement, not by fisheries bureaucrats, but by society as a whole."

Born in Victoria in 1950, Hume is a veteran reporter who's covered BC for the *Vancouver Sun* and now the *National Post*. One of five boys, he was the only one to catch the fishing bug as a child in Penticton.

"It's almost like a fishing gene you inherit," he muses.

As a young teen, he stumbled across the writings of Roderick Haig-Brown in a Victoria library. He eventually decided he wanted to fly fish and write like the Campbell River lay magistrate.

The seeds of a strong conservation ethic were planted. In both of his previous books, *The Run of the River* and *Adam's River*, Hume argue for better stewardship of rivers and more responsible fishing.

Hume gravitated to the Bella Coola River after friend and physician Harvey Thommasen moved to Bella Coola. Thommasen, who wrote *River of the Angry* Moon with Hume, previously compiled and edited two bestsellers about the life and times of Clayton Mack, *Grizzlies & White Guys* and *Bella Coola Man*.

Hume and Thommasen spent many hours walking, talking, and casting into its pools and riffles. Over the years Thommasen catalogued much of the ecosystem's flora and fauna and collected stories from elders about the way it used to be. He realized the Bella Coola and its tributaries were under siege; a meat fish mentality in the sports fishery and a relentless commercial fleet were wiping out the most valued runs. As well, some Nuxalt natives used river nets, targeting the weakest stocks. Silt oozing from clearcuts choked the finest spawning streams.

Hume and Thommasen resolved to write a book that would alert people to the river's plight and counter a local belief the fish "would always come back." *River of the Angry Moon*, subtitled *Seasons on the Bella Coola*, is part lament for what was, yet it also celebrates what remains and what could be again. There is an undercurrent of optimism throughout.

The wild Bella Coola River carves a mesmerizing path through each chapter, linked to the moons of the Native Nuxalt calendar. In spring, yellow stone flies dance off its surface, in winter silvery steelhead rest in deep pools conserving energy for the spawn. We catch the husky scent of skunk cabbage, hear the woof of an agitated grizzly, and watch light caress rainforest. Hume captures the river's own poetry.

> *The river is fed by the sky. It runs over a bed of*
> *shattered mountains, through the dreams of a great forest*
> *and into the mouths of ancient fishes. It starts in*
> *clouds as grey and heavy as the sea and ends in a*
> *windswept estuary haunted by ghosts. It is a place where*
> *white swans dance on dark mud flats and salmon lay fragile*
> *eggs in nests of stone.*

Fly-fishers will appreciate Hume's delight at reading streams and currents, casting the perfect fly imitation – rewarded by the electric surge of fish on line. The two men pull on scuba masks to float the river in neoprene sailboarding suits encountering ghostly columns of dark chinook and rainbows feeding in rapids. Hume seems to become the river itself.

Bulbs

If your bulbs are coming up and you are worried about damage from cold January weather, simply cover the shoots with bark mulch. You can still plant Narcissus, minor bulbs, and tulips for a good spring showing.

January Top Ten List for Gardening

1. dormant spraying of fruit trees, roses and ornamentals
2. weed control
3. start early seeds like pansies, geraniums, and begonias
4. feed wild birds
5. fertilize indoor plants
6. start begonia tubers
7. add gypsum to break up heavy clay areas in your garden
8. aerate lawns and apply dolomite lime
9. spray all indoor plants with an insecticide soap
10. plant trees and shrubs that bloom in January

MARTINI, ANYONE?

Each morning our *BC Almanac* crew gathers to hash over stories we want to put on the radio. When food columnist Don Genova strolls into the room, we never quite know what he'll be carrying — a new BC cheese, fruity dessert, or zesty pesto. One morning it was a tall-stemmed glass containing an award-winning martini. The Dragon's Breath Martini was concocted by a Hotel Vancouver bartender. Needless to say, the story meeting was rather short-lived that morning.

Dragon's Breath
From 900 West, Hotel Vancouver
Winner of the Best Specialty Martini in the Vancouver and International Categories

2 oz good quality gin
Splash of vermouth
¼ oz Cointreau
Splash of blood orange juice

Shake the gin and vermouth with ice and pour into a well-chilled martini glass. Garnish with Cointreau, and a squeeze of juice from a blood orange. Blood oranges have an orange skin,

Hanging listless, drifting where the current takes me,
I lose touch with my body and start to melt into the green
light. Only the sound of my lungs brings me back.

Old-timers' memories and newspaper accounts reveal how overfishing on the Bella Coola was a significant problem even seventy-five years ago. On one fishing excursion, three men killed 732 fish. By the mid-1990s what appeared to be a limitless bounty was virtually exhausted – steelhead stocks reduced from 10,000 to a mere handful. Chinook and coho stocks are also in crisis, the same sombre story played out on river systems from Alaska to Oregon.

Hume reminds us that wildlife managers in the last century outlawed commercial hunting of animals to save them from extinction; he says nature can't keep up with today's industrial harvesting and similar action is required for at-risk fish stocks.

Writing the book was a welcome change from newspaper reporting. "It allowed me to put myself in the story," he says, "tap into my feelings and express myself. As a reporter I can't do that."

The late British Poet Laureate Ted Hughes also provided unexpected inspiration. Hughes had written about fishing BC's famous Dean River and while attending a Steelhead Society fund raiser he was interviewed by Hume. The poet remarked how much he had enjoyed Mark's first book *The Run of the River*. Shortly before his death, Hughes sent a letter encouraging Hume to complete the Bella Coola book.

Hume paid tribute to Hughes at the BC Book Prizes when he accepted the Roderick Haig-Brown Regional Prize awarded to the book that best contributes to the understanding and appreciation of BC.

Originally published in BC Bookworld, Summer 1999.

For my loved one and I, the most romantic place in BC is Dallas Road in Victoria, especially in the spring.

Let me set the scene: brilliant sun in the vibrant blue sky; Juan de Fuca Strait a darker blue, mirroring puffy white clouds; the Olympic Mountains, carved in shades of purple and blue and white against that sky. Then Dallas Road walkway itself: green grass dotted by yellow daffodils, blue camas, and assorted "volunteer" flowers from neighbouring gardens; benches from which to look out over the water; and the beach, covered with smooth, miraculously-coloured stones, giant, gnarled driftwood logs – and everywhere, people of all ages with strollers and bicycles, roller blades, wheel-chairs, brilliant-coloured kites, hang gliders, and windsurfers.

Kelowna

There are joggers, picnickers, sunbathers, birders, and idlers – and everyone is smiling.

Now before I go any further, to help you really understand my romance with Dallas Road, I must tell you that the big, muscular, blond love of my life is a golden retriever, Ulysses. We head for Dallas Road – an "off-leash" section – each day, and once there, we dance the tennis ball waltz, as romantic a dance as the best of Strauss. Ulysses bounces, I bow. I toss the daffodil-coloured tennis ball in a big looping arc against the sky. He hurtles after it, catching it on one bounce. He struts back, macho, proud of his skill, and drops his trophy at my feet. He bounces, I bow.

I see his smile, his flashing bright eyes, and I know I am bringing him enormous pleasure. In return, he fills me with joy. But he doesn't stop with me – Ulysses checks all the benches, watches for wheelchairs and strollers. He obviously believes that anyone sitting still must be needing pleasure. So Ulysses rushes over, drops his ball at their feet, then bounces his first steps in the dance to let them know they too can play. Almost everyone does … and their faces light up and I see more smiles, more pleasure, more joy before Ulysses wags his way back to me.

Dallas Road provides beauty, colour, and the romance of simple pleasures of life for hundreds of people each day. It is the place where Ulysses and I dance our romance with life.

Marsha Mildon

Victoria

but a very red flesh and juice. (You can find them in most grocery stores with good produce sections.)

The Casablanca
From Gerard Lounge, the Sutton Place Hotel (Vancouver)

2½ oz Bombay Sapphire Gin
Hint of Scotch
Olives

Pour gin and Scotch over ice and stir. Strain into a well-chilled martini glass and garnish with olives.

Ultraviolet Martini
From the Four Seasons Olympic Hotel (Seattle)

¹⁄₁₀ oz grappa (Jacopo Poli preferred)
3 drops of Crème de Cassis
⅛ oz Chambord
½ oz Bombay Sapphire Gin
2¼ oz vodka
3 frozen blueberries

Pour grappa into a martini mixing glass; coat the bottom of this glass with the grappa, then dispose of the excess grappa. Then fill the mixing glass with ice, and pour the remaining ingredients over the ice. Spoon stir until ice cold and strain into an ice cold martini glass. Garnish with blueberries.

191

The Ultimate Chill
From Oliver's, the Mayflower Park
Hotel (Seattle)
Winner of Best Seattle and
International Classic Martini

2½ oz Bombay Sapphire Gin or
    Stolichnaya Gold Vodka
¼ oz Cinzano Dry Vermouth
2 large vermouth-marinated
    Italian olives

Start with an empty ice cold martini
mixing glass. Pour the vermouth into
the empty mixing glass. Swirl to coat
the inside of the mixing glass with
the vermouth, dispose of excess
vermouth. Fill coated mixing glass
with ice. Pour the gin or vodka over
the ice. Cap and shake vigorously.
Let the mixture stand approximately
20 seconds. Suspend a skewered set
of the olives over an ice-cold martini
glass. Strain the mixture into the
glass over the olives.

Winter Preserves
BC Newtown Apple Butter

4 lbs BC Newtown (a.k.a. Pippins) or other
    tart apples, quartered with skins and stems
2 cups apple cider
4 cups sugar
3 tsp cinnamon
2 tsp cloves, ground
1 tsp allspice

In a large, heavy, stainless steel saucepan, combine apples and cider. Bring to a boil over medium heat, then simmer 25 minutes until apples are soft. Stir occasionally to make sure apples do not stick.

Once the apples are soft, pass them through a food mill to remove skins, seeds, and cores. In a medium saucepan, combine sieved apples, sugar, and spices. Taste for sweetness, adding more sugar if desired. Heat apple mixture over low heat for 4 hours until very thick and no liquid separates around the edges, stirring frequently to avoid scorching. Ladle hot apple butter into 250 ml sterilized mason jars, leaving ¼ inch (0.5 cm) head space. Wipe jar rims clean. Apply prepared canning lids fingertip tight. Process in a boiling water bath canner 5 minutes. Cool. Sealed lids curve downwards. Store in cool, dry, dark place. Makes 8 250 ml jars. Alternatively, cover tightly and keep refrigerated for up to 3 weeks.

Recipe courtesy BC Tree Fruits.

Reluctant Immigrant

I had no intention of immigrating anywhere. The war was over. We could go to sleep knowing that we would, in all probability, wake up in the morning, and while there was still rationing of some hard-to-get items, in general, life looked good for a nineteen-year-old living in Wimbledon, on the outskirts of London.

Then I met Gord, a research chemist. It was November 1950. He had been living in Canada for a couple of years and had come home for his father's funeral and was going back again in January. Great, I thought, a boyfriend for Christmas and then freedom again. January, February, March and still he had shown no signs of leaving, but I didn't mind. I had grown fond of my tall redhead. At the end of March, he proposed to me. "I'd like to marry you, if you'd like to live in Canada," he said. It sounded like a conditional proposal – it was a conditional proposal. If I said no to Canada, I might as well say no to marriage – to this man, at any rate. I said "yes," although I hated the prospect of leaving my parents. We had a wonderful wedding and four months later we sailed away from Southhampton on the Queen Mary.

We arrived in Edmonton, after hitchhiking from New York. It took us nine days. I was, by this time, two-and-a-half months pregnant and morning sickness dragged on into the afternoon and evening in the guise of homesickness.

There was some regulation in place when we left England, restricting the amount of money we could bring out of the country. I don't think we came close to having that much, as by the time we reached Edmonton, we had five dollars between us. Fortunately, Gord had friends we could stay with for a couple of weeks. He started work the day after we arrived, on Saturday morning, sorting dirty beer bottles for ninety cents an hour and I started work on Monday as a secretary, earning a dollar an hour! It would be the only time I ever earned more than my husband.

We have a lot to be thankful for. My parents, my sister, and Gord's brother all immigrated a couple of years after us. Dad was eighty-six when he died and Mum was ninety-six. We have four children, nine grandchildren, and two great-grandchildren.

As if this country hasn't given us enough, Gord has a Canadian heart beating in his chest. He received a heart transplant four years ago. I often wonder what my life would have been like if I had stayed in England, but I have never regretted my decision.

Pamela Kent

JANUARY EVENTS

Brackendale Annual
Bald Eagle Festival

Falkland International Sled Dog Races

Kamloops Annual Ice Wine Festival

Kelowna Snowfest

Lumby Snofest

Prince George Iceman Competition

Quesnel Sled Dog Race
Championships

Rossland Winter Carnival

Vancouver's Annual
Ice Sculpting Competition

Vancouver Polar Bear Swim

Eric Touche, Fernie

193

Retreating History

Keeping a network of transmitters on the air in a mostly vertical province is a thankless job left to a handful of people most of us who work at CBC never see. They're transmitter technicians and engineers scattered around the province who drive snowcats and snowmobiles up mountainsides (trying not to get stuck) to fix and maintain our 123 AM, FM, digital, and shortwave radio transmitters.

When they finally reach a site (travelling in daylight hours only, in case of breakdown), transmitter shacks are sometimes completely buried in snow. Get out the shovel. If it's spring, that means mud, or porcupines known to eat plywood foundations and floors out of the shacks (they're attracted to the glue). Sometimes they stumble across other surprises — like a marijuana plantation.

Engineer Dave Newbury oversees the crews. He says it takes "an outdoors person" to pull it off, adding that the toughest site to service is Copper Mountain at Terrace. Its elevation and heavy snow make it especially challenging. There's so

During World War II, thousands of Japanese-Canadians were taken from their homes and shipped to internment in the interior. Some of those people relived the experience for the filming in Greenwood of a movie based on David Guterson's bestselling book *Snow Falling on Cedars*. Local resident Nancy Yamamura played an extra; she was seven when her family was evacuated.

Nancy: We were extras in the actual evacuation scene where there were hundreds of us coming down the hill towards the water to board the boats. It was freezing cold with the most uncomfortable shoes, and clothing that wasn't warm enough. It was quite an experience to see the people dressed in the garb of the period. It really did bring back memories.

Mark: I'm sure it did. You were a child in 1942....

Nancy: I was very young; as a child, my memories are a little different from the elderly people and as typical children it was more fun and games for us. It was fun because economically we were all in the same boat, and there was so much togetherness, we always got together and played hard. That was quite an adventure for us, but the stories parents tell are quite different.

Mark: Their whole community was being rounded up and interned. Playing this part, did that make you think about what your parents might have been going through?

Nancy: Yes, we all talked about this a great deal since the movie and we've all thought more about our parents than ourselves. It was a very degrading, traumatic time for our parents. Being put in Hastings Park … having to go to the sugar beets and being treated like that must have been very difficult. Many lost everything materially. We also talked about it in terms that we have to be very proud of our parents because they persevered all this. Even in hard times they got together, learned to be a tailor, a baker, a plumber, a shoemaker. We don't even have those things in Greenwood now, but that just goes to show you that you really don't have to have very much if you want to get ahead and get something going. Many of our young women learned trades in all of this.

Mark: And many stayed – made lives there?

Nancy: Yes, for a number of years. Now there's nothing for our younger folks, and they have to leave town to get education and get jobs. But some of us die-hards are still here. It's our home. We have maybe forty to forty-five people of Japanese descent here still.

Mark: I know it was very difficult for your parents' generation to actually talk about that experience. I've heard in many cases they just didn't. To now be part of this movie, can you describe what it's like?

Nancy: I've talked to other people who were older, who recall very hard times, for the moment it did bring back terrible memories. They all concluded we have to think back on our parents, how they would feel now, what they would like us to be feeling – not to be holding a grudge, that time heals. There's not much point in dwelling on being angry. We all kind of agreed on that. We know it was very difficult for our parents. We can't even begin to imagine what that would be like in this day and age.

Mark: So there you were, standing in the cold, do you want to be a movie extra again?

Nancy: (chuckling) I don't know about that, but I now have a greater appreciation for all extras in all movies.

much white stuff you "enter the building on the second floor."

Copper Mountain transmitter

Some CBC Radio trivia:
First Radio Transmitter: Vancouver, CBU on air January 1, 1938.
Highest transmitter site: Cranbrook FM, located on Mount Baker at 7244 feet or 2207.9 metres above sea level.
Lowest transmitter site: Vancouver, CBU located in Richmond six feet above sea level with the transmitter building on the dyke and the four towers located in the mud flats.
Mostly northerly site: Fort Nelson.
Most southerly site: Metchosin/Sooke.
Most westerly site: Port Clements on Queen Charlotte Islands.
Most easterly site: Sparwood.

AM Transmitters:
Highest power: 50,000 watts.
Lowest power: 40 watts.

FM Transmitters:
Highest power: 100,000 watts radiated power, Vancouver Radio 2 and Prince George Radio 1
Lowest power: 6 watts radiated power, Ocean Falls Radio 1

WHAT'S THE FREQUENCY?

CBC Radio One

Aiyansh	102.3 fm
Alert Bay	105.1 fm
Alexis Creek	93.7 fm
Alice Arm	1150 am
Ashcroft	860 am
Bamfield	540 am
Barriere	104.1 fm
Bella Bella	89.9 fm
Bella Coola	103.5 fm
Blue River	860 am
Bonnington	89.5 fm
Boston Bar	90.7 fm
Burns Lake	99.1 fm
Cache Creek	1450 am
Campbell River	104.5 fm
Canal Flats	91.7 fm
Castlegar	94.9 fm
Chase	860 am
Chemanus	90.5 fm
Chetwynd	93.5 fm
Chilliwack	91.7 fm
Christina Lake	88.5 fm
Clearwater	860 am
Clinton	1070 am
Coal Harbour	540 am
Cooper Creek	1540 am

On a Wing and a Prayer: Peter Wing, the First Chinese Mayor in North America

Charlie Cho

Charlie Cho is a writer and an associate producer with CBC Radio. He contributes regularly to Rice Paper.

With his sharply-combed, shocking white hair, pale blue Hawiian shirt, 6'1" height, and charming smile, you might mistake Peter Wing for the host of *The Price Is Right* or *The Tonight Show*. Instead, his infectious charisma helped make him a born leader. In 1966, he became the mayor of Kamloops – the first Chinese mayor in North America.

Even as one of only five Chinese families in Kamloops, the Wings were part of mainstream society; belonging to the United Church made it easy for them to socialize and integrate. Peter's first memories were also his fondest: going to Sunday School at a Methodist Church with his sister. Peter served on many committees, and even spent twenty years in the choir.

He left school at age sixteen to work in his dad's new grocery store. At the time, in 1930, there were few reasons to stay in school. Chinese were barred from all professions, including mechanics, until 1947.

But it was also in his teens when he met the love of his life. Kim Kwong lived in Revelstoke. Her brother contracted tuberculosis in China, and the only TB clinic nearby was in Kamloops. She was told Peter "was the only one in the Kamloops with a car." (He was actually one of two Chinese guys that owned a car.)

"In those days, of course, it was more matchmaking than love anyways. Our parents decided that if we wanted to, it would happen." They did want to, and when he turned eighteen, he married Kim, beginning a wonderful partnership that continues today. "No one could do what I did without help from behind."

His climb continued through the Kamloops Chamber of Commerce. He joined the Board of Trade in 1934, and became its vice-president in 1953. After rising through the Church and the Chamber of Commerce – and gaining the right to vote and be voted for – Peter Wing was encouraged by friends to go into politics.

After six years as alderman, he smashed through the "yellow ceiling." In the mayoral race, he got as many votes as the other two candidates put together. Becoming Mayor of Kamloops didn't just make a splash in Canada. He became famous around the world. A year later, when he visited Taipei, "I got a wonderful reception. They practically gave me the keys to the city."

Wing's term was a critical one for Kamloops. The city amalgamated with North Kamloops in 1967. Three or four years later, the provincial government forced the amalgamation of the rest of the surrounding area. The population of Greater Kamloops jumped from 40,000 to almost 80,000.

None of that fazed Mayor Wing: "I felt so at home there. It was a natural thing for me. I never felt anything special about it."

Kamloops became the Wing's extended family. "I was giving a speech at the time, and I said, 'My wife and I have no children.' And one of my friends shouted from the back of the hall, 'You and she got more kids than any of us! All the kids in Kamloops are your children!'"

Courtenay/Comox	92.5 fm
Cranbrook	101.3 fm
Crawford Bay	89.9 fm
Creston	100.3 fm
Crofton	90.5 fm
Cumberland	92.5 fm
Dawson Creek	89.7 fm
Deas Lake	98.1 fm
Denman Island	92.5 fm
Donald Station	900 am
Duncan South to Victoria	90.5 fm
Edgewood	860 am
Enderby	92.7 fm
Falkland	102.7 fm
Fernie	97.7 fm
Field	860 am
Fort Nelson	88.3 fm
Fort St James	91.9 fm
Fort St John	88.3 fm
Fraser Lake	102.9 fm
Gold Bridge	860 am
Golden	101.7 fm
Gold River	860 am
Grand Forks	860 am
Granisle	920 am
Greenwood	97.9 fm
Harrison	96.7 fm
Hazelton	1170 am
Holdberg	1490 am
Hope	101.7 fm
Hornby Island	92.5 fm
Houston	102.1 fm
Hudson Hope	940 am
Hundred Mile House	91.3 fm
Jaffray	101.3 fm
Kamloops	94.1 fm
Kaslo	860 am
Kelowna	88.9 fm

Keremeos	1350 am
Kersley	90.9 fm
Kimberley	900 am
Kispiox	990 am
Kitimat	101.1 fm
Kitwanga	94.3 fm
Ladysmith	90.5 fm
Lake Windermere	94.5 fm
Lillooet	860 am
Logan Lake	92.9 fm
Lumby	96.7 fm
Lytton	93.1 fm
MacKenzie	920 am
Masset	103.9 fm
McBride	92.1 fm
Merritt	860 am
Midway	97.9 fm
Moricetown	96.5 fm
Nakusp	900 am
Nelson	98.7 fm
New Denver	740 am
New Hazelton	1170 am
Osoyoos	95.3 fm
Parksville	92.5 fm
Parson	740 am
Pemberton	1240 am
Penticton	93.7 fm
Phoenix	97.9 fm
Port Alberni	98.1 fm
Port Alice	1170 am
Port Clements	102.9 fm
Port Hardy	95.5 fm
Port McNeill	105.1 fm
Powell River	92.5 fm
Prince George	91.5 fm
Prince Rupert	860 am
Princeton	93.1 fm
Quadra Island	104.5 fm
Qualicum Beach	92.5 fm

Meldrum Creek

I arrived two days before school was to begin. The double-wide trailer that was the Meldrum Creek School nestled in front of the modern little teacherage on an acre of dusty meadow protected by a sturdy log fence. Everything was surrounded by a golden poplar halo. The cloud of dust that had shadowed me from Williams Lake tanned me as I stepped out of my Rambler. Logging truck drivers honked, black-eyed susans waved, and deer came to watch. My front window framed the clouded road and the parade of red willow bushes. Brilliant yellow-crowned, checkerboard poplar trunks and clumps of vivid evergreens were set against the hazy blue hills of this little valley.

I was there to educate my thirteen students, but I picked up a few lessons myself that have stood the lifetime test.

One can live very happily without electricity for an entire year. A large bucket of snow will melt down to one litre of water. When the hand pump won't work, there's probably mice stuck in the pipe. As long as you boil it for fifteen minutes and see no mouse hair, the water is clean — no matter if there is scum on it.

You wave at every car when you're driving. No one passes you by when you have a flat or you're in a snowbank. Children can be late for school because they were scientifically following snake tracks in the snowbank. Hunters shoot at children riding their horses beside the road.

Christmas school pageants are the highlight of the winter. The local Santa tells the best mixture of truth and tall tales and will correspond with you for years.

You can fit a post office, general store, and an oil barrel stove in a three-by-four metre shed. By fall, calves are very hard to hold still.

A dance includes all ages. Nobody sits down while a dance is playing. If a single young schoolteacher declines to attend a local dance, the cowboys remove the door of her home and carry her off. Cowboy boots are great protection while dancing a polka. Butterflies will stay on your shoulder for two dances at an outdoor dance. While dancing the "butterfly," the middle person's feet don't get to touch the ground.

Leaving undies on an unsupervised clothesline is extremely dangerous for them. It's fun to hard boil chicken eggs and put them back in the nests on Halloween.

Wave your hand at a plane overhead and it will wag its wings at you or drop flowers. When you sweep the snow off a pond, the texture of the ice is nothing like the Kerrisdale Arena. Well-known radio personalities back out of wild cow riding at the local rodeo if the Meldrum Creek school marm takes up their challenge. A school of thirteen pupils can almost win a tug-of-war with a school of thirty-three. You have to be very careful of any barbwire fences when you toboggan down a steep logging road on an old car hood.

Corn is reasonable bait for ice fishing. Beavers can make or break a hay pasture. Hay doesn't have to be baled to keep through the winter. Moose can gracefully leap over tall school yard fences but get caught in hay corrals. The moment they hit the water, horsehair snakes will untie themselves from any knot they're tied in. Squirrel nests in the Chilcotin have bits of cigarette packages and lots of lice in them. Leaches gently anesthetize your skin where they attach themselves.

When the windshield wipers don't work, you can get almost a kilometre before you have to scoop up more puddle water with your hat. During spring breakup, you only drive when the ruts are frozen. A car can completely freeze up while you're driving it and you have to be very careful how you build the fire under the motor to get it started again. At -56°F, there are three-centimetre icicles growing out of the outhouse seat.

When a Meldrum says we'll keep in touch, we do.

Verna Pigou
Rosedale

Quesnel	90.9 fm
Radium	94.5 fm
Revelstoke	91.3 fm
Rock Creek	94.1 fm
Salmo	740 am
Salmon Arm	96.9 fm
Saltspring Island	90.5 fm
Sandspit	104.9 fm
Sayward	630 am
Slocan	91.7 fm
Smithers	97.5 fm
Sointula	105.1 fm
Sooke/Metchosin	99.5 fm
Sorrento	1080 am
Sparwood	105.7 fm
Squamish	1260 am
Stewart	1450 am
Tahsis	1240 am
Terrace	95.3 fm
Tofino	91.5 fm
Trail/Rossland	94.9 fm
Tumbler Ridge	89.9 fm
Ucluelet	540 am
Valemount	90.3 fm
Vancouver	690 am
Vanderhoof	96.7 fm
Vavenby	91.9 fm
Vernon	106.5 fm
Victoria	90.5 fm
Wells/Barkerville	540 am
Westview	92.5 fm
Whistler	100.1 fm
Williams Lake	860 am
Winlaw	91.7 fm
Woss	92.7 fm
Shortwave	6160 KHz

CBC Radio Two

Lillooet	98.7 fm
Peachland	99.1 fm
Prince George	90.3 fm
Sooke/Metchosin	105.1 fm
Vancouver	105.7 fm
Victoria	92.1 fm
Wells	98.1 fm
Winfield	91.9 fm

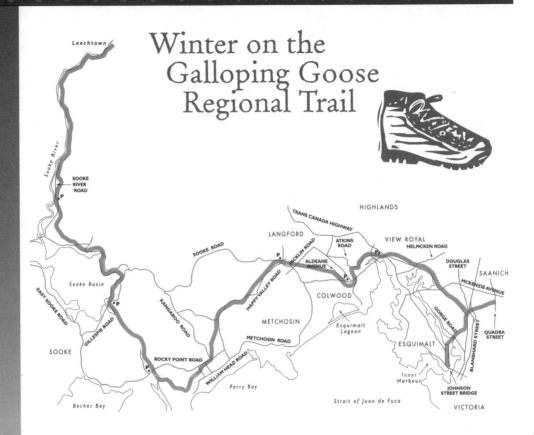

Winter on the Galloping Goose Regional Trail

The Galloping Goose Regional Trail, a fifty-seven kilometre former railway line, starts from downtown Victoria and snakes westward through urban landscapes, pastoral farmscapes, and semi-wilderness coastline out to the Sooke River Valley. This rails-to-trails regional trail is ideal, even in winter, for hiking, strolling, horseback riding, and easy cycling with a mountain bike. Highlights include two tall trestles, spectacular oceanside cycling right beside the Sooke Basin, cool creeks emerging from fern forests, and arbutus-clad, rocky outcrops.

The urban sections are paved, but the western rural and semi-wilderness sections use original hard rail bed. Facilities are minimal, although designated parking and washrooms are found at a few locations. You can also park at any of the many road crossings. Remember to bring your own water.

The Goose is a multi-use trail so hikers should remember to keep right, pass on the left. The trail also passes by private property, so travellers are asked to respect those areas.

During the winter, watch for wet and muddy areas in the western sections of the trail. Strong cyclists can travel the Goose in a day, but most trail users prefer to cycle shorter sections in the more spectacular western area. Plan your day carefully, keeping in mind the early sunsets.

More information can be found at the website: www.crd.bc.ca/parks.

Information courtesy James Muchinock, Information Coordinator, CRD Parks.

BC Mythical Creatures: Caddy

Caddy, a cadborosaurus, is the name given to the west coast's giant seagoing serpent that was first spotted in the 1930s in Victoria's Cadboro Bay and has since been sighted in BC on a regular basis. Like Ogopogo, the creature is thought to be a relic from the dinosaur age. And although there is believed to be several varieties of Caddy, it is usually described as being from five to fifteen metres in length, with a snake-like body, and a head that looks like a sheep or camel. Its body has vertical humps or loops, with strong upper anterior and lower posterior flippers that allow it to swim at reported speeds of forty knots at the surface. It is thought that, similar to garter snakes, the females come to the shores of shallow estuaries to bear their live young. In 1937, flensers at the Naden Harbour whaling station reported that they had found a strange serpentine animal in the stomach of a recently harvested whale. The creature was reported to be ten feet long, with characteristics commonly sighted in the caddy. Mysteriously, however, the tissue samples were stolen from the fisheries station in Nanaimo. There was also a picture of the creature taken by the Naden Harbour whalers, but the details were quite sketchy and inconclusive.

EVENTS

FEBRUARY EVENTS

Clearwater's Wells Gray Loppet (Ski Race)

Fernie Griz Days

Fort St John's Jam Can Curling Tournament

Kamloops Rotary Ice Fishing Tournament

Kimberley Winterfest

100 Mile House Cariboo Cross-Country Ski Marathon

Penticton Mid-Winter Breakout

Prince George Mardi Gras of Winter

Sparwood Snowarama

Whitehorse Frostbite Music Fest

Yukon Quest Dogsled Race, Fairbanks, Alaska to Whitehorse

BC WEATHER EXTREMES

Coldest Temperatrue
-58.9°C
Jan. 31, 1947
Smith River

Most Total Precipitation in 1 year (Rain and Snow)
9,080.1 mm
1997 and 1931
Henderson Lake

Most days, in 1 year, with precipitation
300
1939
Langara

Most average annual precipitation
6,655 mm
Henderson Lake

Most rain in 6 hours
265 mm
0400 - 1000, Jan. 26, 1984
McInnes Island

Most snow in 1 day
127.1 cm
Feb. 10, 1999
Lakelse Lake

Most snow over 5 consecutive days
246.2 cm
from Jan. 14, 1974
Kitimat

The Storm of the Century, December 1996

Jamie McDuff

Jamie McDuff is one of the two Environment Canada weather forecasters who appear on BC Almanac.

We'd planned a party for the night of the twenty-eighth. Of course, we prepared by making hundreds of snacks and laying out extra liquid in case people were thirsty. Our favourite in-laws were in town and planned to leave Sunday afternoon. Needless to say, after hearing the snowfall warnings of fifteen to thirty centimetres and strong winds on early Saturday afternoon, I contacted all the people we invited and told them to think twice about coming. They might not get home! Many of them obviously could not stomach the thought of being trapped with us, so they cancelled. The intelligent thing to do.

Ten people did show up, but as soon as the winds picked up at 11 pm, headed for home. Another informed choice. So we were left with our in-laws and the kids to watch the storm. Sixty-four-and-a-half centimetres of snow in twelve hours, on top of the thirty-seven centimetres already on the ground combined with strong winds: a recipe for shutdown!

Sunday morning, we were shocked to see the amount of snow and height of the drifts. We caught a nice snapshot of our last remaining rose blossom, floating above a sea of white. So much for the aesthetics. My brother-in-law and I had to shovel a path across the deck and into the backyard so the dog could relieve himself. Then we trooped around the house to chop down the three foot snow cornice that ran off the roof over the pathway beside the house.

With hardly any party guests, we had ample snacks left over. To this day my kids will not eat mini-quiche! I think that will be their memory of the Storm of '96.

Greatest Single-Day Snowfall Record
February 11, 1999

Tahtsa Lake received 145 centimetres of snow, a new Canadian single-day snowfall record, but well below the world's record of 192 centimetres at Silver Lake, Colorado on April 15, 1921.

Information courtesy Environment Canada.

Most snow in 1 month
535.9 cm
Dec. 1959
Haines Apps No. 2

Most snow in 1 season
2,446.5 cm
1971/72
Revelstoke (Mt Copeland)

Most average annual snowfall
1433 cm
Glacier (Mt Fidelity)

Most days with blowing snow in 1 year
68
1957/58
Old Glory Mountain

Greatest hourly wind speed
143 km/h
Feb. 20, 1974
Bonilla Island

Longest frost-free period
685 days
1925/26
Victoria

Compiled by Jamie McDuff and Anne McCarthy, of Victoria's Environment Canada weather office.

BRIAN MINTER'S WINTER GARDENING TIPS: FEBRUARY

Pruning and dormant spraying
Prune only fruit, shade, and ornamental trees. Leave roses, evergreens, and flowering trees and shrubs until later. Most of your deciduous trees and shrubs should be dormant sprayed this month. Use four ounces of lime sulphur and one ounce of dormant oil per gallon of water. Use a pressure or trombone sprayer for best results, and remember: three sprayings are necessary to really clean up your trees.

In Oweekeno
Frank Hanuse

Frank Hanuse is the BC Almanac *community correspondent in Oweekeno Village.*

Oweekeno Village is an isolated community located on Katit Indian Reserve # 1, on the north side of the Whannock River in Rivers Inlet, ninety kilometres northeast of the tip of Vancouver Island. The population varies from sixty to ninety depending on the time of year. Oweekeno is only accessible by floatplane, large private boat, or by boat charter service from Port Hardy. There are bi-weekly freight services that will deliver groceries and other supplies to Oweekeno Village. The Oweekeno Elementary School goes from kindergarten to grade seven, then all students from grade eight on must go out to attend school elsewhere.

The fall is one of the most important times of the year for the Oweekeno. The sockeye that migrate up the Whannock River are gill netted then canned, fresh smoked, or barbecued. The barbecued sockeye can be frozen or canned. A family of five needs at least ten cases of canned fish to help them get through the winter. If a feast or potlatch is to be held over the winter months, more fish and other species are canned in preparation. In late fall, the red sockeye are caught and smoked, barbecued and dried. Other species, such as chinook, pink, cohoe, chum, and halibut, are also smoked.

After the fish, hunting is also important – deer, goat, duck, and geese. These are also canned for the winter, as by late November you know if a long, hard winter is around the corner and you have to be prepared.

If you are lucky and have a boat you can get fresh cod, clams, and mussels which

are gathered approximately twenty-five to thirty miles towards the mouth of Rivers Inlet. In the past the odd seal was shot for fresh meat, the fat was eaten with the barbecued and smoked fish.

After all that is over, you just keep the house warm, look out the window, and laugh at the snow. Waiting for spring.

CBC engineer Dave Newbury digging out the transmitter shack at Woss Mountain on Vancouver Island.

Lawn care and preparation
It is important to lime your lawn as soon as possible because of our heavy winter rains, which makes your soil acidic. As some limes contain magnesium, your grass will also green up. If you are concerned about moss, it is still too early to apply moss killer. Aeration, followed by an application of ⅜ of an inch of coarse sand, will improve drainage and help your lawn grasses grow.

Compost on the garden
Try spreading some mushroom compost on your vegetable and flower gardens soon to let the goodness work in and prevent further soil compaction.

Index

Index

Index

Index

Index

Index

Index

Index